A LEGACY

FROM DELAWARE WOMEN

A LEGACY FROM DELAWARE WOMEN

The cover was designed and contributed by Martha Carothers, Associate Professor of Art, University of Delaware.

PHOTO CREDITS

Sincerest thanks to the following for their generosity in providing photographs for this book.

The News Journal Co.: Egri, Blish, Keyser, Leach, Baker, Mullin, Wright, Williams, Leasure, Miller, Rose, McEwing, Preston, Spruance, Vernon, Ginns. Delaware Commission For Women: Theisen, Handloff, Connor, Steele, Freer. University of Delaware Archives: Warner/Robinson, Warner. Wilmington Garden Center: Flower box, Anderson. Brandywine River Museum: Handy. Winterthur Museum: Beldin. Delaware Nature Education Society: Fleming. United States Post Office: Bissell stamp. Delaware State Chamber of Commerce: Mankin. Delaware Army National Guard: Mitchell. Rita Justice: Group photo of women in politics. Jim Rememter: Thompson. Susan Rosenberg: Graham. Margaret Towers: Tull. Bruce K. Turner: Hull.

A LEGACY

FROM DELAWARE WOMEN

Sponsored by
The Chesapeake Bay Girl Scout Council
and
The Women's Center of Delaware Technical and
Community College and the University of Delaware

1987

A Delaware Heritage Commission project
with assistance from the Delaware Humanities Forum

GIRL SCOUTS

We the People
Delaware
...... ◆ ......
Freedom's First

Distributed by The Middle Atlantic Press.

ISBN 0-912608-49-8 (softcover edition)
        0-912608-54-4 (hardcover edition)
Printed in the United States of America

The Middle Atlantic Press, Inc.
848 Church Street, P.O. Box 945
Wilmington, Delaware 19899

TABLE OF CONTENTS

Foreword   vii
Acknowledgements   ix
Women of My Time: An Essay   xi
The New Women: An Introduction   xiii
With Skill and Imagination: Women in the Arts   1
Up the Ladder: Women in Business and Management   17
Spreading the Word: Women in Communications   33
To Help One Another: Women in Community Service   41
Nature's Guardians: Women in Conservation   51
Developers of Minds: Women in Education   59
For the Public Good: Women in Government,
   Politics and Military Service   75
Toward Sound Minds and Bodies:
   Women in Health Care   89
Preservers of Our Heritage: Women in History   101
Purveyors of Faith: Women in Religion   113
On the Cutting Edge: Women in Science
   and Technology   123
Ready . . . Set . . . Go: Women in Sports   131
Significant Dates in the History of Delaware Women   141
Hall of Fame of Delaware Women   149
Delaware American Mothers   151
Schools Named for Women Educators in Delaware   153
Index

KEY TO SYMBOLS AND ABBREVIATIONS

* Biography in *Delaware Women Remembered*
AAUW: American Association of University Women
CPA: Certified Public Accountant
DAR: Daughters of the American Revolution
M.B.A.: Master of Business Administration
NAACP: National Association for the Advancement
   of Colored People
PTA: Parent-Teacher Association

FOREWORD

THIS book was produced by many people as a volunteer effort. As a unique project, the development of the book may be of interest to its readers.

Preparation for *A Legacy From Delaware Women* began over five years ago when the Chesapeake Bay Girl Scout Council received a Delaware Humanities Forum grant to identify and profile women who were making significant contributions to Delaware and the larger world. An earlier book, *Delaware Women Remembered*, published in 1977, had been out of print for a number of years.

Project Director Mary Sam Ward led a major volunteer effort to develop this book as she had done a decade earlier. Women from business, cultural and community groups were recruited to identify candidates for inclusion in the book and to coordinate the research for each chapter. Mary Sam has inspired and guided the research work on this project since 1982.

The biographical files developed for more than 700 women have been accepted by the Historical Society as a contribution to the Delaware historical record.

In 1983, the Women's Center of Delaware Technical and Community College and the University of Delaware agreed to co-sponsor the project and act as the financial clearinghouse for donations from individuals and Delaware companies. The endorsement of the book as a "heritage project" and a publication grant from the Delaware Heritage Commission in 1986 have given the project welcome recognition.

To select candidates for the book, executives in private and public sector organizations were asked to nominate women; newspapers were culled; community leaders and women's clubs were contacted. Choosing the women for the chapters was carried out according to the following criteria: eminent or first in regard to position or attainment in a given field; a founder; a leader for a special concern; honored or recognized by colleagues or the community. Some women from *Delaware Women Remembered* were included because of their historical significance, the outstanding nature of their accomplishments, or because of new achievements. The ultimate criterion common to all selections was that their outstanding effort leaves a legacy in Delaware for the benefit of others, both now and in the future.

Despite the years of effort and the broad involvement of women throughout the state, some women, whose biographies should have been in this book, have probably been missed. This we humbly recognize. Those selected (more than 500) are regarded as examplars of feminine achievement in Delaware society.

Lynn Williams
Chesapeake Bay
  Girl Scout Council

Pamela Morris
Women's Center,
Delaware Technical and
  Community College,
  and the University of
  Delaware

ACKNOWLEDGEMENTS

ALTHOUGH the intent of the book was to chronicle the many accomplishments and contributions of Delaware women, it became clear that we were chronicling as well a legacy of caring, commitment and inspiration shown in the dedicated effort of all who were involved with the project. We are very grateful to the many volunteers who have created this book as their legacy for the women of tomorrow.

Advisors

Helen Balick, Claudia Bushman, Mae Carter, Penelope Cope, Betty Cronin, Irene Dardashti, Rona Finkelstein, Helen Fox, Geri Garvin, Marie Giovino, Lin Herndon, Barbara Herr, Vivian Houghton, Susan Jamison, Ruth Kaplan, Pat Kent, Janet Kramer, Gerda Latham, Paula Lehrer, Nancy Lynch, Ruth Mankin, Annie Lu Martyn, Kathy Meyer, Marion Monet, Frances Naczi, Agnes Nolan, Shirley Patterson, Priscilla Rakestraw, Leah Roedel, Nancy Sawin, Dale Stratton, Gloria Stuber, Emma-June Tillmanns-Skolnik

Photographers

Mary Lowenstein Anderson, Brandywine River Museum, Hagley Museum, News-Journal Company, Jeanette Zipf, and individual owners

Writers

Janine Jacquet Biden, Hazel Brittingham, Betty Burroughs, Isabel Church, Irene Dardashti, Ann Frazier-Hedberg, Geri Garvin, Hilda Grant, Eugenia Gray, Susan Jamison, Ruth Kaplan, Pat Kent, Gerda Latham, Nancy Lynch, Karen Mooney, Frances Naczi, Shirley Patterson, Judith Roberts, Leah Roedel, Katherine Smigie, Christine Talley, Cari DeSantis Tull, Bonnie Wingate

Typists

Phyllis Hamilton, Katherine Hanke, Christine Held, Mollie Hibbard, Ann Marcial, Janet McClennan, Ann Mary Mertz, Emily Robertson

Researchers

Hazel Brittingham, Betty Cronin, Helen Fox, Geri Garvin, Annie Lu Martyn, Ruth Stewart

Chronology

Martha Bayard, Doris Chambers, Geri Garvin, Phyllis Hamilton, Christine Held, Helen Thomas

Librarians

Helen Carnell, Carol Hallman, Jackie Hinsley, Betty-Bright Low, Charlotte Walker

Libraries

Corbit-Sharp Library, Delaware State Arts Council,

Hagley Museum and Library, Historical Society of Delaware, Rehoboth Public Library, Morris Library of the University of Delaware, Wilmington Library, Winterthur Museum

Book Promotion

Stooker & Company, Public Relations, Inc.

We are indebted to the institutions that have sponsored and assisted this project. The Chesapeake Bay Girl Scout Council received and administered the research grant, and its staff gave support services to Mary Sam Ward. Later, its Board of Directors underwrote the publishing process and the staff assisted with pre-publication promotion and sales. We gratefully acknowledge this sponsorship.

Appreciation is expressed to the Delaware Technical and Community College for providing the resources that enabled the Women's Center to be a co-sponsor.

Thanks are given to the Historical Society of Delaware for the use of its facilities as an editorial office and depository for the permanent file of biographies.

A grant from the Delaware Humanities Forum is gratefully acknowledged. It provided the necessary supplies and services for the volunteers in the research stage of this project. It encouraged and supported their effort and goal.

The recent grant from the Delaware Heritage Commission is received with appreciation. Its endorsement of this book as a "heritage project" has also added to the significance of the work.

For contributions of funds to make this publication possible, grateful acknowledgement is given to:

Crystal Trust, Genevieve Gore, Hercules, Inc., Nanticoke Homes, Inc.

Special thanks also go to:

Bank of Delaware, Beta Chapter-Delta Kappa Gamma, Blue Cross Blue Shield of Delaware, Irene Dardashti, Walter C. Deakyne, Jr.-Barcroft Company, Diamond State Telephone Company, Emily du Pont, Carolyn J. Fausnaugh Associates, Clarence Fulmer, GFWC-Hockessin Community Club, Junior League of Wilmington, Inc., Annabelle Kressman, National Council of Negro Women, Inc.-Peninsula Section, National League of American Pen Women, Inc.-Diamond State Branch, Pepsi-Cola Bottling Company of Wilmington, Inc., Professional Secretaries International, Quota Club of Wilmington, Inc., Temple Beth Emeth, Washington Heights Century Club, Women's Alliance-First Unitarian Church, Women's Democratic Club of Delaware

The editorial process of moving a collection of biographies to a book "with one voice" has taken time and devotion. Our sincere thanks to:
Associate Editors: Lyn Herndon, Frances Naczi, Katherine Smigie.
Editor: Susan Web Soltys
Editorial Advisory Committee: Barbara Benson, Chair; Claudia Bushman, Carol Hoffecker.

The undersigned, working as an Ad Hoc Steering Committee, express to all of the above, and to our families and colleagues, our gratitude for their support and encouragement along the way.

Mary Sam Ward, Project Director
Lynn Williams, Girl Scout Project Coordinator
Pam Morris, Women's Center Project Coordinator
Judy Just, Delaware Humanities Forum
   Representative
Cari DeSantis Tull, Publishing Advisor

L to R seated: Susan Soltys, Barbara Benson; Standing: Lynn Williams, Cari DeSantis Tull, Mary Sam Ward, Judith Just, Pamela Morris.

WOMEN OF MY TIME:

An Essay

Mary Sam Ward

DELAWARE has been blessed with women of foresight who saved bits and pieces from the past from everyday life and wove them into our history. As we approach the Bicentennial of the Constitution, there are changes in our socially acceptable behavior patterns, education, and employment opportunities for women. This book about Delaware women has not only discovered valuable insights and identities from the past but points to changes that will carry into the next century.

Over the fifty years that I have lived in Delaware, many women have impressed and inspired me to write these books. I would like to mention a few.

FLORA LOMAX was a saintly kind of woman. She held together the congregation of Saint James Church, Newport, with dignity and love, and literally held one end of the altar rail while the minister built the altar. She nursed an elderly sister with compassion and love, night and day, in that pre-medicare and pre-visiting-nurse time, and prayed to be spared long enough to finish the task. She barely made it but I will remember her love and faith.

ELLA WELDIN JOHNSON, who lived down the street from the Lomax family, had been the Newport postmistress from 1922 to 1931. She never accepted 19804 as a substitute for Newport. She spent her ninety years collecting information about Newport and its people.

As suburbia had not exploded living patterns at this time, almost everyone went to Wilmington to shop. MARJORIE W. SPEAKMAN hired LIZETTE DAVIS, the first black woman in Wilmington to decorate windows, serve customers, and travel to New York as a buyer. She still works at Speakman's in Greenville where she has bought clothes for three generations of children.

MARJORIE W. SPEAKMAN of Smyrna was a leader in education and preservation of historic buildings. At a "pre-Hall of Fame" dinner at Mrs. Speakman's home, Belmont Hall, I met DR. MARGARET HANDY, the first woman pediatrician in Wilmington. My interest in researching the large number of outstanding women in Delaware was piqued that night for the rest of my life. LOUISE DU PONT CROWNINSHIELD, among the guests I met, saved Eleutherian Mills, the home of one of Delaware's most influential families. And I met BELLE EVERETT and DOROTHY ELSTON KABIS, who introduced women to the art of politics.

Hundreds of women have been trained to interpret Delaware's treasures and artifacts in homes and museums. MARGUERITE DU PONT BODEN restored numerous churches and historic houses such as the Hale Byrnes House in Stanton. CATHERINE DOWNING has worked tirelessly on boards and commissions throughout the state and LOUISE

CORKRAN and her assistant RUTH C. STEWART and dozens of women in Sussex County saved the Homestead, one of the cultural centers of the state.

RUTH CANN, civic leader, clubwoman, and WDEL radio personality, kept Delawareans informed of "People in the News" with appeals for public service.

JEANETTE SLOCOMB EDWARDS, a visual artist as well as a poet laureate of Delaware, wrote, in *Songs Against the Dark* (1936):

> I pray one song that I have sung
> when I am dust, will still be young
> And lend to beauty just one jot
> of loveliness that I begot.

DORIS CHAMBERS trained Delmarva Girl Scout leaders for more than a quarter of a century while THELMA ROBERTS, director of Country Center Day Camp, taught staff members and over six thousand girls to appreciate and love the outdoors at the Hockessin Girl Scout camp.

Outstanding teachers were CARRIE DOWNIE, who taught in New Castle for over sixty years and left her entire estate to the Carrie Downie School. GRACE RIGGIN "boarded around" with parents and taught in a rural school for $50 a month. She saved enough to attend summer school until she got a degree and became principal of the Mary C. I. Williams School.

ELLA MIDDLETON TYBOUT (1871–1952) wrote *Poketown People*, also known as "Parables in Black," and captured the hearts of her community; KATHRYN S. CHASE was librarian at Hercules, Inc., for over forty years; and ELSIE WILLIAMS saved a scrapbook of "Washington Chatter" with photographs. She gave it to the Historical Society of Delaware in 1970. NANCY DU PONT REYNOLDS designed more than five hundred religious symbols for kneelers at Christ Church Christiana Hundred.

Dr. John A. Munroe states that there are still "empty quarters" and unexamined areas in Delaware history. I hope that *A Legacy From Delaware Women* will help to correct that score. CAROL HOFFECKER's forthcoming history book for fourth graders is an exciting contribution. *My Brandywine Valley*, by ETHEL LUELLA HAYWARD JONES (1986) will also help fill one of those empty quarters.

In addition to other acknowledgements, I want to thank Harold B. Hancock, who has researched and written about black women's contributions; C.A. Weslager for his insights into the Lenape Indian culture and especially NORA THOMPSON DEAN; W. Emerson Wilson for writing on women in the period of the revolution; John A. Monroe, who has taught Delaware history to so many; Harry Themal, who has encouraged us by his interest in our project and helped with photographs; the James Garvins for their support; and Bill Frank, who has been "beating the drums" for women's accomplishments for half a century. For these friends, and all who have sent information from their personal archives, news clippings, and photographs, I am ever grateful. Thanks to all these wonderful Delawareans.

Mary Sam Ward
Project Director

THE NEW WOMEN:

Introduction

Carol Hoffecker

A decade ago, Americans celebrated the bicentennial of the signing of the Declaration of Independence with an outpouring of patriotic and historical events and activities. Paraders marched, tall ships sailed, concert artists sang and played, fireworks exploded, buildings were restored, and books were written. Ten years later we have memories of that celebration, some recorded for posterity as photographs or on videotape, but only the restored buildings and the books remain as the tangible results of 1976. In Delaware one of the more remarkable legacies of the bicentennial was a book entitled *Delaware Women Remembered*. The volunteer writers and editors who produced the book presented it as "a bicentennial gift to Delaware," and "dedicated [it] to all women whose lives have helped to sustain the spirit of our ancestors who left us a legacy of permanent values, and to those who, by the sharing of their time, love, and creativity, have enriched our lives and culture." Mary Sam Ward, the chief editor of the volume, noted in the introduction her hope "that future historians and students will be inspired to continue to illuminate the contributions and to chronicle the many fascinating stories of creative and capable Delaware women." *A Legacy from Delaware Women* is one fulfillment of that hope.

Delaware Women Remembered chronicled the hitherto unrecorded history of women's involvement in the development of the First State. It recalled the lives and activities of significant women in Delaware from the time when the earliest European settlers encountered the native Americans until the mid-1970s, and included many "firsts" for women in traditionally male fields. The book's topical organization drew attention to the patterns of women's activities outside the home. Although women participants in predominantly male activities such as sports, law, and business were noted, the emphasis was on women's contributions in areas related to their traditional roles in nurturing, home life, and culture. Activities that fit this womanly image included historic preservation, gardening, health care, community service, and education. The biographies described many women whose contributions were as volunteers rather than as paid professionals.

The publication of *Delaware Women Remembered* coincided not only with the two hundredth anniversary of the American Revolution but also with a modern-day revolution affecting the lives of women throughout the industrialized nations of the world. In 1977, when the volume was published, the women's movement was but a decade old. The idea of writing a book on such a theme was itself a manifestation of the resurgence of women's long-standing efforts to achieve more meaningful and useful social roles. In the years since the bicentennial, the women's movement has continued to evolve, and Delawareans, together with other Americans, have become more accustomed to seeing women performing in

xiii

fields where once they were absent or at best sparsely represented. Three examples that illustrate this point are the appearance of women as major party candidates for the office of lieutenant governor and United States representative in 1984 and the selection of a woman to be a judge of the Federal District Court of Delaware in 1985.

Achievements of such striking magnitude are the most visible signs of the continuing shift in women's lives away from the home-bounded world of the past. That is not to say that in the days when the ideal woman's place was in the home, women did not in fact range far beyond it. Low-income women have always been employed outside their homes as farm laborers, factory workers, and servants. Single women, especially those from low- and middle-income backgrounds, also have a long history of participation in the work force, and young unmarried women have traditionally been employed as retail sales clerks, school teachers, and office workers. The modern women's revolution has as yet done little to alter the lives of the pink-collar work force or of those who toil in the households of others. Recent changes have most affected another group: young, well-educated, married women who are entering the work force at professional levels and making the two-income family as much a phenomenon of the upper middle class as it once was among factory workers.

At the turn of the century Delaware's women were just discovering roles for themselves in the public sphere. Emalea Pusey Warner, the president of a Wilmington women's club called the New Century Club, celebrated the arrival of the "New Woman," who was extending her concerns for child care, cleanliness, purity, and morality beyond the home into the world at large. Settlement houses, women's clubs, and the suffrage crusade were but the most visible manifestations of the "New Woman's" expanded role. Many of the reforms launched by the women of that era had long-lasting effects. In Delaware one woman, Sarah Pyle, began the Peoples Settlement Association on the East Side of Wilmington; another, Emily Bissell, raised funds to build a sanatorium for tuberculosis patients. The Christmas Seal campaign that she first undertook in 1907 is still in use today. Delaware's women's clubs played a major role in securing the state legislature's approval to establish the Women's College in Newark, Delaware, in 1914.

The hallmark of the "New Woman" of Emalea Warner's day was her status as both a volunteer and a matron. To be sure, there were professional women in the early twentieth century. Dean Winifred Robinson, who oversaw the day-to-day management of the Women's College, and Edwina Kruse, the long-time principal of Howard High School, are examples, as is Annie Jump Cannon, an astronomer from Dover who spent her career at Harvard University's observatory plotting stellar spectra. Professional women were, however, rare. The typical "New Woman" did not work for a living and few were college graduates. Her husband was a businessman, lawyer, or doctor whose income permitted the family to live in a large and comfortable house staffed by servants who prepared the family's meals, washed and ironed its clothes, and beat the rugs twice a year on the clothesline in the backyard. Because servants performed the most time-consuming household tasks, the "New Woman" was free to serve on the board of managers of a social welfare agency, to listen to a college professor speak at the women's club, or to lobby in the General Assembly on behalf of educational reforms. The wealthy women who devoted themselves to the twin goals of self-improvement and community welfare epitomized what New Womanhood was all about.

Of course, the "New Woman" did not remain "new" for long, but the ideals that she represented inspired the activities of several generations of upper-income women who filled the ranks of such organizations as the Junior League and the junior boards of Delaware's hospitals. The voluntary service undertaken by these women has been of incalculable benefit to Delawareans. In more recent years, they have been joined by legions of their middle-income counterparts who have gone door to door collecting funds to fight disease, served as Girl Scout leaders, den mothers, Sunday school teachers, homeroom mothers, hospital aides, museum guides; the list of tasks and beneficiaries seems endless. In short, women have long filled a host of vital positions in our economic and social life on an unpaid basis.

In the last decade, however, many young women have chosen a different route to community involvement and service, that of the paid professional. This metamorphosis represents both a shift from volunteer to paid staff positions within institutions that hitherto depended on female volunteers and the entrance of women into professional areas that were once closed to them. Today's version of the "New Woman" is either salaried or self-employed. If the volunteer was the principal heroine of *Delaware Women Remembered*, the contributions of professional women are hailed far more often in *A Legacy from Delaware Women*.

This volume, then, describes the lives of significant Delaware women at a time of dramatic change in women's roles. Statistical data from the United States Census Bureau provide a backdrop to set the stage for the women whose careers and accomplishments follow. In terms of gross statistics, the twentieth century has seen the rise of a female majority in Delaware. In 1980 the census takers counted 307,739 First State females. There are currently one hundred females to every 93.1 males in the state. This statistic continues a long-term consistent growth in the ratio of women to men in Delaware. Some day demographers will invest this striking statistical phenomenon with the social significance it deserves.

Women have yet to achieve equality in the workplace. Although women's educational levels are about comparable to those of men, and women account for 43 percent of the state's work force, they make up only 28 percent of those employed in jobs the Census Bureau describes as "executive, administrative, and managerial." Statistics also suggest that the work life patterns for women differ from those for men in that many women who enter the work force in their early twenties leave it some years later during their childbearing years and re-enter once their children reach school age. Doubtless these factors are linked

in the sense that many families continue to emphasize the husband's career over that of the wife. But women are more and more frequently entering well-paid and highly demanding professional fields. The University of Delaware reports, for example, that women presently constitute nearly 53 percent of the students in its College of Business and Economics and 23 percent of those enrolled in the College of Engineering.

The developments of the past decade point to a future in which fewer women of working age will be available to undertake volunteer activities, and more women will be competing for the most highly paid and prestigious positions in the economy. The biographies that follow reveal a society in transition between these two models of successful accomplishment. There is an important social significance to this shift. As accomplishments in paid work gain importance, socioeconomic class recedes as a primary factor in signalling accomplishment. In the heyday of the volunteer, only well-to-do women were free to cultivate the style of the "New Woman." Nowadays, with widespread public access to quality education, middle-income women have achieved equality of access to professional careers. Today any girl with enough talent and drive can aspire to be included among the significant Delaware women of the future.

Carol E. Hoffecker

WITH SKILL AND IMAGINATION:

Women in the Arts

Ruth Egri

The Delaware Theatre Company, Opera Delaware, the Rehoboth Art League, and the Delaware Art Museum are among the many institutions that owe much of their vitality to the women who have helped shape them. Women also contribute to the arts in Delaware as instructors and board members of institutions, as individual performing and visual artists, and as teachers.

Government plays an important role in the arts. Since 1969 the Delaware State Arts Council has supported artists and arts programs, encouraging the arts to develop and flourish throughout the state. POLLY BUCK served as chair of the council until 1974, when she resigned to join the staff of the National Endowment for the Arts. By that time, the council was attracting close to $200,000 in federal funds and over $40,000 in state funds annually. In 1978 the Delaware State Arts Council was reorganized under the state Division of Historical and Cultural Affairs.

Under the administration of JUDITH HECKROTH HOOPES (1938-   ), who chaired the council from 1979 to 1985, state funds more than quadrupled. Therefore, even though federal support began to decline, as it did throughout the nation, total funding grew from $447,900 in fiscal year 1979 to $775,480 in fiscal year 1984. In response to a proposal by Governor Pierre S. du Pont IV, Hoopes coordinated an effort to bring state government together with county and municipal governments, the private sector, and arts organizations in a unified process for allocating funds to cultural programs. By forming grant review panels that include business and civic leaders, the council has assured a broadly based and impartial forum for determining the needs and merits of grant applications. Hoopes, a native of Wilmington and now director of development for the Delaware Symphony Orchestra, has served on the boards of the Historical Society of Delaware, the YMCA, and the Delaware Art Museum.

NANCY BARTOSHESKY LYNCH (1950-   ) also is involved in many aspects of the arts. She became the first executive director of the Wilmington Arts Commission, after serving as its secretary and president. Lynch has worked in community arts

1

Nancy Bartoshesky Lynch

versity of Delaware. She has performed in theater productions and as a solo mime. Devotion to the arts has motivated Lynch to volunteer as an officer of Brandywine Friends of Old Time Music, the Delaware Theatre Association, and Youth Communication, Inc. She has taught drama at Ursuline Academy, Wilmington, where her interest in theater was nurtured by SISTER BERENICE and MARY KATHERINE MULLINS. Mullins taught speech and drama at the school for forty years. She also was a board member of the Delaware Theatre Association.

The restoration of the Grand Opera House in Wilmington has allowed residents of the state to see outstanding performing artists of all kinds. In her book *The Grand Experience: A History of the Grand Opera House* (1976), TONI YOUNG (1946-) describes the enormous undertaking of restoring the Grand Opera House in Wilmington as a center of the performing arts in the area. Continuously since the board formed in 1972, she has served as board member, secretary, vice-president, or president. For five years she wrote an historical column in performance programs on "the Grand" one hundred years ago, stimulating interest in its architecture, acoustics, and performances. Young also serves on the board of the Historical Society of Delaware.

CAROL BALICK of suburban Wilmington was a primary force in establishing the Delaware Theatre Company, the only resident professional theater group in the state, in 1979. Its audience grew quickly, and the company opened a new building on the Christina River in Wilmington in 1985. Balick serves on the executive committee of the Delaware Theatre Company and the boards of the Grand Opera House and Delaware Children's Theatre.

Originally from Brooklyn, New York, Balick owns Artisans III, a store in downtown Wilmington, and is a member of the Downtown Wilmington Improvement Corporation. She has been a member of the Wilmington Arts Commission and the Delaware State Arts Council. Balick paints, but finds little time for it amid her many activities. She believes that "art is one of the most civilizing and humanizing vehicles. . . . It crosses . . . political, national, and racial [lines]. The arts show us how to treat one another, how to share experiences. Everything else is territorial and tends to divide us." Balick received the Chesapeake Bay Girl Scout Council World of Arts Award in 1985.

development for the Delaware State Arts Council, parks, and schools. Delaware's only female mime, Lynch studied theater at the University of Notre Dame, the Wisconsin Mime Theatre, and the Uni-

2

Toni Young

MARIE SWAJESKI was a pioneer in children's theater in Delaware. In 1969 she organized the Wilmington Opera Society, Junior Division. Swajeski directed and choreographed productions and toured schools throughout Delaware to introduce children to opera. She founded the Children's Repertory Theatre and produced and directed the first children's production by Arena Stage in Washington, D.C., which led to the establishment of a children's theater wing there. Swajeski took a cast of thirty children from Delaware to northern Virginia to perform "The Pink Siamese" in the Fourth International Children's Festival at Wolf Trap Farm Park for the Performing Arts. She currently directs the Delaware Children's Theatre.

After starting her career in the Robin Hood Theatre in Arden in 1957, KATHLEEN WIDDOES, a Wilmingtonian, has received international acclaim as an actress. She has performed on stage in Paris, New York, and Stratford, Ontario. In New York, Widdoes has starred in productions as diverse as Joseph Papp's *Hamlet* and Neil Simon's hit *Brighton Beach Memoirs*. She also performs in television.

Delaware women have achieved prominence in vocal and instrumental music. KATHERINE CIESINSKI (1950-   ), a native of Newark, is celebrated in many cities around the world for her mezzosoprano voice and her opera roles. Her moving performance as Erika in Samuel Barber's *Vanessa* brought her into the national spotlight with the public television broadcast of the Spoleto Festival. International recognition followed Ciesinski's debut as Siebel with the Lyric Opera of Chicago production of *Faust*, which was filmed for European and American television. Ciesinski and her sister, KRISTINE CIESINSKI (1952-   ), a soprano, often perform together. They are the only American sisters in this century to have international opera careers. Kristine Ciesinski's career has taken her as far away as Taiwan and back to Delaware, where she performed in the Opera Delaware production of *Tosca* in 1982.

EVELYN DICKENSON SWENSSON (1928-   ) continues to perform, produce, and conduct opera throughout Delaware. Her special interest in opera has made Aldersgate United Methodist Church in Wilmington, where she is director of music, a leader in church drama. Swensson considers opera an

Carol Balick

3

Kristine and Katherine Ciesinski

4

Evelyn Dickenson Swensson

MARGARET STOCKTON STOREY of Dover founded three area choral groups and promoted youth music programs. She organized and directed the Community Singers (originally the Dover Century Club Chorus), which produces musicals; the Choral Society, which performs Handel's *Messiah*; and the Singing Players, which performed concerts until it dissolved in 1986, upon Storey's retirement as music director. In 1976 she cooperated with EVELYN SWENSSON to produce a two-hundred-voice concert of patriotic music in Philadelphia to celebrate the bicentennial reenactment of Caesar Rodney's ride from Dover.

Storey began teaching in the Selbyville school system in 1931 and later became Kent County supervisor of music. She helped start a summer music camp and music festivals for young people. Storey established the Music Department at Wesley College and chaired its Arts Department for ten years. She was president of the Dover Century Club and of the Middle Atlantic Conference, State Federation of Women's Clubs, and served on the board of directors of the Grand Opera House, Wilmington.

Because she believes that music, and young musicians in particular, make an essential contribution to the cultural growth of our civilization, LILLIAN ROSEN BALICK, a prodigy herself, has organized and produced showcase opportunities for musically talented youth for more than twenty years. An Artist-in-Education Coordinator for the Delaware State Arts Council, Balick founded and directs both Commu-

effective means of teaching the Bible. She has conducted more than fifty operas and musicals in Wilmington, including the world premiere of Gian Carlo Menotti's *The Boy Who Grew Too Fast* in 1982 at the Grand Opera House. In 1984 Swensson was the music director and conductor of Festival Two-Hundred, the musical celebration of the two hundredth anniversary of Methodism in America, held in Baltimore.

JUNE M. CASON (1930-   ) is founder and general manager of the Minikin Opera Company, a professional touring company that specializes in one-act operas sung in English. She augmented her degrees in music and music literature with postgraduate studies at the Wharton School of Business. Cason has taught voice students privately and at the Wilmington Music School and is a featured singer in musical theater, opera, oratoria, and solo recitals. She has served as chair of Delaware Pro Musica and the Music Consortium of New Castle County and vice-president of the Resource Center for the Performing Arts.

Margaret Stockton Storey

5

Lillian Rosen Balick

nity Showcase Performances, Inc., which arranges concerts for classical musicians, and the Jewish Community Center Contest for Young Musicians. Balick, a native of Philadelphia, won a musical competition that enabled her to attend Temple University College of Music and later earned a master's degree from West Chester State College. Balick wrote a book on the Delaware Symphony Orchestra and researched the contributions of women to music. She also developed a lecture-recital, "Music and History of the Women's Suffrage Movement," that sums up her belief that music represents "a triumph of the human spirit."

At the age of five, HELEN DECAIRE OKONOWICZ (1947-   ) launched a career at the piano. By the time she was twelve, Okonowicz was a soloist with the Wilmington Symphony Orchestra; she has appeared with them frequently over the years. In 1962, while a freshman at Ursuline Academy, Wilmington, Okonowicz received a scholarship to the Wilmington Music School and was the Eastern Division winner of the Music Teachers National Association annual competition. She appeared on Philadelphia television and made a concert tour to Mexico City. A

native of Toledo, Ohio, Okonowicz graduated from the University of Delaware and taught piano at the Wilmington Music School. She continues to give concerts in the region, although she is now a graduate nurse in obstetrics.

Guitarist, band leader, music store owner, and teacher FLORENCE L. ("SIS") SALTER (1918?-1981) was a vital part of Wilmington's musical life for nearly forty years. She was born and raised in Wilmington and started playing piano at age six. Salter first took up harp and then mandolin before she settled on guitar as her favored instrument in the 1940s. In 1951 she organized a band known as the Wilmington USO's Harmony Tones, which continued independent of the USO and traveled far beyond Delaware's borders for many years. Even before she graduated from high school, Salter joined her father in managing Salter's Music Shoppe in downtown Wilmington. The business was incorporated as a father-daughter partnership. Her father, "Doc," repaired instruments and "Sis" Salter taught guitar to three generations of students. Salter later shared a store in Manor Park with former student ROZ SCHWEBEL until Salter moved to Florida in 1974. There she managed the guitar and band department of a music store until her death.

Hundreds of Delawareans have studied at Marion Tracy Dance Studio, in Dover, Milford, and Smyrna. MARION TRACY (1919-   ) of Camden began dance training at age four. She took classes four days a week during her school years on Long Island, New York, reserving the fifth day for Girl Scouting. Tracy started teaching dance when she was thirteen years old and had studios in three towns by the time she graduated from high school. During her husband's tours of duty with the Air Force, she studied Hawaiian, Japanese, and Indian dance. When the family moved to Delaware, Tracy opened a dance studio to assure a daily class for her daughter. She now employs eight teachers. Tracy organized the Delaware Regional Ballet Company in 1973.

Tracy has also continued to be involved in Girl Scouting. She led troops, raised $3,000 for the Girl Guides in Calcutta, India, and has been the consultant for dance badges in Delaware.

JUDITH MINGUS (1947-   ) is artistic director of the dance company écarté. Born in Wilmington, North Carolina, she studied dance in Florida and at the

6

University of North Carolina and earned a theater degree from the University of Delaware. Mingus studied and performed with Dover Ballet Theatre. She founded Dance Directions in 1977 and écarté in 1981, with associate director GINGER ANGSTADT. Mingus choreographs and teaches modern dance and ballet to children and regional artists. In 1986 she received the Eastern District Dance Merit Award from the American Alliance for Health, Physical Education, Recreation, and Dance.

Delaware women have also made an impact on the visual arts, using a variety of media for self-expression, including painting, sculpture, and metalwork. Within an environment of increasing recognition and appreciation of women's art, a feminine artistic perspective is developing and expanding in Delaware.

A number of artists have formed groups for mutual reinforcement. Three friends, EUGENIA RHOADS, MILDRED EDINGER, and MARION HOWARD founded the Studio Group in Wilmington in 1935. They brought in eight more members, JEANNETTE SLOCOMB EDWARDS, MARGERY PYLE, ANN BENNETHUM, BETTY BOYD, CLARA FINKELSTEIN, MARGARET CALLAHAN, ELIZABETH DAVIS, and IRENE LENHER. They rented studio space and hired a teacher a few days each month. In addition to helping members develop their own work, the group fostered local talent through their Clothesline Fair. Beginning in 1937, the outdoor fair attracted the public for thirty-five years. Delawareans became aware of local artists and bought their work. The Du Pont Company and the Hotel du Pont purchased many paintings to hang in their buildings. Proceeds from commissions were used to make gifts to the University of Delaware and the Delaware Art Museum. The fair eventually became part of the Wilmington Flower Market, but the Studio Group is still active.

For decades a gentle force in the art community, EUGENIA ECKFORD RHOADS (1901-   ) was a founding member of the Studio Group and is now its honorary president. She was also a charter member of the Rehoboth Art League and is a member of the Visual Arts Committee of the Delaware State Arts Council. Rhoads, a native of Dyesburg, Tennessee, paints in an impressionistic style. Her association with the Delaware Art Museum spans almost fifty

years. She held many posts and chaired numerous committees, joined the board of trustees in 1958, and became president in 1980. Two years earlier, in recognition of her distinctive participation in the museum's activities, the museum mounted a retrospective of her watercolors, oils, and pastels. In 1982 the American Hollies Foundation honored Rhoads for "her dedication and contribution to the civic and arts communities."

Although she was born in Rye, New York, IRENE LENHER (1907-1986) spent her childhood in South Africa and studied art in London and Paris. In 1929 she returned to the United States, married, and settled in Wilmington, where she continued to paint and exhibit her softly representational paintings. Lenher was a charter member of the Studio Group, a former president of the Diamond State Branch, National League of American Pen Women, and a member of the Delaware State Arts Council. She organized the first Regional Art Exhibition at the University of Delaware, from which she received an honorary master of arts degree in 1968. Lenher was honored with an exhibition of the Special Collections of the University of Delaware in Spring 1986.

FLORINE HUGER ("TUA") HAYES (1916-   ) was president of the Studio Group in the mid-1950s. A native of Anniston, Alabama, she has left her mark on the cultural life of Wilmington, not only through her subtle, simplified representational oils and watercolors but also in her drive to expand the artistic community. As a trustee of the Delaware Art Museum from 1962 to 1980, Hayes started the Women's Committee (the volunteer arm of the museum now known as the Museum Council) and the Downtown Gallery, a branch of the museum that functioned for several years in downtown Wilmington. She was a member of the New Castle County Beautification Board from 1967 to 1973 and continues to serve on the board of directors of the Hilton Head Art League on Hilton Head Island, South Carolina, where she spends the winter months.

Among the nationally known holdings of the Delaware Art Museum is the John Sloan Collection. The archival material was given by HELEN FARR SLOAN (1911-   ), widow of John Sloan (1871-1951), famed painter and member of The Eight, popularly known as the "Ashcan School." Now a Wilmington resident, Helen Sloan began her association with the museum when she commuted from New York to do research. She contributes several days a week to assist in sorting and cataloguing the art work, personal papers, and books that make up her donation. An artist herself, Sloan first met John Sloan when he was her teacher at the Art Students League in New York City. She edited his book *Gist of Art* (1939). Helen Sloan headed the art departments of several New York high schools and has exhibited, lectured, and written widely.

LOUISE CHAMBERS CORKRAN (1882-1973) founded the Rehoboth Art League in 1938. Friends worked with her to develop the organization into a cultural center for Sussex County. They purchased an old building, moved it to Corkran's property, and renovated it as an art studio. The group built additional buildings and expanded programs as the membership grew from fifteen to more than one thousand. The Rehoboth Art League mounts exhibits, offers classes and lectures on the arts, and operates a sales gallery for members' work. Corkran, a native of Kentucky, was trained as an interior designer in Philadelphia.

The Council of Delaware Artists (CODA) was founded in Arden in 1955 to bring together artists of competence and serious intent. The group is limited to sixty professional artists, chosen by an admissions committee on the basis of their work and resumés. The artists, who work in diverse styles, frequently exhibit as a group.

Former President of CODA and vice-president of the Diamond State Branch, National League of American Pen Women, IRENE CARMEAN HILL PONSELL of Wilmington paints primarily in oil and watercolor. Strongly influenced by the cut-out designs of Henri Matisse, she balances strong, distinctive, abstract shapes in flat color areas. Since 1967 Ponsell has exhibited her paintings in Delaware and Pennsylvania. In addition to preparing for numerous one-person shows, she lectures on "How to Appreciate Modern Art."

Women are the major art subject for RUTH EGRI (HOLDEN) (1911-   ). She places abstracted, sometimes faceless silhouettes against the geometric lines and stark blackness of their environment. Egri portrays women's foibles and strengths, their ordeals, and their capacity for tenderness, whether they are seated awkwardly under hairdryers, sharing confidences, or experiencing the loneliness of old age. Born and raised in New York City, Egri and her two brothers were encouraged to become visual artists by their father, a poet and editor. Starting in her mid-teens, she studied at the National Academy of Design and the Art Students League. During the Great Depression, Egri worked as a muralist and illustrator for the WPA Art Project. She moved to Wilmington with her husband in the late 1940s. At one time, Egri felt compelled to sign her canvases "R. Egri," pretending to be a man in order to sell. But she persevered, and has sold widely and exhibited her work in major museums. Egri's work has won eight first prizes at the Delaware Art Museum.

The Delaware Center for the Contemporary Arts (DCCA) was founded in 1979 to promote the growth of contemporary arts in the state. GINA C. BOSWORTH (1938-   ) of suburban Wilmington, president from 1979 to 1981, wrote the by-laws and initiated systems for financial reporting, membership, and gallery exhibitions. Later, Bosworth helped locate and acquire permanent exhibition space for DCCA in downtown Wilmington and negotiated lease of the space from the city. She has served DCCA as development director and later as artists' representative. As president of the Delaware Crafts Council, Bosworth developed public exhibitions for the group. In 1985 she was a founding member of Arts Aware in Delaware, an association of visual and performing arts groups organized to promote the arts in the state.

A native of Los Angeles, JOANNE GROSS studied art at the University of California, Los Angeles, and continued her studies in Philadelphia after she moved to Delaware. Her paintings, done in acrylic and pencil on canvas, are linear geometric abstractions with subtle, flat color areas. Gross is a member of the Council of Delaware Artists, the Delaware Center for the Contemporary Arts, Philadelphia Artists' Equity, and a group of mostly Pennsylvania and New Jersey women known as "Markings." Her work has been exhibited in Delaware, Pennsylvania, and New York City and is included in numerous corporate and private collections on the East Coast.

A measure of the strength of the arts in a community is not only the number and caliber of professional artists, but also the role art plays in the lives of amateurs and non-artists. MARION F. T. JOHNSON (1911-   ) believes that art is for all people, not only the talented few, and she has spent her life promoting the aesthetic and cultural values of the arts. Her thirty-five years as education director of the Delaware Art Museum, from which she resigned in 1978, represent an outstanding contribution to the Wilmington arts community. She became interested in museum art education while studying with Victor D'Amico, education director of the Museum of Modern Art, and Joseph Albers, who taught there. Johnson went to the Delaware Art Museum in 1943 to establish an education program of scholarship classes for children. She expanded that program to include classes for adults as well as for children. Enrollment reached one thousand students annually and included workshops for teachers, film and lecture series, traveling exhibitions, and special programs for the general public. Johnson encourages students to develop the confidence to express themselves in some art form and to cultivate an awareness and enjoyment of art in their lives.

Johnson's interest in making ceramics led to building the museum's reputation as a leader in the exhibition and collection of contemporary American crafts. She also helped start the Delaware Crafts Council. Johnson has been executive director of the Chester County Art Association and art education coordinator of Absalom Jones Community Center near Wilmington. She helped form the Chester County Chapter of the Pennsylvania Guild of Craftsmen and is an instructor and consultant to the University of Delaware's Academy of Lifelong Learning.

Wilmington artist and educator MARIE J. SANTORA KEANE (1931-   ) was born in New York City and studied education, drawing and painting, and art history. Keane taught art and religious education for the Catholic Diocese of Wilmington and Archmere Academy. In 1984 and 1985, under an Artists-in-Education grant from the Delaware State Arts Council, she taught art to handicapped children and adults at Charles Bush School, the Mary Campbell Center, and Wallace Wallen School. For the general adult public, Keane has taught painting and lectured on art history at community sites. A member of the Council of Delaware Artists and the Studio Group, Keane exhibits drawings and paintings and contributes designs for advertising and literary publications.

PEGGY KANE aims to affect those who view her art, whether or not they like it or understand it. In the studio behind her house in Magnolia, she employs paint, collage, and printmaking techniques to prove that "there is more to existence than what we see with our physical senses." Kane began taking private art lessons when she was seventeen. She exhibits her work in Delaware, Maryland, and Pennsylvania and teaches children and adults. Kane demonstrates the use of a nineteenth-century loom and a printing press as a museum aide for the State of Delaware's Division of Historical and Cultural Affairs.

After graduating from Hollins College with a music history major, MARY PAGE EVANS became interested in painting. She studied with Chester County artist Tom Bostelle after she moved to Delaware and also studied with Gene Davis and Grace Hartigan. Evans is best known for semi-abstract garden scenes and landscapes, painted in bright acrylic colors with loose brushstrokes that belie the discipline and effort that go into them. She exhibits regularly in Wilmington, Philadelphia, and Washington, D.C.

Once her face entered American kitchens on the Yuban coffee label, but ever since CAROLYN BULLIS BLISH (1928-   ) became an artist, it is her popular paintings and prints that have made their way into homes across the country. Blish began painting in 1955, when she balked at paying the high prices demanded for works to decorate her house and decided to try to make something herself. She sold her first paintings at the Clothesline Fair in Wilmington for $5.98 each. Blish, who grew up on Long Island, New York, painted spectacular landscapes such as sunsets, but when Otto Dekom's review in the News-Journal papers called them "calendar art" she took the criticism to heart. Realizing "that the obviously beautiful is not what you should paint," Blish turned to understated subjects like dunes and daisies that reflected her deepening interest in the spiritual world. Her watercolors and oils sold so well that in 1968 Blish began selling limited-edition prints of her paintings with great success.

Carolyn Bullis Blish

Margo Allman

Painter, printmaker, and sculptor MARGO ALL-MAN has shown her work professionally for more than thirty years in the eastern United States. Trained at Moore College of Art in Philadelphia and by noted abstract expressionist artist Hans Hofmann, she began a lifelong interest in psychology and philosophy at Smith College. Allman made her reputation in the Delaware Valley for her woodcut prints, which were collected by the Delaware Art Museum and the Philadelphia Museum of Art. In 1966 she began more than a decade of work on abstract sculpture in wood, Cor-Ten steel, and stone that received top Delaware and national awards from the National League of American Pen Women. By the seventies she had turned to marble and ferrocement. At one time, Allman painted flat, hard-edged color fields, but since 1979 she has produced highly active, often enormous, black-and-white expressionistic images on Teflon® Allman paints heads, figures, couples, childbirth, and the slaughterhouse, searching for ways to articulate universal, elemental truths.

Prints and shaped paper works by ROSEMARY LANE (HOOPER) of Bear are included in the permanent collections of museums from Denmark to Oregon. She creates complex, subtly mysterious work in soft colors, often using unusual techniques. A bichromate process on vinyl makes it possible to adhere many negatives to the same surface, giving the collage a lifelike relief. Lane treats full or partial human forms as icons or sacred vessels housing the life force. She joined the faculty of the University of Delaware Art Department in 1974 after earning a master of fine arts degree from the University of Oregon. Lane won the Delaware State Arts Council Individual Artist Fellowship for an established professional for 1985-86.

Prints by graphic artist ROSEMARIE ("ROSIE") BERNARDI (1951-   ) of Newark have been included in more than sixty national juried print exhibitions, often taking prizes. They may be found in the permanent collections of the Philadelphia Museum of Art, the New Orleans Contemporary Art Center, and other institutions throughout the country. Bernardi has received many competitive fellowships, including one from the National Endowment for the Arts. She holds a master of fine arts degree from the University of Cincinnati and joined the University of Delaware in 1981. Bernardi's printmaking technique combines hand-manipulated photo etching with collaged photography. She juxtaposes familiar imagery and a realistic approach with abstraction to jog the viewer's awareness of the philosophical ramifications of photography and printmaking.

Graphic and book designer MARTHA CAROTHERS (1955-   ) of Newark also came to the University of Delaware Art Department in 1981. At Pennsylvania State University, where she earned a master's degree, Carothers learned to combine type and image into a cohesive whole. In both design and bookmaking, she employs a wry wit and an invitation for the viewer to become involved by touching and turning the works. Her work is represented in the Artists' Book Collection of the Museum of Modern Art.

JEAN BATTLES IRVIN (1941-   ) of Wilmington refers to her mixed-media drawings as "femmage," a term coined by New York artist Miriam Shapiro to describe "collage by women." The technique represents the artist's personal life and thoughts through items that women often collect, such as lace, buttons, strings, feathers, thread, old stamps, photographs, and ticket stubs. Irvin integrates these bits and pieces with symbols like stars and stripes,

11

checkerboards, rainbows, and hearts and with drawn and painted lines. The result is delicate yet bold, highly personal but with glimpses of experiences shared by many women. Born in Pittsburgh, Irvin earned an M.F.A. in drawing, painting, and print-making at the School of the Art Institute of Chicago and taught on the college level before moving to Delaware in the late 1970s. She teaches art at Tower Hill School, Wilmington, and the Delaware Institute for Arts in Education.

NANCY KISSEL CLARK has won local, regional, national, and international recognition for her sculpture, yet she did not turn to three-dimensional work until middle age. For fifteen years, she painted in oil and watercolor. Experimentation, she believes, is often necessary for an artist to find his or her best medium. Clark's welded sculptures often incorporate scrap parts. "Bald Eagle," constructed from metal knife stampings, won a top award in New Jersey and was purchased for the Municipal Building in her hometown, Joplin, Missouri. Clark has exhibited her work in Sweden and China and has received commissions from Africa. In addition to executing selected commissions, Clark teaches serious students privately and lectures for the Academy of Lifelong Learning of the University of Delaware. She was an artist in residence at the Rehoboth Art League.

ANNE SLOAN OLDACH (1948-   ) believes that many women struggle to free their emotions. It is this emotional freedom that she seeks to convey in her figurative sculpture. Oldach, who was born in Wilmington, studied anatomy and art history at the University of Pennsylvania and the Pennsylvania Academy of the Fine Arts. She earned master's degrees in art history from both the University of Pennsylvania and the University of Delaware. In 1967 Oldach learned to work in bronze as an apprentice to Delaware sculptor Charles Parks. She has exhibited in Wilmington and the Philadelphia area and won many prizes and awards.

Whether she is creating figurative or abstract sculpture, MARGARET SCOTT KINCANNON (1941-   ) is interested in exploring, developing, and utilizing the optical properties of the materials with which she works. Kincannon often carves pieces from acrylic material or constructs pieces from aluminum sheet material. Both media have reflective and refractive

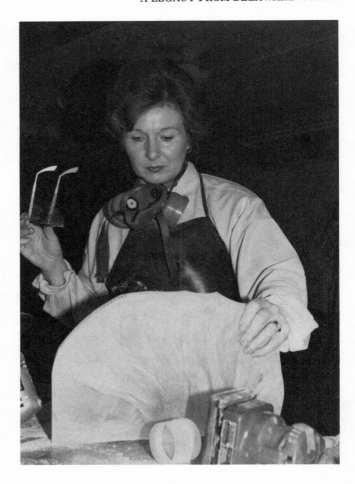

Margaret Scott Kincannon

properties that become an integral part of the sculpture. Kincannon was seven when her family emigrated from England to California. Later they moved to Delaware, where she completed high school at Ursuline Academy, Wilmington, and became a citizen of the United States. Kincannon earned bachelor's and master's degrees in art from the University of Delaware, where she continued post-graduate studies under Joe Moss. Kincannon's work has progressed from jewelry and other small pieces to larger-scale works. She has received many awards and her work is included in a number of private and corporate collections. She sculpted an acrylic trophy for a national tennis tournament sponsored by the Du Pont Company.

12

ANNE KROHN GRAHAM (1942-   ) was influenced by her aunt, Ruth S. Koach, a nationally known jeweler whose leadership in the field strongly impressed Graham. She holds degrees from the universities of Minnesota, Northern Iowa, and Iowa (M.F.A.). Graham has headed the jewelry and metals area of the University of Delaware Art Department since 1972. She also teaches in public and private schools as a visiting artist. Although Graham creates one-of-a-kind jewelry pieces on commission, she prefers to make objects and "sculptured combination" jewelry pieces because their larger size offers her more options in form and scale. She works

with the processes of fabrication or construction, casting, electroforming, and anodizing of titanium and aluminum. Graham's jewelry and other metal objects have been displayed in major juried and invitational exhibitions in New York and other art centers.

Natural shapes, particularly the organic forms of the sea, provide inspiration for distinctive metalwork by BETTY HELEN LONGHI (1937-   ). Living in Seaford, she has become interested in contrasting the textures and colors of shells with highly polished metal and often incorporates the shells into her jewelry. Holder of a bachelor of science degree from the University of Wisconsin, Longhi also attended Cranbrook Academy of Art. From her home, she conducts lectures, workshops, demonstrations, and special programs for school children. She taught workshops at the University of Delaware and participated in the Artist-in-Education program of the Delaware State Arts Council. Longhi exhibits work at important regional juried shows. She feels that jewelry should enhance the wearer and at the same time make a strong statement in itself. To this end, she designs stands to hold many of her pieces when they are not being worn, enabling them to succeed as sculptures as well as ornaments.

VERA E. KAMINSKI (1949-   ), a professor of art at the University of Delaware, creates mixed-material fiber fabrications, using traditional textile construction methods to develop non-traditional sculpture and architectural work for interiors. She also acts as a consultant on textile program development and lectures on her own works, historical textile traditions, and the contemporary art fabric movement.

ALICE CAFFREY ADELMAN (1924-   ) of Hockessin admires the directness, simplicity, and freshness of children's art and tries to capture those qualities using paint and clay. Her intuitive art has also led her into the human potential movement, the interpretation of dreams, and to leading dream workshops at the Tressler Center for Human Growth in Wilmington. Adelman's acrylic and watercolor paintings are non-representational or loosely based on landscape. She has shown her work in solo and group shows in Delaware and New York City.

Anne Krohn Graham

For fifteen years, SALLY W. COHEN (1943-   )

has made the arts accessible to people through community arts and lifelong learning programs. In the early 1970s, she was the first chair of Gallery 20, a community arts space in Newark where local and regional artists' work is exhibited. More than ten years later, Cohen serves as director of Gallery 20 while working full-time at the University of Delaware. She helped initiate the arts activities at Newark Community Day, an annual celebration for city residents. Cohen's interest in the arts helped her take an innovative approach to her work as manager of a career-oriented program for economically disadvantaged people. To provide work experience for some of them, she developed the New Castle County Band, a photography workshop, and a textile shop to make Bicentennial costumes for members of the band.

Cohen is chair of the City/County Arts Advisory Commission, of which she has been a member since 1984. She has served on the grants panel for the Delaware State Arts Council and on the evaluation team for the Artists-in-Education program. She helped create the statewide arts advocacy group Arts Aware in Delaware. Cohen is regional editor of the national art periodical *New Art Examiner.* Since 1979 she has received over fifteen grants for projects about traditional and contemporary art. Motivated by a strong interest in marketing the arts, Cohen has produced posters, brochures, and other publications to promote exhibitions, artists, and the concept of the visual arts as an integral part of daily living. In the early 1980s, Cohen became active in the American craft movement. She published two books documenting Delaware craftspeople and has become a resource for those interested in local craftspeople and the national craft scene.

The line between "craft" and "art" has become indistinct as artists seek out all kinds of materials to express their ideas. Similarly, many artists use their skills and interest in art to do various kinds of work in addition to making objects.

MARJORIE DEAN ANDRUK (1922-   ) of Wilmington emphasizes "originality of eye and thought." This approach enables her to exploit the possibilities of oil, acrylic, charcoal, pastel, clay, metal, and collage, continually "searching for original solutions to problems of expression." Andruk, who was born in Norfolk, Virginia, received a master of fine arts degree from the University of South Carolina and

later studied in Mexico. She taught drawing and painting at the University of South Carolina and at the Gertrude Herbert Art Institute in Augusta, Georgia. Andruk has conducted art seminars in Mexico and Venezuela as well as in Delaware and Georgia.

HELEN MASON (1926-   ) has been chair of the art department of the Tatnall School, Wilmington, since 1973. A graduate of the Rhode Island School of Design, Brown University, and the University of Delaware, she works mainly in ceramics, especially raku, and in metal and enamelling. Mason exhibits in Delaware and New Jersey and has received many grants and awards, including the National Endowment for the Arts/Delaware State Arts Council Individual Artist Grant for 1986-87.

WYNN BRESLIN (1932-   ) has exhibited her prints, drawings, sculptures, and oil and watercolor paintings. She has won many awards, including the national award from the American Federation of the Arts for watercolor. After earning an M.A. from the University of Delaware, Breslin taught art in schools. She resigned to devote more time to her own art, though she continued to teach privately. Breslin, a member of the Council of Delaware Artists, has held offices in the Diamond State Branch, National League of American Pen Women, and the Delaware Association for Art Education and served on the education committee for the Delaware Art Museum.

Mary Clark Keyser

MARY CLARK ("BOOTS") KEYSER of Yorklyn was the only woman in a class of fifty at the University of Pennsylvania School of Veterinary Medicine. She was licensed in Pennsylvania in 1944 and became the first female veterinarian in Delaware. Keyser retired from practice in 1962 to spend more time with her children and to pursue a career in art. Because of her veterinary background, Keyser's paintings of dogs and horses are lifelike and she has received many awards. Her paintings, primarily in oil, are in many corporate and private collections. Two were chosen as covers for Delaware Trust Company calendars.

JUDITH McCABE (1930-   ) uses her talent and interest in art to serve as volunteer advisor to state and national advisory committees and as an entrepreneur of art-related businesses. McCabe is a member of the Delaware Art Museum board of trustees, arts advisor for St. John Art International in New York, and a member of the City/County Arts Advisory Committee of Wilmington and New Castle County. She was appointed to the Advisory Committee on the Arts at the John F. Kennedy Center for the Performing Arts in 1982. In 1974 McCabe combined her devotion to art with a love of plants to establish The Blooming Arts, Inc., a freelance decor-

ating business that sold plants, paintings, and sculptures for home accents. She was a partner with CAROL BALICK in Artisans III, a Wilmington retail shop that specializes in handcrafts, from its founding until 1981. McCabe now owns Pot-Pour-Ri Plants and Gifts.

REBECCA RAUBACHER (1954-   ) won the Delaware State Arts Council Individual Artist Fellowship in the "emerging artist" category in 1984. She has exhibited widely in Delaware and Maryland and has had two one-person exhibitions in New York City. Raubacher owns the Raubacher Gallery in Dover.

DOROTHY TRUMAN (1925-   ) operates Truman Gallery in New Castle. She has shown leadership in showcasing local talent since she took over the Ware Gallery in Arden after its founder, Hamilton D. Ware, died in 1968. Truman, who was born in Connecticut, has won prizes for her own oil and watercolor paintings and has been active in many state art and cultural groups. She has been active in the Diamond State Branch, National League of American Pen Women, and the Brandywine Arts Festival.

Daughter of Delaware artist Walt Stan, CYNTHIA STAN (1953-   ) teaches art at Wilmington Friends School while she actively pursues her art career. She has exhibited collages and paintings regularly since 1974 and has received many awards. Stan was

Judith McCabe

Cynthia Stan

15

granted a fellowship in 1976 to pursue a master's degree at Pennsylvania State University. In 1982 she was one of twelve artists selected to exhibit in the National Print Competition of the Los Angeles Print Society and was awarded an Individual Artist Fellowship from the Delaware State Arts Council.

Delaware's art scene owes much to its location. Close to New York City, with its ever-changing ex-perimental trends, the state maintains strong ties to Brandywine Valley realism and the vitality of regional performing arts. Delaware women, drawing from both of these centers, are active as individual performing and visual artists. They perform, create works of art, and teach and direct others. Women continue to be leaders in the many groups that promote the arts and bring them to the people of Delaware and the region.

16

UP THE LADDER:

Women in Business and Management

Jyotsana Dhiren Patel

Many women have entered the field of business in recent years as it has become more open to them. Women in the past usually entered business because the death or lack of a husband deprived them of financial support. Traditionally limited to being secretaries (though sometimes with a good deal of unacknowledged influence), women have only recently begun to attain positions of power in significant numbers in all types of businesses.

A traditional business role for women is farming, where a wife shares responsibilities with her husband. SARAH S. PRATT (1909-   ) grew up on a farm in Ohio. She graduated from college during the Great Depresssion and could not find a job in her field. She then earned a nursing degree, but, as she says, "ended up nursing baby chicks." She and her husband established a hatchery between Middletown and Odessa that was the first in Delaware to dispense eggs to customers from an automatic vending machine. Pratt was a charter member of the Middletown chapter of the American Association of Univer-sity Women (AAUW) and has been an active member of the Cooch's Bridge Daughters of the American Revolution (DAR) and the Business and Professional Women's Club in Middletown.

Since 1923, when CECILE LONG STEELE (1900-1940) of Ocean View revolutionized the "spring chicken" system by incubating chickens the year round, women have continued to be a major factor

in one of Delaware's fastest-growing industries. For her contributions, Steele was selected for the Hall of Fame of Delaware Women in 1983. SANDRA LAYFIELD of Dagsboro is typical of the modern-day woman who manages the broiler houses while her husband oversees the rest of the farm work. Instead of incubating the chickens as Steele did, Layfield receives deliveries of 73,000 two- or three-day-old chicks at once from large hatcheries. They also bring the chicks' feed, which is stored in large automatic feeder bins. The broilers are usually White Plymouth Rocks, sometimes mixed with Barred Rocks or New Hampshire Reds, because they tend to grow rapidly. Layfield monitors the thermostat, changes from starter to finisher feed, keeps the water cool, and sweeps the floors. If she is lucky and no disease has been carried into the chicken house, the birds are ready for market after about seven weeks.

Real estate is another business in which large numbers of women are employed. Hours are flexible, so work can be juggled around raising children and maintaining a home. Most women sell residences, using their domestic experience to sell buyers on the livability of a certain house. However, there is greater earning potential in commercial real estate and in real estate development. A few women have entered those fields.

The first woman in Delaware who received the Certified Commercial Investment Member (CCIM)

17

designation was BECKY PAUL ABEL (1948-   ) of Wilmington. Only 1 percent (approximately 1,500) of all real-estate sales agents in the country are CCIMs. Abel entered real estate by accident rather than by plan. After two years of teaching school, she worked as a secretary for a real-estate firm before earning her real-estate license in 1973. Now an investment specialist for B. Gary Scott Realtors, she teaches courses in selective financing for the University of Delaware's Continuing Education program. She is a member of the New Castle County Board of the Delaware State Association of Realtors and serves on the City of Wilmington Rental Housing Task Force. Abel also invests in real estate.

BONNIE M. SHERR (1946-   ) is principal and vice-president of City Systems, a Wilmington real estate development company that specializes in renovating, leasing, and managing certified historic buildings. Sherr grew up in Philadelphia and took courses in marketing, accounting, and business at the University of Delaware. Her job as a sales and relocation associate with Sachs and Associates Realtors made her aware of the potential market for

Bonnie M. Sherr

urban residences for transplanted executives. Passage of the state's Financial Development Center Act of 1981 brought more people from larger cities to Wilmington and increased the demand for such housing.

Sherr left a position in commercial real-estate sales to establish City Systems with a partner in 1981. The firm's projects include developing and managing small apartment buildings in Quaker Hill and Trolley Square, a European-style hotel on Market Street, a garden apartment complex in North Wilmington, and office condominiums in the Christina Gateway. Sherr has received the Braunstein Young Leadership Award of the Jewish Federation of Delaware.

Vice-president of P. Gerald White, Inc., Realtors, JANICE M. TRAYNOR (1953-   ) negotiates leases for offices and industrial space throughout New Castle County for commercial clients. She began her career in the departments of Planning and Development and Real Estate and Housing of the City of Wilmington and subsequently worked for the

Sandra Layfield

18

Janice M. Traynor

JENNIFER THOMPSON (1945-   ), a Lewes resident, has combined a lifelong fascination with science and art into a career as an architect. She has managed her own architectural firm for twelve years and now works from offices in her Victorian home. She finds this a satisfying way to combine a career with caring for her children.

When Thompson received her degree in architecture from the University of Virginia in 1968, she was only the second woman in its history to do so. She has designed private residences, townhouses, and commercial projects in Sussex County and Maryland. Thompson's public service includes work with the Rehoboth Art League and the Rehoboth Co-op Nursery School. She chairs the building committee for the Delmarva Easter Seals Rehabilitation Center in Georgetown and is a member of the Planning Committee for the Historical District of Lewes.

MARGARET ("PEGGY") MERVINE (1933-   ) of Greenwood began building houses when her husband John started a backyard project that quickly became too large for one person. They built their

Wilmington Economic Development Corporation. In 1984 Traynor became the first female director of commerce for the city. During the year she spent in that position, she negotiated three Urban Development Action Grant (UDAG) loans resulting in $20 million of investment and obtained foreign trade zone status for the Port of Wilmington. Traynor serves on boards and committees for Wilmington Women in Business, the Salvation Army, Read Aloud Delaware, and the YMCA, and is on the Mayor's Tax Incentive Task Force for Wilmington.

Delaware women also excel as architects and designers. VICTORINE DU PONT HOMSEY (1900-   ), an architect, established an architectural firm in Wilmington with her husband in 1935. The designs of Victorine & Samuel Homsey, Inc., include the Delaware Art Museum, the Pavillion addition to Winterthur Museum, churches and schools throughout Delaware, and the houses for the U.S. ambassador and deputy chief of missions in Teheran, Iran.

Samuel and Victorine du Pont Homsey

19

Margaret Mervine

prise now operates twenty-four plants throughout the world. Gore, corporate secretary-treasurer, has been deeply involved in the development, evolution, and direction of the company. In addition to being profitable, the business has been hailed for its distinctive management style, using a task-force approach to solve problems. The company is a family affair, with one son as president and three daughters and the other son as directors.

In spite of the satisfaction of working with associates all over the world, Genevieve Gore still considers caring for her family her primary career. "For a woman, that's most important." She grew up on a cattle ranch in Wyoming, rode horseback to school, and developed a self-sufficiency that enabled her to deal with problems independent of outside assistance. Gore serves on the board of Newark Senior Citizens and the Newark School Council and is an active participant in music and sports. She received the Medal of Distinction from the University of Delaware in 1983.

first building in a chicken house. Nanticoke Homes, Inc., was started in 1971 to find better ways to build and sell houses. The result is a company that produces modular houses, built from components made on an assembly line. Peggy Mervine has done almost every job in the company, purchasing materials, drawing plans, accounting, figuring the payroll, and selling the houses, and is presently secretary/treasurer. Mervine believes that women bring distinctive gifts such as dedication, patience, and sensitivity to any role that they undertake. She is also active in her community and church. She declares, "This is the land of opportunity. . . . It does take hard work and determination to solve the problems you're going to have along the way [but] it's worth it all. . . . Only in America can what happened in my backyard happen."

A growing number of women, like Mervine, own their own businesses. GENEVIEVE WALTON GORE (1913-   ) is co-founder of W.L. Gore & Associates, Inc., of Newark. Her late husband, Wilbert, developed Gore-Tex fabric, a waterproof material used in parkas, flight suits, tents, and skin grafts. When the business, established in 1958, outgrew the basement of their house, they bought the nearby cornfield and built their plant for the manufacture of PTFE, insulated wire and cable. The high-technology enter-

LOZELLE DeLUZ is president of DeLuz Management Consultants and co-owner of two McDonald's restaurants. She has a Ph.D. in urban affairs and public policy from the University of Delaware and was vice-president and editor-in-chief for the language arts division of J.B. Lippincott Co. and a teacher and principal in the Washington, D.C., public schools.

DeLuz is involved with numerous professional and civic associations, including the National Coalition of 100 Black Women and the Minority Business Association of Delaware. She is a member of the boards of Christina Cultural Arts Center; the Wilmington Music School; the Children's Bureau of Delaware; and United Way of Delaware and is a trustee of the Medical Center of Delaware. DeLuz has served on the State Personnel Commission and the Mayor's Advisory Council for the City of Wilmington, among others. She received the Brandywine Professional Association's Outstanding Achiever among Entrepreneurs honor in 1983 and the Annual Award of the Delaware Region, National Conference of Christians and Jews in 1985. The latter award was given to DeLuz for "being an exemplary model to small business people, for her positive force and her active leadership . . . serving the youth of Delaware . . . and for her visible commitment to the vision of

Wilbert and Genevieve Walton Gore

human dignity, equity, and a community working together."

Delaware's delegate to the White House Conference on Small Business, JYOTSANA DHIREN ("JYO") PATEL (1945-   ) owns the Jyo Patel Network, including two travel agencies, a motor coach tour company, and a travel school. After receiving a master's degree in advertising and public relations in her native India, she worked for Air India in Bombay. Patel combined being a mother with developing her career after she made the difficult decision to come to the United States. She taught at the University of Texas and at a private school in Houston before she reentered the travel business in Texas and North Carolina. She managed travel departments for Farmers Bank and Bank of Delaware before starting her own business. Patel helped found the National Association of Asian-Americans of Indian Descent and served on the boards of directors of Soroptomist International of Wilmington, the Inter-

national Air Transport Association, the American Civil Liberties Union, and Wilmington Women in Business. She is a member of the Governor's International Trade Council.

Carter Alan Ltd., a jewelry design store, opened in Kennett Square, Pennsylvania, in 1983 with CHERYL CARTER-PIERCE (1948-   ) as president. She founded Delaware Gem Exchange and is studying gemology. Carter-Pierce's bachelor's degree is in psychology. Her community service includes proposing and administering a project for battered women and their children at a shelter for battered women in Arden.

MARGARET E. ("PEGGI") MITTEN (1948-   ) represents her Delaware family's fourth generation of female entrepreneurs. Although Mitten did not learn of this history until she already owned her own business, she believes she was influenced by coming from a long line of independent women. Mitten

21

Lozelle DeLuz

her goals and had a good grasp of her strengths and weaknesses, two attributes she considers necessary for anyone planning to go into business. Her achievements as a business leader will be featured in a book on female entrepreneurship by California writer Joanne Pugh; Mitten is one of only two Delaware women so honored. She served on the board of directors of the League of Women Voters, both in Wilmington and in Sussex County, and on the Brandywine College Executive Alumni Council.

The specialty clothing store owned by MARTHA MORGAN has become a popular place for New Castle County businesswomen to buy their working wardrobes. She opened Morgan's in 1979 in the Trolley Square area of Wilmington, a desirable location according to market research. Morgan had acquired nearly eight years of business and marketing expertise in Allied Stores and Macy's/Bamberger's. To increase her skill in fiscal management, she took special training at the Amos Tuck School of Dartmouth College. Morgan often speaks to youth groups about the importance of hard work.

Marketing, an increasingly important tool in operating a profitable business, is a field many women have entered. DIXIE JANE THOMPSON DE RIEMER (1919-   ) founded the market research firm of Jane De Riemer Associates in 1981. Originally a home economist, she spent eleven years with the Du Pont Company, followed by a period of teaching home economics and working in a women's specialty store. When De Riemer returned to Du Pont in the Textile Fibers Department, she helped develop new marketing and merchandising techniques for three new synthetic fibers. De Riemer's retail training program grew in size and scope as she taught other specialists to assist her. After a period of homemaking, she worked as an independent marketing research analyst on contract with Du Pont and then founded her own company. De Riemer has been a member of the boards of the Mental Health Association and the American Cancer Society and is co-founder of Delaware's Reach-to-Recovery program. She was presented with the American Cancer Society's Teresse Lasser Award in 1982.

For Winterthur Museum and Gardens, TERRY LEARNED (1924-   ) oversees marketing of the shop, catalog, and antique reproduction program. She worked in retailing while raising two children

started her business in the middle of an economic recession with only the $3,000 she had earned by working as a temporary secretary. Wordtech, Inc., Wilmington's first word-processing service bureau, opened in February 1981 in rented office space, with rented equipment and Mitten as the sole (unpaid) employee. She had only enough money to pay three months of expenses, but by then the business was paying for itself. Mitten soon hired a staff, moved to larger quarters, and bought the building that contained her offices as well as other tenants. She sold the business in 1986.

Wordtech was not founded on a whim. A feasibility study and months of planning, along with her own hard work, turned a potentially risky business into a solid financial venture. Mitten was sure of

22

and two stepchildren and believes the secret of combining family and career is "a good housekeeper and a good secretary." When Learned's husband died, she moved to take advantage of diverse opportunities in order to support her family. She rehabilitated buildings, designed the merchandising plan for a shopping center, was executive director of an environmental organization, and owned a country store that specialized in New England handcrafts. Learned designed the merchandising strategy for the "Treasures of Tutankhamen" exhibition at the Seattle Art Museum. This experience led to work as a catalog consultant to museums throughout the United States and Canada and ultimately to Winterthur.

JAN JESSUP (1948-   ) works for Everfast, Inc., as director of marketing for its seventy Calico Corners retail stores and managing director of the Everfast Decorating Program division. Jessup, from Glendale, California, had been employed at an advertising agency in Portland, Oregon, before accepting a position with Wilmington-based Everfast. She notes that "instead of job-hopping outside this company, I have progressed by expanding my responsibilities within the company." Jessup is a founding member and former president of Wilmington Women in Business and member of the Delaware Business Council for WHYY and of the Junior League Community Advisory Board. She serves on the board and is chair of the Properties Planning Committee for the Chesapeake Bay Girl Scout Council. Jessup is on the Wilmington Arts Commission and the Physical Planning Advisory Board for the City of Wilmington, where she lives. She has served on the Steering Committee for Common Cause of Delaware and on campaign committees for Governor Michael Castle and Wilmington Mayor Daniel Frawley.

KATHLEEN M. MEYER (1943-   ), a marketing specialist with the Du Pont Company, was also a founding member of Wilmington Women in Business and of the Delaware Association of Professional Women. She is the founder and current president of People-to-People International, Delaware Chapter. During 1985 she led an official state delegation to the People's Republic of China under the auspices of People-to-People. She will lead a second delegation to China in 1987 at the invitation of that nation's Foreign Ministry.

*   *   *

Women, long involved in banking, are moving into higher-level positions. LINDA N. OUTLAW (1948-   ), vice-president and commercial loan officer for the Bank of Delaware, lives in Wilmington. She has worked for the bank since 1970 and has taught finance at Drexel University. Outlaw is a member of the Bank of Delaware Speakers Bureau and of the Wilmington Women in Business Budget Committee and is a past president of the Wilmington Chapter of the American Institute of Banking. She was treasurer of the Minikin Opera Company.

DOROTHY J. WHITE (1945-   ) of Twin Oaks, Pennsylvania, is vice-president, Human Resources Group manager for the Bank of Delaware. She was promoted steadily in the bank from her first position as a teller. White placed third in a national public speaking contest sponsored by the American Institute of Banking in 1977. She serves on the board of the Wilmington Youth Development Corporation and has held leadership positions with United Way of Delaware, which presented her with a civic award in 1983. In 1986 White began a term as president of the board of the Delaware Lung Association,

Dorothy J. White

23

the first woman and first layperson to serve in that position since EMILY P. BISSELL, early in the century. Two groups that White leads under the auspices of her church, are the "passions" of her life. She explores the relevancy of the Bible in modern lives with her women's Bible study group and meets with a group of nineteen high-school girls after school.

ELEANOR DUGUID CRAIG (1938-   ) is also involved in the field of finance. Since 1962 she has been on the faculty of the University of Delaware economics department, where she is an associate professor. The College Council of Business and Economics named her Outstanding Teacher in 1973 and in 1981. Craig has written frequently for economics, financial, and banking journals.

Eleanor Duguid Craig

Under Governor Pierre S. du Pont IV, Craig was chair of the Delaware Economic and Financial Advisory Council, which provides the state's official revenue forecasts and offers economic advice to the General Assembly and the governor. She is still a consultant to du Pont. Craig also serves on the board of the Bank of Delaware and Swarthmore College. Craig has held advisory positions on boards and councils for women's issues, desegregation, public utility regulation, and tax law changes.

Accountants help entrepreneurs and individuals manage their resources effectively. TATIANA BRANDT ("TANYA") COPELAND (1941-   ) is president of Greenville-based Tebec Associates Limited, a consulting firm in the field of national and international taxation. The company is engaged in tax planning and financial and investment advice to individuals, trusts, estates, and corporations in Europe and the United States. Copeland holds an M.B.A. from the University of California at Berkeley and is a C.P.A. Her previous experience was in international operations, capitalizing on her background as the daughter of Russian parents, born in East Germany and educated in South America and California, and on her fluency in six languages. As manager of the International Department, Copeland coordinated the business analysis and internal reporting of the Du Pont Company's worldwide operations.

In 1981 President Ronald Reagan appointed Copeland to the Presidential Advisory Committee for Trade Negotiations, the only woman among twenty-four members. She is a fellow of the Aspen Institute for Humanistic Studies. Copeland has a special interest in music (the Russian composer Rachmaninoff was a relative) and serves on the boards of the New York City Opera, the Delaware Symphony Association, the Grand Opera House, and the Wilmington Music School.

CAROLYN J. MANN FAUSNAUGH (1944-   ), a C.P.A., owns the accounting firm Carolyn J. Fausnaugh Associates. Previously, she was a partner with Whisman & Associates and manager of the Accounting Department of Avon Products, Inc. As a member of the Small Business Committee of the Delaware State Chamber of Commerce, Fausnaugh advises the committee and legislators on legislation that affects taxation of small businesses. She has been a moderator for the White House Conference of

Small Businesses. Fausnaugh is assistant treasurer of the New Castle County Economic Development Corporation and is involved with Newark Housing for Senior Citizens and the City of Newark Development Block Grant Advisory Committee. Fausnaugh came to accounting by accident, her interest kindled by a required introductory accounting course in college. Since then, she has earned a master's degree in taxation from Widener University and has taught in the College of Business and Economics of the University of Delaware.

ANN TAYLOR TANSEY (1944-   ) is a partner in the Wilmington accounting firm Cover & Rossiter. She is a past president of the Quota Club of Wilmington and an officer in Quota Club International, and has held national and local offices in the National Organization for Women. Tansey has served on committees for the YWCA, Goldey Beacom College, the United Way of Delaware, New Castle County Head Start, and Developmental Child Care, Inc.

JERELINE A. COLEMAN is a senior accountant

Jereline A. Coleman

Faith A. Wohl

with Delmarva Power and Light Company. She has taught accounting at the University of Delaware. Coleman was the first black woman to become a C.P.A. in Delaware and has served as president of the American Society of Women Accountants. She has contributed her talents to local organizations such as the Wilmington Parking Authority, Delaware Alliance of Professional Women, Wilmington Women in Business, Christina Cultural Arts Center, and the United Way of Delaware.

Many female corporate employees work in the field of communications. FAITH A. WOHL (1936-   ) of Landenberg, Pennsylvania, is director of Corporate Affairs, a division of the External Affairs Department of the Du Pont Company. She is responsible for the company's internal and external publications, employee communication services, the annual report, annual meeting, staff functions that involve corporate contributions, and special community projects. Before becoming a Du Pont employee in 1975, Wohl held communications positions in New York State. She serves on the YWCA board of directors. Wohl has concentrated her energies on what she calls her "two clear (and sometimes conflicting) priorities," her job and raising her three children. She believes they are her contribution to the community. In 1980 Wohl received the YWCA Tribute to Women and Industry Award.

As vice-president of the Delaware State Chamber of Commerce, RUTH L. MANKIN (1932-   ) is

Ruth L. Mankin

26

responsible for public affairs and community relations and is editor of the *State Chamber News*. She coordinates the activities of the chamber's environmental affairs, business and economic development, foreign trade, and employee relations committees. Mankin has a degree in speech. From 1976 to 1981 she was press secretary and special assistant to former U.S. Representative Thomas B. Evans and managed his successful 1980 congressional campaign. In 1978 she was a Republican candidate for the Delaware General Assembly. Between 1981 and 1983, Mankin was public affairs director for the regional office of the U.S. Department of Health and Human Services in Philadelphia. She has served on boards or committees of Wilmington Waterways, the March of Dimes, the Child Care Connection, Leadership Delaware, Wesley College, and the Public Relations Roundtable of Delaware.

IRENE E. SHADOAN (1946-   ) is public affairs manager, petrochemicals, in the Public Affairs Department of the Du Pont Company. She is responsible for all public affairs needs of the Petrochemical Department, writing speeches and press releases and managing media relations. Her previous Du Pont

Irene E. Shadoan

position, as the first woman corporate coordinator for Delaware economic development, included serving on local boards involved in economic development. Shadoan was the second female gubernatorial press secretary in the nation when she held that post for Governor Sherman W. Tribbitt from 1973 to 1977. She has worked in broadcasting and for the Associated Press in Dover and Dallas.

When Shadoan was starting her career in the late sixties, she found that "women were treated as temporary workers who would work for a few years until marrying and having children. . . . Women in general had to convince employers that they wanted careers, not temporary work." She believes that, although women "have made great progress, equality is not yet ours." Shadoan was the first woman to serve on the Metropolitan Board of the YMCA in New Castle County. She was named "Young Career Woman" of the Delaware Federation of Business and Professional Women's Clubs by the Dover Chapter in 1974, "Delaware's Outstanding Young Woman for 1973" by the Washington, D.C.-based Outstanding Young Women in America Program, and has been honored by the Delaware State Chamber of Commerce for efforts on behalf of economic development in the state. Shadoan is a reader for Recording for the Blind and has served on the boards of Wilmington Waterways and the Wilmington Economic Development Corporation.

When Wilmington Women in Business was launched in 1979, LINDA C. DRAKE (1948-   ) was a founding member of the women's network. With an M.A. in communication from the University of Massachusetts and experience with local firms, she is now with Blue Cross/Blue Shield of Delaware. Drake serves on the board of directors of United Way. She won the Trailblazer Award of the Delaware Alliance of Professional Women in 1983.

ARLENE ("DALE") BERGER STRATTON (1933-   ) brought a technical background to her corporate position. She was vice-president and director, Research Products, for New England Nuclear Corporation, a division of the Du Pont Company. Stratton, who holds an M.S. in mathematical statistics from Rutgers University, received the Society of Photographic Scientists and Engineers' Service Award in 1968. She has served on the Technical Service Board of the Graphic Arts Technical Foundation

27

Evelyn Callahan

and the Industry Advisory Committee of West Virginia Institute of Technology. Stratton is a Presbyterian elder and a volunteer reader for Recording for the Blind.

Awarded the National Business Leadership Silver Award in 1986 by Junior Achievement, EVELYN CALLAHAN saw Junior Achievement of Delaware grow from 371 to 6,300 members in her twelve years of service. She is a purchasing agent for Hercules, Inc.

MOIRA KATHERINE DONOGHUE (1951-   ) was the only woman corporate officer of Delmarva Power and Light Company. She was elected assistant corporate secretary by the board of directors in 1983. In 1981 Donoghue was the first woman hired in the company's Legal Department; she is now manager of the Real Estate Division. Donoghue grew up in Alexandria, Virginia, and attended Marshall-Wythe School of Law, College of William and Mary. She was president of the board of directors of the YWCA of New Castle County. Donoghue served on the Wilmington Planning Commission and the Wilmington

Economic Development Corporation and is active in Wilmington Women in Business.

Like Donoghue, many lawyers use their legal skills as corporate executives. Others are judges or work in government, non-profit organizations, or in private law firms. When SYBIL WARD and EVANGILYN BARSKY passed the Delaware Bar examination in 1923, they became the first Delaware women to enter the legal profession.

More than two hundred women have been admitted to the Delaware Bar since then, including, in 1977, the first black woman, PAULETTE SULLIVAN MOORE. Significantly, more than one hundred fifty women have joined the profession within the past six years, reflecting both the national thrust toward careers in law and growing acceptance of women in the field. A number of women have made significant contributions to law in the First State.

ROXANA CANNON ARSHT (1915-   ) was the first and only female judge in Delaware throughout her twelve-year tenure on the bench, 1971-83. Five women are now judges in the state. Arsht, who was born in Wilmington, attended the University of Pennsylvania Law School and was admitted to the Delaware Bar in 1941. She spent the next two decades raising her family and participating in community activities. In 1962 she began nine years as a master of Family Court, working full time without pay. When funds became available in 1971, she was appointed a full judge. In a speech honoring Arsht, Vincent J. Poppiti observed that "she developed [a] unique talent of expressing the sense of the law so that those who appeared before her not only understood and accepted the decision rendered, but also saw the workings of the system and felt a part of the process." Arsht comments, "Of the lawyers . . . who appeared before me in Family Court, the women, on the average, were better prepared, more conscientious, and more personable than the men. These women are making it easier for their daughters and younger sisters to enter and achieve in whatever field they may choose." Arsht was chosen for the Hall of Fame of Delaware Women in 1986.

HELEN SHAFFER BALICK (1935-   ), Delaware's second female judge, began her legal career as a secretary for a law firm after high school. For ten years she did work that is usually done by a

Helen Shaffer Balick

paralegal today. With encouragement from her husband and friends, Balick was admitted to Dickinson School of Law despite her lack of a formal college education. She was the first female probate administrator of Girard Trust Bank, Philadelphia, and the first woman staff attorney for the Community Legal Aid Society in Delaware before becoming a master of Family Court. Balick became a bankruptcy judge for the U.S. District Court for the District of Delaware in 1980, after serving as both judge and magistrate beginning in 1974. She has been president of the board of trustees of the Community Legal Aid Society and a member of the Citizens Advisory Committee of Wilmington and the Wilmington Board of Education. Balick received the Trailblazer Award of the Delaware Alliance of Professional Women in 1984.

PEGGY L. ABLEMAN (1950-   ) has been associate judge of Family Court since 1983. She was born in New York City but grew up in Wilmington and worked as an associate in the law firm of Connolly, Bove & Lodge. Before becoming a judge, Ableman served as an assistant United States attorney for the District of Delaware, the first woman to hold that position in this state. She has held several offices in the Delaware State Bar Association, is a

board member of the Chesapeake Bay Girl Scout Council, and has assisted with fundraising events for the American Cancer Society and the American Heart Association. Ableman was inspired in her pursuit of a law career by her father. He began law school while she was in high school, just five years before she entered Emory University School of Law.

JANE KELLOND RICHARDS ROTH (1935-   ) became the first female judge in the U.S. District Court for the District of Delaware when she was confirmed by the United States Senate in 1985. After five years of foreign service with the U.S. Department of State, Roth earned a law degree from Harvard University. In 1965 she passed the bar examination and entered private law practice in Wilmington with the firm Richards, Layton & Finger. There she specialized in defending physicians and hospitals in malpractice suits. Roth also campaigns for her husband, U.S. Senator William V. Roth, Jr., in election years and makes speeches for him when he is not available. She was president of the Delaware Chapter, Arthritis Foundation, for almost ten years, is a trustee of the Historical Society of Delaware, and assists the Delaware Learning Center, the Chesapeake Bay Girl Scout Council, and Delaware Library Associates.

Another trailblazer in the federal government is BRERETON STURTEVANT (1921-   ) the first woman appointed to the Board of Appeals, U.S. Patent Office. She has been examiner-in-chief since 1971. Before moving to Washington, D.C., where she grew up, Sturtevant lived in Wilmington for over twenty years. Following law school at Temple University, she worked as a research chemist for the Du Pont Company. Sturtevant became the first female law clerk for the Delaware Superior and Supreme courts in 1950 and subsequently specialized in patent and trademark litigation as a partner in the law firm Connolly, Bove & Lodge.

Other women work in state government. During the term of Governor Pierre S. du Pont IV, BATTLE RANKIN ROBINSON (1938-   ) of Georgetown became the first woman to serve as assistant counsel to a Delaware governor. A recognized expert on the constitutional powers of the governor, Robinson was also the first woman to run for lieutenant governor of the state. She was appointed a Family Court judge by Governor Michael Castle in 1985. A graduate of Yale Law School, she became the first woman to serve as a trial attorney with the Civil Rights Division of the U.S. Department of Justice in the 1960s. In the early 1970s, Robinson was the first female attorney for the Republican caucus in the Delaware House of Representatives.

She was also the first woman admitted to practice in Sussex County. Robinson was selected Woman of the Year by Delaware Business and Professional Women in 1979. She was president of the Sussex County Arts Council.

REGINA M. MULLEN (1948-   ) of New Castle has been a deputy attorney general with the Delaware Department of Justice since graduation from the University of Virginia School of Law in 1973. In 1979 Mullen was the first woman appointed to the Board of Bar Examiners of the State of Delaware. That same year she was named state solicitor and served on the senior staff of the attorney general. Mullen managed a staff of thirty-five in the department's Civil Division (at that time the largest law firm in the state) and was responsible for providing legal services to all state agencies.

In 1981 Mullen presented a case before the United States Supreme Court. She also became the first woman from Delaware to serve as a delegate to the Judicial Conference of the United States Court of Appeals for the Third Circuit. Mullen, a native of Cambridge, Massachusetts, became chief of Delaware's Financial Services Unit in 1983.

NANCY JANE MULLEN (1946-   ) specializes in criminal law, a field in which there are few women. She is an assistant public defender in the Office of the Public Defender, the first woman to hold that position. Mullen chiefly defends people accused of felonies and has been counsel of record for several capital defendants. She has been involved in the litigation resulting from Delaware's death-penalty statute, enacted in 1977. Mullen has taken part in litigation challenging mandatory sentences, commutation of sentences, and other sentencing matters.

She was also a deputy attorney general in the Delaware Department of Justice. Mullen, a native of Washington, D.C., was a drug counselor in the Delaware Office of Substance Abuse before attending George Washington University School of Law. Mullen serves on the Court Long-Range Planning Committee for Delaware and on the Supreme Court Rules Committee, which make recommendations on operating the courts more efficiently. In 1982 Mullen received the New Lawyer's Distinguished Service Award of the Delaware Bar Association. She has been a board member of the Mental Health Association of Delaware and is on the board of the Community Legal Aid Society.

MARY M. McDONOUGH (1953-   ) is the first female executive director of the Community Legal Aid Society. She is responsible for administering a statewide law firm that provides civil legal services to low-income, elderly, and handicapped Delawareans. While attending New York University School of Law, McDonough assisted in creating the Public Interest Law Foundation, which subsidizes public-interest projects nationwide. She also handled the federal class-action suit that sought removal of lead-based paint from public housing.

McDonough, a Wilmington native, is a board member of the Ministry of Caring, the corporation that operates the Emmanuel Dining Room, and of the Mary Mother of Hope Houses, which are emergency shelters for homeless women. She lives in Hope House II, where she is a counselor. A contributing editor to the *Women and the Law Handbook*, McDonough received the Delaware Bar Association New Lawyer's Distinguished Service Award in 1983 and the Community Builder Award from the Delaware Region, National Conference of Christians and Jews, in 1984.

AIDA WASERSTEIN (DOROSHAW) (1948-   ) worked for the Community Legal Aid Society as staff attorney, acting director, and deputy director. A native of Cuba, she immigrated to the United States alone at the age of thirteen. After learning English, Waserstein graduated *cum laude* from Bryn Mawr College and then from the University of Pennsylvania Law School. Upon leaving the Community Legal Aid Society, she was staff attorney for the Education Law Center in Philadelphia, where she worked on cases dealing with special education, school finance, and bilingual education. In 1979 Waserstein began working for a private Wilmington law firm; she started the partnership Waserstein & Demsey with CHRISTINE DEMSEY in 1984. Waserstein is active in the Delaware State Bar Association and is a member of the board of the National Women's Law Center.

Aida Waserstein

CHRISTINE McDERMOTT HARKER (1947-   ) is executive director of the Delaware Council on Crime and Justice, a private, nonprofit agency dedicated to improving the quality and effectiveness of Delaware's criminal justice system. She has been assistant city solicitor and chief prosecutor for the City of Wilmington and executive director of the Delaware Criminal Justice Planning Commission. Harker has served on numerous criminal justice committees for the state and region, on the Wilmington City Charter Revision Commission, and on the YWCA board of directors.

She was one of the developers of Womanpower, a program that trains women for jobs in heavy industry. The program has received a national award and has been cited as a success by President Ronald Reagan. Harker has taught criminal justice administration, criminal law, and social policy in the Department of Sociology of the University of Delaware. She began working toward a Master of Public Administration degree in the Department of Urban Affairs in 1983 while continuing to be employed.

Some Delaware women are in private practice. Native Wilmingtonian JOANNA REIVER (1946-   ) is a partner with her husband, Robert E. Schlusser,

in the Wilmington law firm of Schlusser & Reiver. Prior to forming their own law firm in 1982, they were directors of the law firm of Murdoch & Walsh. Reiver specializes in estate planning and estate administration. She has served as secretary and as vice-chair of the Delaware Bar Association Section on Estates and Trusts and as a member of the board of directors of the Estate Planning Council of Delaware. She is a member of the Chancery Court Fiduciary Rules Advisory Committee. A frequent speaker and writer on the subject of estate planning, Reiver attended the University of Delaware and West Virginia University and received a law degree from the Catholic University of America in 1976.

Delaware's outstanding women lawyers work in the private sector and government, civil and criminal law, and on cases of national, state, and local importance. Women have worked to extend legal service to poor people; many are active in community service. Despite growing ranks of female lawyers, there are still relatively few in high-level positions. Those women who are judges and in other prominent positions are demonstrating their competence and opening the way for more women to follow them and make an impact.

Joanna Reiver

31

In the business world, the fields of real estate, banking, and stockbroking have been friendly to women of talent. Large corporations, however, have been particularly slow to accept female managers. Male-dominated social structures and networks have hampered the efforts of qualified women to attain high-level positions.

Generally, farming and other family businesses afford a degree of flexibility in combining career and family that more rigid corporations do not allow. Entrepreneurs may also be able to tailor their business responsibilities to their personal needs, particularly if they can afford to forego immediate profits in exchange for the ability to allocate some of their time to family. FAITH WOHL observes that juggling family and career "is perhaps hardest of all in the [corporate] business world, which, almost by definition, is relatively structured, and also a group endeavor. Those women who choose the arts, or professions like medicine or law may have more choices as to allocation of their time and may also be able to work in a variety of ways. . . . Those of us who work for corporations may not have those options." On the other hand, business jobs usually pay higher salaries than many other types of work, which enables women to hire help.

Women have entered virtually all types of business and have made significant progress in being accepted for the work they do. They are learning to build networks and to undertake the challenges of success.

SPREADING THE WORD:

Women In Communications

Georgi Marquisee

Verbal, written, and visual communication is an important aspect of human endeavor. It is a component of the work done by many of the women in this book. In this chapter, however, the medium of communication is the career.

Many women write poetry and fiction. EDNAH DEEMER LEACH (1907-1983), appointed first poet laureate of Delaware by Governor Walter Bacon in 1947, began writing poetry when she was twelve. She believed that "there is a poem in everything we see," and over the years filled notebooks and dresser drawers with simply written poems and humorous verses that have been a source of fun and amusement for many Delawareans. Leach was so busy giving poetry readings, serving as a volunteer for the Traveler's Aid Society and the Governor Bacon Health Center, and working for over thirty years as chair of the Toy for Every Tot campaign, that she never sought publication for many of her poems.

ANTONIA BISSELL LAIRD (1932-   ) revels in nature, explores relationships, and captures the subtleties of social situations in her poetry. Her poems have appeared in magazines as diverse as *Ladies Home Journal, Gourmet, Ski,* and *Delaware Today. A Melody of Words* (1978) and *Echo of My Heart* (1982) are among her published volumes of poetry.

She gives poetry readings under the auspices of Artistic Productions, Inc. Laird, a native Delawarean, has given many hours of service to others on the boards of the University of Delaware, Wilmington Institute Free Library, and the Historical Society of Delaware and as a member of the Junior Board of the Wilmington Medical Center.

HELEN V. GRIFFITH launched a writing career when she took a course on writing for magazines at the University of Delaware. For twenty years Griffith had denied the urge to write, but she was encouraged when she sold one of the non-fiction articles written for the class. Griffith preferred fiction and began writing books for children. *Mine Will, Said John* was selected as a Children's Choice of 1981 by the International Reading Association and the Children's Book Council. Griffith's pets, Alex, the dog whom she declares was still a puppy at age twelve, and Malkin, the unexcitable cat, became characters in her next book. *Alex and the Cat,* named Best Book of Spring 1982 by the *School Library Journal,* was also a Junior Literary Guild selection, as was *Alex Remembers.* She followed with *More of Alex and the Cat.* A native of Wilmington and secretary-treasurer of S.G. Williams & Bros. Co., a building products distributing company founded by her grandfather, Griffith has also written *Georgia Music* (1986).

33

Ednah Demmer Leach

BARBARA MITCHELL (1941-   ) writes books to help children "see beyond cold, historical facts into the hearts of people." *Cornstalks and Cannonballs*, a tale of Lewes in the War of 1812, was published in 1980 and received a star review, the highest rating given by the American Library Association. Mitchell has also written *Tomahawks and Trombones* (1982), set in Bethlehem, Pennsylvania, in 1775, during the French and Indian Wars; *The Old Fasnacht* (1984), a collection of Pennsylvania German folk customs of Berks County in the 1850s; and *Click!: A Story about George Eastman* (1986). Mitchell's books are for beginning readers. Her urge to write was born when a third-grade teacher read MARGUE-RITE deANGELI's books to the class. Mitchell now belongs to a Philadelphia writers' group with de-Angeli, still one of Mitchell's favorite writers. Born

in Chester, Pennsylvania, Mitchell taught in the Glenalden, Pennsylvania, public schools. Although she left the school system when her daughter was born, Mitchell has taught private clarinet lessons in her home in Claymont. Many of her students have taken solo chairs in the Delaware all-state bands.

SANDRA SEATON MICHEL (1935-   ) of Wilmington is a poet, journalist, editor, and writer of books. They include *From the Peninsula, South* (1980) and *Thomas, My Brother* (1981). She has written for *Delaware Today* and *New Directions for Women*. Michel's poems are included in *World Poetry Day Anthology* (1970), *International Anthology on World Brotherhood and Peace* (1978), and *Wordcraft* (1983). She is the co-author of two plays, has done Poet-in-School workshops in public and private schools in Delaware and Pennsylvania, and has taught creative writing courses at the Du Pont Country Club, Wilmington. Michel, who was born in Hancock, Michigan, was a social studies teacher and co-owner and editor of Lenape Publishing.

Many of Delaware's print journalists have written for the News-Journal papers, the largest publisher in the state. HELEN McCAULEY BARRETT SMEAD wrote for the company from 1924 to 1953 under the byline "Helen Barrett." At that time, women were hardly accepted in newsrooms. She was limited to covering society, shopping, and religious news and doing occasional theater and music reviews. She was also a "re-write reporter" who took down stories from reporters over the telephone. Smead also did news broadcasts for WDEL radio in Wilmington. Born in Cecil County, Maryland, she made costumes for the Wilmington Drama League and was a charter member of the Wilmington Pilot Club.

A female pioneer in the previously all-male newsroom, BETTY BURROUGHS (1916-   ) retired in 1981 after more than thirty-six years with the News-Journal papers. Her column "Of This and That" in the *Morning News* reminded the public of the plight of the elderly and of the vulnerability of children and lost animals. Burroughs, who was born in Hartford, Connecticut, attracted a devoted readership and won numerous awards for writing stories about subjects that are often overlooked in favor of more glamorous themes. She was honored by the American Cancer Society, the American Red Cross, the U.S.

34

Department of Health, Education, and Welfare, and the Humane Society of the United States.

SUSANNE PISKO CORTY (1925-   ) writes for the "Opinion" page of the News-Journal papers as well as writing the column "Health Views" (as "Sue Corty") for the *Sunday News Journal*. Corty, born in Austria into a family of publishers and journalists, believes that "in order to benefit from today's opportunities, a woman as well as a man must be raised to have a feeling of self-esteem and faith in his/her capabilities. Without these personal qualities, no person can get ahead and reach whatever potential he or she may have."

PENELOPE BASS COPE (1949-   ) reports on visual arts and music for the News-Journal papers. Since earning a master's degree in art history from the University of Delaware, she has progressed from free-lance writer to staff member, in the process promoting greater awareness of the arts.

Since she joined the News-Journal staff in 1979, BETH MILLER has covered almost every amateur and professional sport, including the Winter Olympic Games in Sarajevo, Yugoslavia, in 1984. She had planned to attend law school, but a course in journalism and work on the student newspaper at Wheaton College, which she attended after graduation from Mt. Pleasant High School in Wilmington, reshaped her career plans. As a sports writer, Miller works almost exclusively with and writes mostly about men, but benefits from today's greater acceptance of female sports journalists.

EILEEN CAMERON SPRAKER (1920-   ) has been religion editor for the News-Journal papers for the past twenty-five years. She also has won five awards from the National Garden Association Writers for her weekly gardening column. She is the only woman on the nominating committee for the Delaware Bar Association's annual Liberty Bell Award, presented to citizens who have strengthened the Bill of Rights and the U.S. Constitution. Spraker, who was born in Dorchester, Illinois, was the first president of Delaware Press Women and has received their annual award for feature writing.

CYNTHIA SHEPPARD MITCHELL SMALL (1956-   ) was the first female managing editor of

Helen V. Griffith

the *Delaware Coast Press*, the weekly Rehoboth newspaper for which she began working in 1980. Her journalism career began at Cape Henlopen High School, where she won the annual Excellence in Journalism Award from the *Delaware Coast Press*. After studying journalism at Delaware Technical and Community College, Small worked for the Lewes *Whale* and the *Milford Chronicle*. During her tenure at the *Delaware Coast Press*, she won awards in editorial, photographic, and energy reporting from the Maryland-Delaware-D.C. Press Association and the Maryland Utilities Council and in publication design from Atlantic Publications.

Wilmington's CRYSTAL NIX, daughter of LULU MAE NIX, made history in 1984 when she was the first black and the second woman given charge of Princeton University's campus newspaper, a 107-year-old, independent daily. She was chosen by seventy staff members from six candidates. Nix found

35

Frances Naczi

that her education and newspaper experience at Friends School in Wilmington gave her an excellent start. She worked as an intern for the News-Journal papers during vacation in 1982. Nix attended the Woodrow Wilson School of Public and International Affairs at Princeton to prepare to work in economic development in the Third World.

FRANCES DAILY NACZI's (1917-) book *Without Bombast and Blunders: An Executive's Guide to Effective Writing* (1980) is culled from her forty-five years of experience as a journalist, public relations specialist, and marketing director. Her father, Francis P. Daily, a prominent editor in Washington, D.C., influenced her to choose a career in journalism. Naczi, who was born in Philadelphia, became a reporter for the Atlantic City *Daily World* at age eighteen. Three years later she was editor and publisher of the Atlantic City *News*.

In Wilmington, Naczi worked as an advertising agency copy writer and as editor of the women's page of the *Sunday News*. Positions in public relations preceded a nine-year career as director of marketing for First Federal Savings and Loan. She opted for early retirement in 1980 but continues to write and to teach writing. Naczi is an honorary life member of the National Press Club and was a charter member of Delaware Press Women and the Brandywine Press Club. Naczi was president of the Diamond State Branch, National League of American Pen Women, 1982-84. Encouraging a group of handicapped adults at the Mary Campbell Center to find self-expression through creative writing is her most rewarding experience.

ANN FRAZIER-HEDBERG (1940-), president of Delaware Press Women, works as a free-lance writer and as a public-relations consultant specializing in writing brochures, press releases, and speeches. In New York, her native state, Frazier-Hedberg worked for daily newspapers in Oneonta and Utica as an editor, columnist, features writer, and photographer. She lived in Massachusetts and New Jersey before moving to Delaware in 1978. Frazier-Hedberg was a public relations officer for the Historical Society of Delaware and a contributing editor to *Delaware Today* magazine, where her articles have won press awards.

LISE MONTY (LEARY) (1937-) admits to being curious about anyone and anything from which she

Lise Monty

can learn. Her interests include human behavior, the arts, and food. Since April 1986, she has been managing editor of *Delaware Today*. By age seventeen, Monty knew she wanted to be a writer. Her first years as a reporter were spent covering everything from cultural events to fires for the Barre, Vermont, *Daily Times*. A five-year stint as a reporter in the Boston Bureau of Fairchild Publications led to her appointment as bureau chief in 1965. She was the first woman to head a major bureau in the company's seventy-five-year history. In that capacity, Monty supervised ten reporters and a dozen stringers.

Monty's insightful profiles, usually about Delaware women, appeared in the *Sunday News Journal* from February 1976, soon after she arrived in Delaware, until May 1981. Her weekly columns in the News-Journal papers on a wide variety of foods, including their history, nutritional values, and food preparation, earned first-place awards from Delaware Press Women for two years. Monty has been restaurant critic for *Delaware Today*, public-relations consultant to Welcome Aboard Travel, public relations officer for the Delaware Art Museum, and editor of newsletters for Wilmington Women in Business and Newark Holy Family Parish.

Delaware women also communicate through public relations. As the first full-time executive director of the Arthritis Foundation, Delaware Chapter, ANNE EVANS CLENDANIEL (1918-   ) used her writing skills to develop and establish public, professional, and patient education programs for the entire state. She published *Rheumatology Update* for physicians and allied health professionals and edited *Arthritis Report*, which is distributed to six thousand state chapter members. "I'm Fighting! How About You?" and "I'm Helping! How About You?" are two of the boldly illustrated interest bulletins that Clendaniel created and distributed with arthritis fact sheets at numerous public speaking engagements.

Clendaniel, a resident of Wilmington for many years, was born in Harrington. Her mother's family received their Kent County land as a grant from the Duke of York. Her husband, H. Edgar Clendaniel, is a Sussex County native. Anne Clendaniel wrote poetry with JEANNETTE SLOCOMB EDWARDS' First State Writers group when her son and daughter were young. Later, she took courses in communications at the University of Delaware and at Goldey Beacom College. From 1963 to 1973, she was a member of the Bishop's staff of the Episcopal Diocese of Delaware; she started the diocesan newspaper, *Communion*. Clendaniel was president of the Quota Club, 1977-78, and worked to make funds available to museums whose guides were trained to communicate with the deaf using sign language. She also encouraged the Deaf Woman of the Year award luncheon, which has become an annual event. A former member of the Professional Staff Association of the Arthritis Foundation, Clendaniel is also an active member of Delaware Press Women.

Seaford resident ANNE CLAYTON NESBITT (1920-   ), a graduate of the University of Delaware, has inspired the competitive spirit in thousands of American women. A home economist, Nesbitt developed promotional programs for the Delmarva Poultry Industry while she was teaching in Seaford. She "hit the jackpot" when she developed and di-

Cari DeSantis Tull

rected the National Chicken Cooking Contest. The event grew so large that it is now administered by the National Broiler Council. Twice honored for outstanding service as director of the contest, Nesbitt retired in 1978. She is now the editor of *The Peninsula Pacemaker*, a monthly publication that entertains and informs residents of the Delmarva Peninsula by featuring events, recipes, and history.

Native Wilmingtonian CAROL ANN DeSANTIS ("CARI") TULL (1953-   ) has worked for ten years in many aspects of communications. Now the senior public relations representative in the Wilmington office of New-York-based Stooker & Company Public Relations, Inc., Tull started her career as editor of *Delaware Today* magazine at age twenty-four. She was editor of the short-lived *Delaware Monthly* magazine and the first director of public relations and graphics for the Delaware Art Museum. Tull managed the first major advertising and marketing communications campaign by Blue Cross/Blue Shield of Delaware. Her advertising campaign for the HMO of Delaware won first place in the national competition sponsored by the National Federation of Press Women. She took an eighteen-month leave from the field to open the ice cream and dessert shop Sweet

38

Seasons with her husband in 1985. Tull was president of Delaware Press Women and an officer in the Delaware Alliance of Professional Women.

Film and video production is a growing field. ELEANOR ANN BETTING ("GEORGI") MARQUISEE (1945-   ) and her husband have guided their company, Arden Films/Video, through a transition from producing only films to producing slide-tape shows, radio spots, and video programs. Their clients include the Du Pont Company, the Delaware Humanities Forum, Container Corporation of America, the League of Women Voters of the United States, and "Sesame Street." Marquisee organized a media workshop for nonprofit organizations in 1982 and has taught classes and seminars in film and media.

After obtaining an art degree, Marquisee started a school art program in Rolla, North Dakota, her home state, and taught art to grades 1-12. She did psychiatric art therapy with emotionally disturbed children at the Terry Children's Psychiatric Center when she first came to Wilmington and later worked as a magistrate/justice of the peace for the State of Delaware. Marquisee served on the Public Education Committee of the American Cancer Society, Delaware Division, and as a board member of Cityside, Inc.

SUSAN WARNER (1941-   ) has her own audiovisual production and special-events business, Warner & Co., founded in 1980. After earning a bachelor's degree from Northern Michigan University, Warner worked at a television station doing news and cinematography, did freelance work, and was director of public relations for the Freedom Valley Girl Scout Council. She taught classes while she pursued a master's degree in film and television production at Temple University. Warner also taught workshops on producing audiovisual programs on small budgets for community action agencies and was founding president of the Women's Media Alliance.

SHARON KELLY BAKER (1950-   ), Newark, uses audiovisual media as a powerful ally in making a point. She and her husband Frank own Teleduction Associates, an audiovisual production company. Sharon Baker was the host of "Newstalk," a radio call-in show that aired every weekday on WILM in Wilmington from 1975 to 1982. It was the longest-

Sharon Kelly Baker

running talk show in Delaware. In 1983 she produced "This Week," a half-hour program on trends affecting residents of the Delaware Valley, for WHYY-TV.

Baker enjoys the range of work she does for her company, including writing scripts, shooting and editing film, and working with clients. She feels strongly about making the world a better place and has put her convictions into practice by participation in peace vigils while she was a student at the University of Delaware. Teleduction Associates often donates services to nonprofit organizations with an important mission. Baker works with the Private Industry Council, a government agency that assists in training hard-core unemployed people.

SALLY VANDECAR HAWKINS (1922-   ) contributes to the field of communications as president and general manager of WILM radio in Wilmington. When Hawkins became manager of the AM station following the death of her husband, she changed to an all-news format, unusual for a listening area the size of Wilmington. A native of Grand Rapids, Michigan, Hawkins has worked in broadcasting for twenty-five years. Her career began in radio sales and included writing commercials and producing radio and television programs for syndication. She was elected to the board of directors of the National Association of Broadcasters in 1984. Hawkins serves

Sally Vandecar Hawkins

on the boards of area businesses and the Delaware State Chamber of Commerce Committee. She is also on the United States Commission for Civil Rights and the boards of the Grand Opera House and Brandywine College. The Chesapeake Bay Girl Scout Council gave Hawkins the World of Today and Tomorrow Award in 1985.

Delaware women use their communications skills to inform the public and promote products through newspapers, books, films, and publicity materials. They also entertain readers and explore the emotions and events around them by creating poems and works of fiction.

TO HELP ONE ANOTHER:

Women in Community Service

B. Ethelda Mullen

Concern for the welfare of others and the desire to improve the human condition have long been concerns of women who have reached out to help people in need. One who still follows in this tradition of personal caring is ALVA LYNCH (1889-   ), a role model of pioneer-type community service and sharing in the town of Roxanna. Devoted to her home, neighbors, and church, she is known for her self-sufficiency and inspiration.

In similar fashion, HILDA PARKER (1905-   ) has served her church and the Lewes community with special concern for racial integration and the elderly. She was appointed to the Heritage Commission for the 350th anniversary celebration of the town of Lewes.

Increasingly, Delawareans have joined together to serve their communities in organized groups. In the nineteenth century, women's groups initiated many charitable projects and took an active role in the reform societies that multiplied at the time. Many of these groups had links to the Society of Friends, in which women stood on an equal footing with men. MARY FRAIM, who worked for the Salvation Army for twenty-five years, and JEAN KANE FOULKE DU PONT, who was a leader in prison reform, are among the Delaware women who aided their communities significantly.

Since the end of the nineteenth century, federal, state, and local governments have been forced to assume responsibility for a growing portion of social service, primarily because of the increasing complexity of problems and their solutions in an urban industrial and post-industrial society. Today, women serve their communities as paid professionals as well as volunteers. Despite the move toward more professional careers for women, volunteers continue to serve on commissions and advisory boards, participate in human resource groups and charitable agencies, and help in the day-to-day operation of state institutions. Many areas of education, social welfare, women's rights, community safety, community improvement, recreation, and even foreign relations depend on participation by hundreds of volunteers.

Community service is no longer the domain of the

41

Alva Lynch

wealthy, middle-aged, white woman. Today, volunteers represent many areas of interest and expertise, economic sectors, races and ethnic groups, and all ages. A growing number take on volunteer commitments in addition to paid employment. For example, over half of Girl Scout volunteers are employed elsewhere.

Because of women's strong identification with family, it is natural that many are involved in programs to help children and families. B. ETHELDA MULLEN (1886-1980) was Delaware's first professional social worker. After working as a kindergarten teacher, she became a "visiting worker" with Associated Charities in 1917 and the executive secretary one year later. As head of that agency, Mullen helped to establish the Family Court of New Castle County, the Visiting Nurse Association, the Children's Bureau of Delaware, and the Needy Family Fund Campaign sponsored annually by the News-Journal papers. Because Mullen recognized that handouts rarely reach the root of family problems, she worked to move social work beyond mere charity. Robert M. Weaver, former executive director of

Family Service of Northern Delaware, credits her with paving the way for the modern social agency system in Delaware.

In 1974 MARTHA VERGE ("MUFFIN") DU PONT founded the Delaware Council of Agencies for Children and Youth, which sought channels of help for young Delawareans. She subsequently established CHILD, Inc., a private agency dedicated to the care and treatment of abused and neglected children and to sheltering battered wives. Du Pont received an award from Abused Women's Aid in Crisis in New York for her aid to battered women.

ELISABETH STROUD ("ELISA") POOLE (1941-   ) of Wilmington has devoted her energy to helping children in many ways. She served with and became president of the Visiting Nurse Association in the early 1970s. From 1973 to 1976, she was director of the Salvation Army's Wee Care Day Care Center and joined its advisory board in 1978, the year she became president of the Junior League of Wilmington. As president, Poole participated in a study of the foster care system in Delaware and proposed and lobbied for legislation to create a Foster Care Review Board. She founded and is president of READ-ALOUD Delaware, an organization that promotes reading aloud to preschool children on a regular and sustained basis to foster a love of books and reading. In 1984 she was the first female United Way campaign vice-chair. Her leadership style elicits the best efforts of everyone working on a project. The United Way of Delaware named Poole outstanding volunteer of the year in 1987.

As director for special services with the Chesapeake Bay Girl Scout Council, NAOMI GAINES WINCHESTER of New Castle developed programs for diverse populations such as the handicapped, the rural poor, migrant workers, and Spanish-speaking communities. Prior to her involvement in scouting, she served as director of the Methodist Action Program for five years and worked to eradicate racism in Wilmington. Now a minister, Winchester serves the Peninsula Methodist Homes Conference in developing programs for the elderly.

JAY H. HUKILL (1934-   ) of Harbeson has been a volunteer leader for the Hollymount 4-H Club since 1969 and president of the Sussex County 4-H Leaders' Association since 1980. She has been local project leader for the Feeder Lamb Project since 1972 and has initiated, organized, and executed the Feeder Lamb and Sheep Breeding Projects for the Delaware State Fair since 1974. Hukill represents Delaware at national and regional 4-H conferences and serves on the Delaware 4-H Advisory Board and the Livestock Advisory Board.

BARBARA TAYLOR of Seaford, an outstanding 4-H leader for the past thirteen years, takes a special interest in the children she leads. Eight of them have attended the National Congress, two have won scholarships, and another was a runner-up.

Children and the whole family suffer the effects of domestic violence. MARJORIE LORENZ established the Families in Transition Center in Milford in 1978 to help victims of domestic violence in Kent and Sussex counties. The program, which seeks to educate community members and influence legislation on domestic violence and women's issues, grew out of one she designed as a requirement for an associate degree in human services from Delaware Technical and Community College. A native of Brooklyn, New York, Lorenz moved to Milford in 1968 and is a member of the Milford Housing Corporation and a former member of the Kent County Catholic Social Services Board.

GERTRUDE LOWELL has served senior citizens for twenty-five years as a lobbyist, as a member of several state and municipal advisory councils, and as editor of the newspaper *Delaware Senior Citizen*, which is delivered to 15,000 senior citizens in the state. She is a liaison for the elderly with Community Action of Greater Wilmington. Lowell was instrumental in organizing the Delaware Employment-over-60 Program. She has received awards from the National Council of Christians and Jews, the U.S. Department of Health, Education, and Welfare, and Wilmington Mayor William McLaughlin. Lowell entered the Hall of Fame of Delaware Women in 1987.

WILHELMINA ("MINA") MILLER (1908-   ) had already lost her friends, family, and husband and was about to lose a teaching position as a result of her alcoholism when she committed herself to Delaware State Hospital. She succeeded in conquering her problem and now works full time to combat alcoholism in paid professional and volunteer capacities. She directs the Wilmington Council on Alco-

Gertrude Lowell

holism, teaches in the University of Delaware Summer Institute on Alcoholism, lectures to student nurses, and counsels at the Delaware Alcoholism Services Center. Miller served on the Delaware Commission on the Status of Women. In 1974 she received the Alcoholism Service Certificate for outstanding service from Governor Russell W. Peterson.

MARKA TRUESDALE DU PONT (1910-   ) has helped raise public consciousness of mental health problems by serving on state boards for mental health. As president of the National Mental Health Association, she lobbied for increased state funding of mental health centers. In 1971 the institute on human behavior at Delaware State Hospital was named in du Pont's honor.

A few months after DELORES J. BAYLOR (1936-1983) assumed her duties as warden of the Women's Correctional Institution, eight men were transferred to her building and she became the first warden of a co-ed prison in Delaware, an experiment that lasted four years. Baylor introduced programs for the prisoners to develop basic skills and to train them for employment in food service and health care. In 1979 she was commended in a State Senate resolution as "a fine example of a state official who combines patience, great common sense, and dedication."

Delaware women help people who have handicaps of many kinds. NAN KENNEDY FOOKS CAMPBELL (-1965) did more than any other Delaware woman to awaken public interest in improved care for the mentally retarded, according to Dr. M.A. Tarumianz, former superintendent of the Stockley Center. Campbell had a long association with the old Delaware Commission for the Feebleminded and was the last chair of the commission. She later served on the board of directors at Stockley Center and a facility there was named for her. In 1957 the Laurel Chamber of Commerce presented Campbell with the Outstanding Citizen award. BEATRICE YERKES MONEY, past president and an active member of the Stockley Center Auxiliary, has carried on Campbell's tradition of service to the mentally retarded.

Although handicapped children traditionally have been educated at specialized facilities, MARIE MUNIS (1907-) favors mainstreaming, allowing them to be in the public schools with their peers. In 1930 she was the first blind graduate of a New Castle County high school. Munis had attended Overbrook School in Pennsylvania, where blind students were educated, but returned to Delaware in the eleventh grade to enroll at Wilmington High School. After her graduation from the University of Pennsylvania with a major in speech therapy, she worked in that field with retarded children. Munis began working with newly blind adults in 1935. In 1982 she was named president of the Delaware Association for the Blind, the second blind person ever to serve as president.

FRANCES ELMA NORRIS ("PUNX") WINGATE, Rehoboth, has been an advocate for the physically handicapped since the early 1960s. Because of a handicapped friend, she volunteered at the Easter Seals Rehabilitation Center in Georgetown, where she is now on the advisory board. Wingate has served on the board of the Easter Seals Society of Del-Mar since the early 1970s. She was an original appointee to the Governor's Architectural Accessibility Board. Wingate also serves on the board of

Frances Elma Norris Wingate

directors of the Delaware Association for Retarded Citizens and the Governor's Advisory Council on Mental Retardation.

As a member of the Sussex County Committee for the Employment of the Handicapped and the Committee to Aid the Handicapped, she helped establish ramps and parking for the handicapped in Rehoboth. Wingate is descended from a long line of Delawareans, although she grew up in Massachusetts. She has represented the Episcopal Churchwomen of the Diocese of Delaware at two Women's Triennials and participated on the Committee to Promote the Ordination of Women.

ELLEN WILLIAMS of suburban Wilmington served on the board of the Delaware Association for Retarded

Citizens for many years. She founded Hanover Pre-school for retarded children and Jefferson Pre-school for emotionally disturbed children, whose needs were not met by state services at the time. Williams's first volunteer position was working in the nursery school at the West End Neighborhood House, a project sponsored by the Junior League. She also has served on the State Service Center advisory council since 1974.

IVY M. HUDSON, Camden, has been a psychologist, a teacher, and a counselor for testing and placing the handicapped for more than thirty years. She served on the council for the Foster Grandparents Program for over fourteen years.

DOROTHY D.W. ("DREX") JONES established Delaware Day School, Delaware's first school for physically handicapped children, in 1948. It was the forerunner of both the Opportunity Center and the John G. Leach School.

MARTHA ZIMMERMAN SHIPE (1921-   ), born in Sunbury, Pennsylvania, grew up in a Pennsylvania German home during the Great Depression, when hard work was necessary in order to survive. Continuing to work hard to improve her community, Shipe initiated a swimming program for the physically handicapped children at the John G. Leach School and helped start the Mary Campbell Center, a home where handicapped people can live together.

She also founded the Delaware Food Bank and was a leader in starting the Hope Lutheran Church Day Care Center in New Castle. Shipe was appointed by Governor Charles Terry as Delaware's representative for Women's Highway Safety Leaders and has been reappointed by each succeeding governor. As regional director of the National Association of Women Highway Safety Leaders, she has directed safety programs in five states. She is also secretary of Delaware Highway Users and a director of the Delaware Safety Council.

Shipe is only one of many Delaware women who perform community service in several different fields. SONIA SCHORR SLOAN of Wilmington has combined community service with a science career. She was the first female graduate of Jefferson Medical College, where she earned an M.S. in microbiology

Sonia Schorr Sloan

in 1950, and was also the first woman on the staff of the Du Pont Company's Chemical Research Department. Sloan has been president of the New Democratic Coalition in Delaware. While on the board of directors of the Delaware Chapter of the American Civil Liberties Union, she helped publish the first edition of *Women and the Law*. She was president and is Public Affairs Committee chair of Planned Parenthood of Delaware and has been a leader of the Delaware Pro-Choice Coalition.

Sloan, an active volunteer in the Wilmington Jewish community, received the Hannah G. Solomon award from the National Council of Jewish Women in 1981. On that occasion she was quoted as saying, "When there is injustice, you have to be willing to stand up and be counted, no matter what the cost or the consequences." The Delaware Region, National

Conference of Christians and Jews, gave her the Community Builder Award in 1984.

Through the League of Women Voters (LWV), JOYCE P. JOHNSON (1928-   ) of suburban Wilmington has helped people exercise their right to vote. For twenty-five years she has provided nonpartisan information on issues, candidates, and voting rules and monitored voting regulations to make them equitable for all citizens. She was state president of the LWV and is a lobbyist and a member of the state board of directors.

Johnson has also been active in environmental affairs, serving on the state Environmental Advisory Council and task forces on low-level radioactive waste and solid waste regulations. As a volunteer with the state Division of Consumer Affairs, she helps consumers solve problems ranging from car repairs to landlord-tenant disputes.

ELIZABETH H. ("LIZ") RYAN (1919-   ) of suburban Wilmington has made an impact on many organizations and issues, especially in the areas of government and criminal justice. As state president of the League of Women Voters (LWV) during the school desegregation controversy, she was an effective force in ensuring a peaceful transition. In order to clarify the state government process for the public, Ryan, a native of Forest Lake, Minnesota, edited the LWV book *Delaware Government* (1976, revised 1981, addendum 1985), the first book published on Delaware government. She lobbied for the Equal Rights Amendment, gun control, and the Bottle Bill. Ryan was co-chair of Common Cause of Delaware, a legislative chair and lobbyist for the AAUW, and state manager of John Anderson's campaign for the presidency in 1980.

Through the LWV, Ryan became involved in developing a more effective criminal justice system. From 1981 to 1983, she was president of the Delaware Council on Crime and Justice, which assisted the Bureau of Juvenile Corrections in developing a treatment and classification system, training staff, and implementing the new system. Ryan served on the Delaware Sentencing Reform Commission and the Governor's Advisory Board on Corrections. She also works directly with prisoners at the Women's Correctional Institution, Claymont, and with boys at Ferris School, whom she tutors weekly. Ryan serves on the board of Planned Parenthood of Dela-

ware. The Delaware Region, National Conference of Christians and Jews, honored her as a Community Builder in 1981. She entered the Hall of Fame of Delaware Women in 1987.

MARGARET ROSE HENRY (1944-   ) has worked in a professional capacity for many social service agencies. As senior allocations associate with United Way, she worked closely with volunteers. Henry was director of Girls Club of Delaware and administrator-counselor of the Job Corps for the YMCA. She now works for the New Castle County Economic Development Council. Henry was the first black to join the Junior League of Wilmington.

CANDIDA DIAZ McBRIDE uses her position in the Wilmington Latin American community to help the city as a whole. A native of Guatemala, she formed the Puerto Rican Association and the Latin American Center. McBride was the first Hispanic on the United Way Planning Council and among the first Catholics in Church Women United. One of the original members of the Urban Coalition, she represented the Hispanic community and was the only woman of more than fifty members. McBride secured funding from the Delaware Presbytery to start the first newspaper in the area for Hispanics and blacks, *El Noticiero/Informer*, and became the volunteer editor.

During the civil rights riots of the 1960s, McBride housed and fed twenty-five children from the burned-out area in addition to her own eleven. Her relief effort after a devastating earthquake in Guatemala in 1976 led Wilmington to adopt one small town, San Jose Sacatipequez, as a sister city. McBride was also active in the project to build a replica of the Kalmar Nyckel, the ship that brought Swedish settlers to Delaware in 1638. She has ventured into the business world by acquiring FM radio station WBNJ in Cape May, New Jersey.

OLGA RAMIREZ has worked for more than ten years to make the criminal justice system more responsive to Hispanics. She is former president of the board of the Latin American Community Center and has been honored by the Delaware Region, National Conference of Christians and Jews.

WANDA BLAZEJEWSKI LARSEN has dedicated her life to improving international cooperation. An

46

Olga Ramirez

active member of the Delaware Council for International Visitors (DCIV), an organization that hosts representatives from other nations, she was honored for improving Polish-American understanding and for achieving better relations among ethnic groups in America. Larsen, who grew up in a Polish immigrant family during the Great Depression, left school at an early age to work to help her family. She graduated from the University of Delaware in 1973, when she was in her sixties, and has continued her studies at Polish universities.

ANNETTE GRUBER, Newark, was one of the founders of DCIV. She also serves on the boards of the Greater Wilmington Convention and Visitors Bureau and of the Sister Cities program. Gruber was state president of the AAUW and was the first woman elected to the St. Paul's Lutheran Church Council. She is active in Church Women United. Gruber was an early member of Friends of the Newark Library, has served on the board of the Newark Symphony Society since its inception, and has received the Community Award from the University of Delaware.

Women also work to improve their local communities, making them more attractive and stimulating places in which to live. HATTYE MAE BETTS

Hattye Mae Betts Biddle

BIDDLE (1915-   ), born in Harrington, is a community organizer who served as chair of "Old Dover Days," a tour of historic houses and public buildings. She was Mother of the Year in 1976 and has been president of Delaware Mothers. After owning and directing a preschool for nineteen years, Biddle operates a bed and breakfast inn, one of the first in Delaware, and is a museum aide for the Division of Historical and Cultural Affairs in Dover.

HELEN WALLACE chairs the Odessa Women's Club Community Improvement Project to restore Old St. Paul's Methodist Church for a town museum and cultural center. The club saved the historic building, fostered its restoration, and placed it on the National Register of Historic Places. An advocate of strict zoning to preserve Odessa's historic district, Wallace became a member of the steering committee that wrote a comprehensive zoning plan for the town in 1969. She was president of the State Federation of Women's Clubs and was the first woman elected to Odessa's town council.

47

MARJORIE K. LOVEN started the Odessa Day tours in 1949 and directed them until 1959. In 1967 the Odessa Women's Club held its first "Christmas in Odessa" tour of the town's historic homes, which Loven co-chaired. The tour raises thousands of dollars for scholarships and charities and encourages the restoration of historic homes in and around Odessa. Loven has been a member of the committee to choose Delaware Mother of the Year for eight years, has judged the Miss Delaware contest, and is on a local committee for Delaware Junior Miss.

MARTHA HART NEWLON (1918-   ), who grew up on a farm in Ohio, was sensitive to the lack of trees when she moved into the new Fairfax development north of Wilmington in 1950. She did research on tree varieties and cost and presented the civic association with her plan, which is responsible for a green neighborhood. She organized Delaware Friends of Bikecology and agitated for safer bicycle and pedestrian facilities. Petitions to the governor led to improved planning of future roads, upgrading of present roads, and the Governor's Bicycle Task Force, which Newlon chairs.

To ensure adequate school libraries for her six children, Newlon marshalled support from the Parent-Teacher Association (PTA), the AAUW, and the School Library Association to have a professional study conducted which resulted in improved libraries, additional employees, and increased book purchases throughout the state. She also participated in successful efforts to have TV Channel 12 licensed for educational purposes.

SARAH SIMPSON WEBB of Houston earned two master's degrees and became a home economics teacher in order to help others. She served as president of the Harrington Teachers' Association and later on the board of People's Place II, a community counseling service in Milford. Webb is a member of the Foreign Study League Homestay Program. She also takes into her home students who have "taken a wrong turn" and rehabilitates them. Her philosophy of life can be summed up in a favorite quote from Bernard Malamud: "One must not withdraw from the task if he has some small thing to offer. He does so at the risk of diminishing his humanity."

Many Delaware women have taken Webb's philosophy to heart and contributed to their communities. In 1966 MARY OWEN BASS (1920-   ) was appointed to the state Committee on Education, which was assigned to inform the public about the Wolcott Report on Delaware education. At the time, she was president of the state AAUW. Later, Bass became involved in student exchange programs. She has been president of the Delaware Council for International Visitors and now serves on its board of directors.

VIRGINIA LODGE BRITTINGHAM, a native Sussex Countian, was employed in the Personnel Department of the Du Pont Company before her marriage. While caring for three children, she served on the executive board of the Sussex Gardeners for twenty years; has served as state chair of the Good Citizens Committee; and was vice-regent of the DAR. Brittingham, the bookkeeper for the Lewes Dairy, was active in the Bethel United Methodist Church, Lewes. Her family hosted an exchange student from Germany in 1961. She was selected as Delaware's Mother of the Year in 1981 and was president of Delaware Mothers in 1986.

BARBARA CHASE HERR (1920-   ), born in Waterbury, Connecticut, has rendered outstanding service to the citizens of Delaware as chair of the Governor's Commission on the Status of Women. Since she assumed leadership in September 1977, the commission has sponsored successful workshops throughout Delaware, a speaker's bureau, a general listing of all women's organizations in the state, and a periodical bulletin on items of interest to women. In Sussex County, a rape crisis center was created. The commission has published booklets on nontraditional work schedules and occupations for women, the *Resource Booklet for Families in Crisis*, *Facing Crisis*, and a new edition of the *Legal Handbook for Delaware Women*.

Herr served on the advisory committees of the Delaware Displaced Homemaker Center and the YWCA Battered Spouse Shelter and on steering committees of the Victims' Coalition and of Women's Unity Day in 1975. She serves on the state Foster Care Review Board and is a board member of the Delaware Council on Crime and Justice. Herr received the Trailblazer Award of the Delaware Alliance of Professional Women in 1982.

Because she values a pluralistic community,

48

SHIRLEY GRAEFF HOROWITZ (1929-   ) works for school desegregation, fair housing, and civil and human rights. Although she lacked a college education, she developed skills in public relations, fundraising, and lobbying through study and experience. Horowitz, born in Harrisburg, Pennsylvania, was a member of the Human Relations Advisory Board during New Castle County school desegregation. She received the Brotherhood Award from the Delaware Region, National Conference of Christians and Jews, in 1973 and was named Outstanding Woman of the Year by the National Council of Jewish Women in 1976. Horowitz was a member of the U.S. Civil Rights Commission for six years. She was director of public relations for Planned Parenthood of Delaware and executive director of Common Cause of Delaware. Horowitz directs the Pro Bono Project of Delaware Volunteer Legal Services, the Delaware Bar Association's effort to provide legal services to indigent clients.

IRENE JORDAN DARDASHTI (1940-   ) became the first executive director of the Delaware Commission for Women in 1982 and organized Women's History Week, held at Hagley Museum in 1984. Born in Wilmington, Dardashti worked on social issues, especially those related to women, for the AAUW. In 1974 she received the Gertrude Fogelson Award, a national prize for craft excellence, in recognition of her weaving.

After holding political positions in the governments of New Castle County and the City of Wilmington, JORENE JAMESON (1947-   ) was appointed by Governor Pierre S. du Pont IV to head his Office of Labor Relations. Interested in public issues concerning children, and a former Girl Scout in Philadelphia, Jameson became executive director of the Chesapeake Bay Girl Scout Council in 1985. She serves on the state Council on Public Health, the Children's Trust Fund, and the Commission on Work and the Family and, through a W. K. Kellogg Foundation Grant to the Girl Scouts, is studying public policy regarding day care and working mothers.

As executive director of the YWCA of New Castle County, CONSTANCE G. BERESIN (1935-   ) has led the organization through an extensive planning effort and into a new era of community involvement. The major goal of the YWCA has changed somewhat, from meeting the needs of members only to meeting the needs of women in the community. The agency's program is directed toward crisis alleviation, nontraditional job training, child care, physical fitness, and self-development. It now incorporates the Women's Center, which provides information and referral, social-service screening, and career counseling.

After she received a master's degree in social work from Bryn Mawr College in 1974, Beresin supervised a social-service team at the Child Care Service of Delaware County, Pennsylvania, and later became director of the Delaware County Division of the Community Services Planning Council of Southeastern Pennsylvania.

Jorene Jameson

49

PATRICIA JOHNSON PRESCOTT vowed to devote her life to animal welfare in 1927, when a puppy kept her company through a long illness. She founded the Delaware Humane Association in 1957, housing stray and unwanted animals in her own and her friends' houses until the shelter was built. Prescott has served on the national board of the American Humane Association.

BERTHA ("BERTIE") GRIMES, a Red Cross volunteer for more than twenty years, originated a pet therapy program for the elderly in cooperation with the state Society for the Prevention of Cruelty to Animals. Animals are brought to visit senior citizens, who thrive on the love and companionship.

These women are typical of many who make their state and local communities better places in which to live. They serve as advocates for children, the elderly, handicapped people, and animals and work to improve mental health and the general quality of life in Delaware.

NATURE'S GUARDIANS:

Women In Conservation

Women have long been associated with nurturing growing things. Traditionally, most women managed a home vegetable garden out of necessity. With increased affluence and leisure time, women were able to spend time and energy cultivating ornamental gardens. They formed garden clubs to enhance their knowledge of plants and their cultivation and to beautify their communities. Women were in the vanguard of volunteer projects to educate the public to the joys of nature and the need to conserve natural resources.

The environmental movement, which began in the 1960s in Delaware and in the United States at large, was fueled in large part by those people, and by many environmental groups which formed as an outgrowth of heightened interest in ecology and in response to threats to the natural environment.

Many women have felt the need to become increasingly political in order to find viable solutions to the problems of pollution and encroachment on wildlife habitats. As in other fields, growing numbers of women now hold positions of responsibility, paid or unpaid. They serve on governmental boards, hold political office, work as professional horticulturalists, and direct conservation organizations.

Garden clubs were among the first organized groups of women to share their interest in nature. The Garden Club of Wilmington, founded in 1918, is the oldest garden club in Delaware. Like members of other garden clubs around the state and the nation, its members educate themselves as well as working to beautify the community. Among other projects, the club has restored the gardens of historic buildings in the state using plant materials appropriate to the time period of each building. Many members of the Garden Club of Wilmington have served as officers of the Garden Clubs of America. LOUISE DU PONT CROWNINSHIELD (1877-1958) was president of the Garden Club of Wilmington and vice-president of the Garden Clubs of America. The Garden Club of Wilmington is unique in having two members, GINA BISSELL and GENEVIEVE ESTES ("BUNNY") DU PONT, who served consecutive terms as president of the Garden Clubs of America.

The club was also involved in starting the Wilmington Garden Center, which provides gardening information to the public. KATHRYN S. ANDERSEN (1928-   ) served on the original board of directors of the Center and as president from 1981 to 1982. She is well known as a grower and hybridizer of daffodils. In 1982 she received the Mary Marsh Award, given to the Wilmington Garden Center member who is "committed to the field of horticulture in the community and has given his or her time, skills, and interests in support of horticulture."

MARY MARSH (1895-1987) "loved every blooming thing." An avid gardener, lecturer, judge, and guide, she promoted gardening and the appreciation wildflowers in naturalized settings for over fifty years.

BARBARA T. HEENAN (1935-   ) is a master flower show judge and design instructor for the National Council of State Garden Clubs. Since 1979 she has put her skills to work for roadside beautification as chair of the Delaware Federation of Garden Clubs' "Operation Wildflower," a project that promotes the use of native wildflowers as the ground cover along roadways.

Kathryn S. Anderson

The most important step in protecting endangered natural resources is raising public consciousness to value the environment. Many Delawareans were influenced by VIOLET FINDLAY, elementary-school science supervisor in the Wilmington public schools during the 1920s. She taught natural history, wrote environmental education booklets, and inspired many of her pupils to pursue careers in environmental fields or to become active in conservation.

When a group of sportsmen met in Dover to found the Delaware Wildlife Federation in 1947, GRACE PREST (1917-   ), the only woman, became its secretary. Over the years, she was involved in many organizations with public education goals. Prest worked in the office of the Brandywine Valley Association in its early days and was a charter member and conservation chair of the Delaware Ornithological Society in the early 1960s. She also planned monthly programs and field trips for the Delaware Society of Natural History.

When Delaware Wildlands began its conservation work in 1962, Prest volunteered to keep the records. In 1964 she served on the board of the Delaware Conservation Education Association, a group dedicated to bringing environmental education to classrooms in Delaware. Her work laid a strong foundation

for the environmental movement that began to grow and make an impact in Delaware in the 1960s and 1970s.

Many women have found a focus for their concern for conservation in the Delaware Nature Education Society (DNES), founded in 1964 as the Delaware Nature Education Center. NANCY FREDERICK (1929-   ) was in the first group of volunteer guides and has supported DNES as a guide, trainer of guides, teacher, naturalist, and board member for twenty years. Frederick, who often lectures to horticultural groups and garden clubs, is now vice-president of DNES. She is also a member of the boards of the Hagley Museum and Library and Bryn Mawr College and serves on the garden advisory committee of Winterthur Museum. Frederick and her husband, William, who operates Private Gardens, Inc., a firm that specializes in residential garden design, received a citation from the American Horticultural Society in 1984 for "outstanding contributions to local horticulture."

The DNES guided tour program, with which Frederick worked over the years, was developed by ANN RYDGREN and SALLY ROBINSON. In 1984 the volunteer corps received the National Voluntary Service Award from the National Recreation and Park Association.

LORRAINE M. FLEMING (1933-   ) is DNES research coordinator and manager of the society's office of preservation. She has written *Delaware's Outstanding Natural Areas and Their Preservation* (1978) and many articles on preserving natural diversity in the environment. Fleming is chair of the state Low-Level Radioactive Waste Policy Task Group and vice-chair of the Governor's Advisory Council on Environmental Control. In 1984 she received the Chesapeake Bay Girl Scout Council World of the Out-of-Doors award for her outstanding contributions to protecting Delaware's natural resources.

The Delaware Audubon Society has played an important role in citizen education and conservation lobbying since LYNNE FRINK (1946-   ) started it in 1976. She saw the need for another organization after an oil spill from a tanker spread into marshes along the Delaware River in 1976. Although Frink quickly marshalled people to help, many birds died. In order to save birds from similar disasters,

Lorraine M. Fleming

she began Tri-State Bird Rescue and Research, Inc., a group of over four hundred well-trained volunteers with a steadily increasing record of success in saving injured or orphaned wildlife. In 1982 Frink established a grant to pay doctoral candidates in veterinary medicine to work with the group. After a major oil spill in 1985, Tri-State Bird Rescue saved every goose and duck brought to them, although they lost the cormorants.

Frink has won many awards and has been invited to speak about oiled-bird rehabilitation to such varied groups as the International Society of Petroleum Industry Biologists, the University of Pennsylvania School of Veterinary Medicine, and the American Ornithological Union. She is on the board of directors of the National Wildlife Rehabilitators Association and wrote the chapter on oiled-bird rehabilitation for the standard veterinary text *Current Veterinary*

Therapy, edited by Robert Kirk. Russell W. Peterson, former president of the National Audubon Society and former governor of Delaware, cited Frink for her "singular leadership ability in the field of wildlife conservation. She stands out," he concluded, "as an example of what one concerned citizen can accomplish."

GRACE WAGNER ("BUBBLES") PIERCE (1926-   ), president of the Delaware Audubon Society, works to protect wetlands throughout the state and serves on a committee studying hazardous waste dump sites in Delaware. For several years she spoke for Watch Our Waterways and she chaired the organization from 1978 to 1980. Pierce also chaired the East Coast Environmental Leadership Conference in 1974. She spent the next three years as an issues specialist for the Wilderness Society in Washington, D.C.

A resident of Dover, Pierce has served as president of the Junior Board of Kent General Hospital, where she was a member of the board of directors from 1971 to 1976. She has held numerous Republican Party posts and was national environmental director of the National Unity Campaign for John Anderson in 1980.

One usually thinks of conservation in terms of wilderness or less developed areas, but natural resources are an important ingredient in the city, too. SARA ("SALLY") FRELICK O'BYRNE (1952-   ), (daughter of JANE HAYDEN FRELICK), developed an ecological approach to regional planning while studying for a master's degree in planning from the University of Pennsylvania. Since returning to Wilmington in 1979, she has applied her knowledge to promote urban approaches that include both human and environmental concerns. As president of Cityside, Inc. (1981-85), O'Byrne fostered many projects and festivities that enhance and celebrate city living. She and her family are active urban homesteaders who have rehabilitated four houses in downtown Wilmington.

From 1979 to 1981, O'Byrne and PRISCILLA THOMPSON coordinated Reclaim Our Waterfront (Project ROW). Participants produced an inventory of the historical, cultural, and physical resources of the Wilmington waterfront; a public school education program; a museum exhibit; and a promotional brochure. Wilmington Waterways, an organization that resulted in part from the interest generated by Project ROW, and on whose board of directors

Priscilla Thompson

O'Byrne continues to serve, works to make the Wilmington waterfront more attractive and encourage recreation there. Efforts have focused on the Christina riverfront and have sparked interest that resulted in Christina Park and the improved appearance of buildings along the river.

Many women have turned to the political arena to accomplish their conservation goals. When the Wetlands Protection Act was before the Delaware General Assembly for consideration in 1973, LYNN JANKUS (1928-   ) was head of the legislation committee for the Federation of Business and Professional Women. She spent many hours lobbying for the act in the legislature, giving speeches, and collecting signatures on petitions in favor of the bill, which became law that year. A resident of Wilmington and Angola-by-the-Bay, Jankus later became president of the federation and continues to support protection of natural resources and coastal wetlands. She was executive secretary for the Kiwanis Club of Wilmington. Jankus also is active in the Civic League for New Castle County.

Other women play important roles in conservation of wildlife and resources. JEAN COLBERT (1928-   ) of Wilmington has worked on issues of air and water quality control, land use, energy conservation, coastal management, and waste disposal at the local, state, and regional level since she moved to Delaware in 1965. While on the League of Women Voters Interleague Council of the Delaware River

Basin, she took an active part in the Tocks Island Study and gave resource information, workshops, and public presentations on the Hazardous Waste Study of the Delaware River Basin.

Because she had served on several technical coordinating committees for the Water Resources Agency of New Castle County for more than a decade, Colbert was appointed in 1981 to the Comprehensive Water Management Committee and to the Advisory Council on Environmental Control in the Department of Natural Resources and Environmental Control.

PAMELA COPELAND (1906-   ) has been a director of the Delaware Nature Education Society (DNES) and is president of the Red Clay Reservation, a land trust formed by her late husband, Lammot du Pont Copeland, and Henry B. du Pont. The trust owns the six-hundred-acre site and buildings occupied by Ashland Nature Center, the DNES site in New Castle County, and has provided DNES with substantial grants for operating funds. Copeland chaired the publication committee and helped fund the DNES publication *Wildflowers of Delaware and the Eastern Shore* by Claude Phillips. In 1983 she established the Mt. Cuba Center for the Study of Piedmont Flora on her estate. The center fosters appreciation of the beauty and diversity of piedmont flora and encourages their use in man-made landscapes by selecting and promoting superior forms.

RUTH PETIT JOHNSON of Frederica has applied the precepts of Quaker religion to life-long activities promoting peace, international goodwill, and stewardship of the earth. As an active member of the Dover League of Women Voters, she has promoted responsible management of coastal waters, the air, and solid waste. Working with Delawareans for Energy Conservation, she presented slide talks on energy problems to service clubs and schools and contributed to the establishment of the Delaware Department of Energy.

Johnson has headed the International Relations Committee of the Dover branch of the AAUW. In that capacity, she presented programs on the Law of the Sea treaty, South Africa, China, the United Nations, and a hunger-simulated meal that contrasted First-World and Third-World diets.

SUSAN MOERSCHEL LAPORTE (1955-   ) promotes proper care and wise use of Delaware's parks, recreation facilities, and natural heritage as a recreation resource planner for the Delaware Division of Parks and Recreation. During 1983 and 1984, she coordinated research for "Delaware Outdoors," an update of the State Comprehensive Outdoor Recreation Plan (SCORP) that recommends action to achieve long-range objectives for outdoor recreation and conservation. The plan was written partly to assure Delaware's eligibility to receive federal Land and Water Conservation Fund money. Laporte coordinates and heads SCORP's Technical Advisory Committee, which reviews the state outdoor recreation plan to identify issues and define policy. For the Office of Natural Preserves, Laporte oversees the registration of natural areas and nature preserves under the Natural Areas Preservation System. She also has coordinated studies on rare and endangered plants of the Delmarva Peninsula, on the impact of recreation on Delaware's economy, and on park visitor satisfaction with facilities and services.

JUNE D. MacARTOR of suburban Wilmington became involved in solving environmental problems through the League of Women Voters. As water resources chair of the local branch, she helped form the Inter-League Council of the Delaware River Basin about 1960. The council helped establish the Delaware River Basin Commission, the first interstate-federal approach to water management. To deepen her knowledge, MacArtor took technical training in pollution control at the University of Southern California. She found the technical field closed to women, but added a law degree from Villanova University, hoping that qualifications in two closed fields would translate into opportunity. MacArtor became head of the environmental group in the Delaware attorney general's office. For nine years she provided the legal expertise for the Delaware Department of Natural Resources and Environmental Control.

In her work, MacArtor prepared regulations for beach preservation and for wetlands protection, shepherded a program to keep public lands for public use, and handled court cases establishing the right of administrative agencies to administer legislation protecting the public interest in environmental matters. She believes that wise land use decisions in this era of attention to wetlands, hazardous waste disposal, and coastal area use are vital for Delaware's future. MacArtor was president of the League of Women Voters of Greater Wilmington and of the state of Delaware and served on the New Castle

County Merit System Committee, Governor's Crime Commission, and the Water Resources Association Board. She has taught environmental law at Delaware Law School. MacArtor now works in the state Division of Consumer Affairs, where she is coordinator of investigations and counseling.

NANCY M. NORLING (1940-) of Wilmington has been chair of the Delaware Public Service Commission since 1984 and a member since 1979. The commission, which regulates rates and services of investor-owned public utilities in Delaware, must maintain a balance between fair return for the utilities and affordable rates for consumers. Utility regulation can also promote energy conservation. During Norling's tenure on the commission, it has become a more professional organization, able to grapple with the complex questions that arise from changes in technology.

Norling, who is originally from Connecticut, has been actively involved in conservation organizations since she became a charter member and officer of Delawareans for Energy Conservation in 1975. Norling did civic work with the League of Women Voters and felt that advanced study would enable her to work more effectively. In an internship for her master's degree in urban affairs and public policy at the University of Delaware, Norling helped the New Castle County Water Resources Agency to develop a system for determining interjurisdictional costs for regional sewage collection and treatment and participated in planning to improve water supply and quality for the county. She has completed the course work for a Ph.D. from the University of Delaware, concentrating on the economic aspects of environmental policy and urban economic development. Norling chairs the water committee of the National Association of Regulatory Utility Commissioners. Despite the responsibilities of her job and academic pursuits, she continues to be involved in community service. She is an officer of the Delaware YMCA and Delaware Vassar Club, co-chair of annual fundraising for the Wilmington Friends School, and an active member of the First Unitarian Church, Wilmington.

JOANNE PASSMORE (1927-) was elected secretary of the National Grange in 1985, the first woman to hold a major office since the organization was founded in 1867. However, Passmore points out that the Grange has always given women an equal voice, recognizing their importance to the success of

55

a farm and as an influence in raising and educating the children. The Delaware State Grange elected JANE T. MITCHELL (1929-   ) of Lewes master of the Grange in 1987.

Passmore works with her husband, Wills, on their farm outside Townsend and served as his backup at meetings and conferences when he was Delaware State Grange Master. As an early 4-H Club Conservation Project leader, Joanne Passmore hosted state farm conservation tours to make members aware of the need for the best land management practices for farmland and agricultural projects. She advocated farmland preservation through her periodicals and books. Passmore, a native of Wisconsin, was co-editor of *Diamond State Granger*, Delaware's major farm periodical, from 1968 to 1972 and editor from 1980 to 1986. She wrote *Three Centuries of Delaware Agriculture* (1978) and *History of the Delaware Grange and the State's Agriculture, 1875-1975* (1975). Passmore was a member of the Governor's Study Committee on Aluminum Can Deposit Exemption in 1983 and of the core group of the Delaware Environmental Legacy Symposium. She has served on the board of trustees of Friends School and on the Corbit-Calloway Library Board for eight years, four as president.

MATILDA ("TIL") PURNELL (1921-   ) of Millsboro, League of Women Voters state environment chair, is a staunch proponent of clean water in Sussex County and throughout the state. Since 1976 she has worked with Friends of Herring Creek to improve water quality and to oversee changing land use along waterways. An active citizen advocate for protection of the Inland Bays for many years, Purnell has been in the forefront of groundwater protection in Sussex County. She is a member of the board of the Delaware Nature Education Society. Purnell is a member of the Possum Point Players and of the Eastern Shore Fibre Guild, and often demonstrates dyeing, spinning, and weaving skills at special craft events.

LEAH ROEDEL (1916-   ) of Wilmington received the first Delaware Nature Education Society Advocacy Award of Excellence in 1984. She was cited for "dedication for more than twenty years to improved environmental quality, the protection of natural resources, and the quality of public recreation opportunities in Delaware." A graduate of the University of Michigan, Roedel is well known for her leadership on local, state, and national commissions and

Leah Roedel

councils on the environment and as a trustee of the National Parks and Recreation Association. She is chair of the Delaware River and Bay Shoreline Committee and was a delegate to the National Conference on Groundwater Protection in 1984. Roedel is a former president of the Chesapeake Bay Girl Scout Council. She has helped bring tall ships to Delaware to focus attention on recreational use of state waterways and is working to set aside land for state parks.

NANCY B. TIEMAN, former mayor of Wyoming, is an advocate of soil conservation. She is the first woman president of the Delaware Association of Conservation Districts, part of a nationwide organization that supports and promotes practices to control soil erosion. Contour farming, grassed waterways, cover crops, crop residue management, natural windbreaks, and no-till techniques are encouraged (but compliance is voluntary) because they maintain and enrich the soil. Under Tieman's leadership, six ad hoc committees were formed to study the primary areas of concern: soil erosion; water management; forestry; fish, wildlife, and recreation; organic waste disposal; and land use.

PATRICIA TODD (1934-   ) became involved in League of Women Voters water-quality issues when she was reviewing the problems of disposing of hazardous wastes and their effect on water resources. Beginning in 1976, she represented the League on the Coalition against Non-returnables (Delaware CAN), an alliance of more than fifty organizations that advocated recycling resources and reducing litter. The coalition supported the Delaware Bottle Bill, which sought to impose five-cent deposits on beverage bottles and cans. Todd contributed long hours lobbying for the bill, which in 1982 was finally adopted in a weakened form due to bottling industry pressure. Todd, who lives in Wilmington, returned to school for another degree and now works in accounting. Among her most pleasant experiences are teaching Sunday school and serving as a Girl Scout leader.

CAROLE WALSH (1937-   ) of Newark is noted in Delaware and surrounding states for her knowledge of air pollution control and is often called upon to inform the public on progress in attaining clean air. She has represented the League of Women Voters in air quality programs since 1972 and participated in a national league conference on reauthorizing the Clean Air Act. Walsh is secretary of the executive board of the Mid-Atlantic Section of the Air Pollution Control Association, a professional organization of people involved in industry, education, research, and environmental protection in the air pollution field.

LYNN WILLIAMS (1932-   ), the first president of the Delaware Nature Education Society (DNES), has been in the forefront of Delaware conservation for more than twenty years and has received many honors for her exemplary work in conservation. In 1976 she was appointed to the state Coastal Zone Industrial Control Board. She also serves as a board member of DNES, Delaware Wildlands, and the

Lynn Williams

Christina Conservancy and as a member of Woodlawn Trustees. Williams considers her involvement with the Girl Scouts, which began when she was seven years old, a continuation of her commitment to conservation. In 1982 she received the first World of the Out-of-Doors Award from the Chesapeake Bay Girl Scout Council and became president of its board of directors in 1984. Williams voices the sentiment of thousands of women throughout Delaware and the nation when she concludes, "I feel strongly about the responsibility of protecting the environment and that comes through [in] everything I do."

DEVELOPERS OF MINDS:

Women In Education

Susan Alexis Thomas

Education has been one of the few fields in which women could find "respectable" paid work while raising a family. It is also one of the few fields where women could assume positions of greater responsibility and leadership.

EMALEA PUSEY WARNER (1853-1948) worked to establish a state college for women. With the support of women's groups, the Women's College Bill passed the General Assembly in 1913. WINIFRED J. ROBINSON (1868-1962) was dean of the college from its dedication in 1914 until 1938. She grew up in Battle Creek, Michigan, and did not earn her bachelor's degree, from the University of Michigan, until she was thirty-one years old. However, she went on to earn an M.A. and a Ph.D. in botany from Columbia University and to teach at Vassar College before coming to Delaware. Robinson was named one of four outstanding deans of women's colleges in 1930. The Women's College merged with the men's Delaware College to form the University of Delaware in 1944.

Warner, in addition to her leadership in higher education, was active in elementary and secondary education. She helped introduce manual training such as carpentry into Wilmington public schools in the 1890s and raised funds to maintain kindergartens and provide cafeteria lunches. For her importance in education, the women's suffrage movement, and starting the Family Court of New Castle County, Warner entered the Hall of Fame of Delaware Women in 1982.

Blacks have been faced with even greater obstacles to obtaining education than women. A few blacks educated themselves or attended schools established for them by the Quakers. The Free School Law of 1829 set up a system of state-supported free schools grouped into school districts, though no state funds went to black schools until 1881. Not until 1907 was school attendance (just three months per year in

Emalea Pusey Warner and Winifred J. Robinson

59

rural areas) made compulsory in Delaware. With the Free School Law, public schools soon sprang up in Wilmington and in other populated areas around the state, but not in rural areas, where most of the black and poor population lived.

Under the auspices of an association dedicated to promoting education of blacks, EDWINA B. KRUSE (18? -1930) was responsible for organizing many schools. In 1876 Kruse, born in Puerto Rico and raised in Connecticut, became the first black principal of Howard High School for black students in Wilmington. Until her retirement in 1921, she maintained high standards for the compulsory academic curriculum that made it one of the best schools in Wilmington. Many of the women who graduated from Howard High School during those years became school teachers. Kruse attracted an outstanding faculty, including ALICE MOORE DUNBAR-NELSON (1875-1935), who wrote an unpublished novel based on Kruse's life.

Until kindergarten became mandatory in Delaware in September 1985, many children received their introduction to formal education in the elementary grades. Elementary-school teachers often set the tone for a student's future success in school and provide a firm foundation of skills.

Among the first women to receive a degree from the University of Delaware, ELIZABETH MAY B. LEASURE (1899-1980) began teaching in Salem, New Jersey, in 1918. She later taught at Glasgow School and then moved to the Eden School in Bear. This school, renamed in her honor in 1975, had only one room when Leasure arrived in 1930. She was on the district building committee in 1956 when the school grew to eight classrooms, with a library and a cafeteria/auditorium. Responsible for many "firsts" in Delaware schools, Leasure organized parent-teacher associations at Glasgow and Eden schools; she started a 4-H Club at Glasgow School, and in 1924 she was the first teacher to have a community doctor examine all of the children in the school.

Leasure received a teaching medal from President Calvin Coolidge and was a guest at the White House in 1926. She was awarded a medal from the Freedoms Foundation of Valley Forge in 1963 for "exceptional service in furthering the cause of responsible citizenship, patriotism, and a greater

Elizabeth May B. Leasure

understanding and appreciation of the American way of life."

TERESA G. CAREY, a lifelong resident of Sussex County, revised the Indian River social-studies curriculum to make learning exciting. She uses a box of artifacts to help teach history and has developed units on fairy tales and on the values of a free-enterprise system. Carey was chosen Delaware Teacher of the Year in 1984.

The majority of classroom teachers in Delaware are women, but women hold only 26 percent of the administrative and supervisory positions in the state. (In 1928, 55 percent of all elementary school principals in the United States were women, in contrast to 18 percent in 1978.) BESSIE DEVINE (?-1946) was assistant superintendent of the Wilmington Public Schools until her death. Three times during her long and successful career she was appointed acting superintendent of schools when the male superintendent died, received a better position elsewhere, or moved out of town. But she was never tapped for the top position herself. Her sisters were also educators. MARGARET DEVINE taught at School #30 and SARAH DEVINE was principal of Harlan School. There are still no female school superintendents in Delaware.

MURIEL CROSBY (1908-) became assistant superintendent of elementary education for the Wilmington Public Schools in 1951. She not only received recognition for her expertise in developing curriculum for elementary schools in a changing society but also for promoting racial understanding to insure a smooth transition during the years that the school system achieved integration.

After teaching elementary school in Delaware for over twenty years, EDITH I. C. SCOTT became the principal of a school in Selbyville. At that time, only two other blacks in town had earned college degrees and neither was employed in Delaware. In 1955 Scott began teaching mentally retarded nine- to twelve-year-olds. A native of Boydton, Virginia, who was educated in Virginia, Scott, who has been retired since 1970, lives in Milford. She served on the Interracial Committee of the Delaware State Education Association and was president of the National Council of Negro Women, Peninsula Section, for eight years.

A Sussex County teacher and later principal of the North East School in Wilmington, ARRIE J. HARRISON (1922-) also was active in implementing desegregation in the Wilmington schools. The first black woman to serve as director of elementary education for the Wilmington public schools, Harrison is the only woman on the New Castle County Parks and Recreation Advisory Board.

There are many distinguished Delaware secondary-school teachers of the past and present. A 1921 graduate of Ursuline Academy, Wilmington, CATHERINE

D. GAUSE (1903-1982) taught at Wilmington High School for more than forty years. She took a special interest in the World War II refugee children who arrived in Wilmington from Europe and privately tutored many of them in English. She also served as an officer of the University of Delaware Alumnae Association, the Ursuline Academy Home and School Asociation, the Catholic Diocesan Book Forum, the Wilmington High School PTA, and the Wilmington New Century Club. At the 1973 Ursuline Academy commencement ceremony, Gause was named "first alumna" of the school and was awarded an honorary diploma and a medal of excellence for "long years of dedication and service." She was named Alumna of the Year at the fiftieth class reunion of the University of Delaware Women's College in 1975.

AMY GUEST LLOYD FARRAND (1905-1982) began her teaching career in a Wilmington elementary school in the late 1920s. Upon receiving a bachelor's degree from the University of Delaware in 1931, she joined the faculty at Wilmington High School, where she developed a guidance program. Later, at Pierre S. du Pont High School, Farrand also taught social studies and wrote the American history curriculum. Farrand, who retired in 1970, was a recognized master teacher.

The influence of a good teacher casts a long shadow. This is the case of MABEL CLOUGH WRIGHT HENRY (1911-), the director of dramatics in the Wilmington public school system from 1934 to 1972. Among the many students she influenced is CHERYL YVONNE JONES, who wrote and performed in the one-woman production "Great Women of Color" during New York City's Black History Gala in January 1983. Henry earned an M.A. and a Ph.D. from Teachers College, Columbia University, in theater "despite low salaries and a teachers union that fought against extra education." When she was growing up in Wilmington, women typically chose either to marry or to teach; she did not marry until she was fifty years old. Henry directed the Children's Theatre of Wilmington High School. She also uses her talent as a writer to inspire others to employ drama as a teaching tool.

BLANCHE MILES FLEMING has been a classroom teacher, a principal, a curriculum specialist, and a director of teacher education programs for the Wilmington public-school system and for the University

61

Harriet Beach Donofrio

Blanche Miles Fleming

of Delaware. In 1980 she developed a tutoring center at La Biblioteca del Pueblo, a branch of the Wilmington Institute Libraries; she has conducted meetings on bilingual education for the Wilmington community.

Fleming is a board member and chairs the education committee of FAME, a program launched by the Du Pont Company to encourage the advancement of minorities in engineering. She is a member of the Methodist Action Program's public assistance task force, a member of the steering committee of Common Cause of Delaware, and chair of the State Council on Volunteers, Division of Consumer Affairs. Fleming was born in Salem, New Jersey, graduated from Delaware State College, and earned a doctorate in educational administration from Antioch College.

CAROLYN B. NACZI (1942-   ) was principal of Ursuline Academy High School and president of Ursuline Academy, Wilmington, her alma mater, from 1978 to 1984. As an Ursuline nun, she earned a master's degree from the University of Notre Dame and served as assistant principal at the Ursuline

School, New Rochelle, New York. Naczi was director of the Beacon Retreat Center and served the inmates of the maximum security prison in Stormville, New York. She also worked as assistant to the director of the New York Archdiocesan Office for World Justice and Peace. In 1986 Naczi applied for dispensation from her religious order. She teaches at a high school in Tuckahoe, New York.

Two Delaware high school teachers have been among the top four national finalists for Teacher of the Year. HARRIET BEACH DONOFRIO (1945-   ), state Teacher of the Year in 1983, teaches tenth-grade biology and advanced courses in oceanography, radioisotopes, and scientific instrumentation at Cape Henlopen High School in Lewes. Donofrio

62

also designed a marine environment and animal life course for gifted third and fourth graders. She conducts seminars for other teachers on units that she designed for the University of Delaware project COAST. Donofrio was honored as the Outstanding High School Environmental Educator for the state because her environmental programs (for kindergarten through grade twelve) are used throughout Delaware.

Donofrio also received awards from the Delaware Nature Education Society and was appointed to Governor Pierre S. du Pont IV's Task Force on Education for Economic Growth. She serves on the steering committee of the State Science Olympiad and assists with development of the marine science curriculum at the University of Delaware. A native of Mardela Springs, Maryland, Donofrio lives near Frederica.

SUSAN ALEXIS THOMAS (1946-   ), a chemistry and physics teacher at Delcastle Technical High School, Marshallton, was named Delaware Teacher of the Year in 1985 and was a national finalist. She developed courses in applied science and advanced earth science and a chemistry course for cosmetology students at Delcastle. Thomas serves on the principal's advisory committee and was vice-president of the New Castle County Federation of Teachers. Thomas gives credit for her success to the nurturing atmosphere at the old Wilmington High School in Wilmington, where she began teaching. She believes it is important to teach the entire student and raise his or her self-esteem by cultivating a positive self-image. While studying at the University of Delaware, Thomas organized the university's first Black Awareness Week. She has helped found drama and athletic groups for youth and adults. These experiences and nine years teaching at Howard Career Center, the Upward Bound program at the University of Delaware, and Shaw Junior High School in Philadelphia, her birthplace, have contributed to her growth and appreciation for education.

NORMA IVONNE ANTONGIORGI (1951-   ) heads the Red Clay Consolidated School District bilingual program. She set up programs for migrant workers and Hispanics and instituted systems to identify children who need special help because of language. About four hundred students are in the district bilingual program and uncounted English-speaking students have Spanish-speaking parents. Antongiorgi helps design curricula to meet these children's needs and organizes meetings of Hispanic parents to assist them in understanding and cooperating with the schools. Antongiorgi, who came to Wilmington from Puerto Rico in 1973, has been vice-president of the Latin American Community Center and a member of the Hispanic Coalition of Delaware.

LINDA F. WINFIELD (1948-   ) of Wilmington was the first black woman to receive a Ph.D. degree from the University of Delaware College of Education. After supervising research and reporting for New Castle County schools, she spent a year as a visiting scholar with the Educational Testing Service, Princeton, New Jersey. Winfield teaches in the College of Education at Temple University and is a research associate in its Center for Research in Human Development in Education.

RUTH MITCHELL LAWS began teaching adult education in Wilmington in 1936 after teaching high school in her native North Carolina. She moved into administration in 1966, serving as state supervisor of home economics and state director of adult and continuing education before joining Delaware Technical and Community College. She is retired from her position as vice-president for research and development there. Laws has held offices in professional associations, civil-rights associations, her church, and the Dover-Kent County YMCA and has served on the Delaware commissions on Children and Youth and on Aging. She helped develop the state Head Start program in the 1960s. In 1972 Laws received the Outstanding Vocational Educator Award of the State Department of Public Instruction and in 1974 the Diamond State Award for meritorious service to education and government, the first woman and the first black to receive it. She was in the first group of women inducted into the Hall of Fame of Delaware Women in 1981.

In 1977 former teacher and administrator LUCILLE PONATOSKI TORO (1936-   ) created New Work Roles for Women, a program that trained Sussex and New Castle County women in skilled trades and helped them find apprenticeship and employment. The program was funded through the Comprehensive Employment Training Act (CETA) and sponsored by the Delaware chapter of the National

black given a full-time contract on the University of Delaware faculty (1965) and helped establish the University Writing Center in 1966 to assist students in developing writing skills. A native of Washington, D.C., with a Ph.D. from the University of Chicago, she later taught English at Wilmington College.

After teaching in colleges in North Carolina and Alabama, Davis came to Delaware to work in the mental health field in the 1950s. In 1958 she was one of six Delawareans named to the White House Conference on Education. Presidents Lyndon Johnson and Richard Nixon appointed her to commissions on the needs of black women and secondary school finance. In the course of over fifty years in the National Association of University Women, Davis served as president and treasurer and was chosen Woman of the Year by the Wilmington branch in 1970. She was the first female senior warden of a mission in the Episcopal Diocese of Delaware and served on the national board of the YWCA. Davis was inducted into the Hall of Fame of Delaware Women in 1986.

When ELIZABETH E. ("BETTY") BOHNING (1915-   ) joined the faculties of Delaware College and the Women's College to teach scientific German in 1942, it was unusual for a woman to teach classes of men, as she did. A native of Massachusetts, she was attracted to the schools because they were pioneers in Junior Year Abroad programs. Since her retirement, Bohning has maintained her interest in foreign study and travel as a means to promote friendship between nations and has been an advisor to foreign study programs in Germany and Austria and president of the Delaware Council for International Visitors. In 1982 the American Association of Teachers of German and the Goethe House, a U.S. organization of centers of German culture, honored Bohning with a certificate of merit. She has served on the board of the University of Delaware Library Associates.

ANNA JANNEY DE ARMOND (1910-   ), who joined the University of Delaware faculty in 1935, was the first female professor in the English department. She became a full professor in 1968. De Armond was the first faculty member to receive the Excellence-in-Teaching Award of the University of Delaware twice, in 1954 and in 1972. She wrote *Andrew Bradford, Colonial Journalist* (1949), the first book pub-

Eugenia M. Hintze Slavov

Organization for Women (NOW). Toro was national chair of the NOW Education Discrimination Committee, which was concerned with discrimination in vocational education and the enforcement of Title IX in public schools. Toro is program officer of Public/Private Ventures, Inc., which implements training programs throughout the country for women in the construction trades.

Among the many distinguished female college teachers, those who teach English and foreign languages have been outstanding. HILDA ANDREA DAVIS (1905-   ) of New Castle was the first

lished by the University of Delaware Press. De Armond continues to teach at the University of Delaware's Academy of Lifelong Learning.

The parents of EUGENIA M. HINTZE SLAVOV (1925-   ), refugees from Bolshevik Russia, valued a good education because, as her grandfather said, "Nobody can take that from you." Slavov, who was born in France and grew up in Bulgaria, received her doctorate from the University of Rome in 1954. She was a reporter for Radio Free Europe in Rome, 1952-56, and freelance correspondent for Radio Liberty in Munich in 1956. Slavov taught languages at Tower Hill School in Wilmington from 1957 until 1964, when she began teaching at the University of Delaware. Since then, she has taught Italian, French, German, Spanish, and Russian language and literature courses, including scientific Russian. In 1982 Slavov won the Excellence-in-Teaching Award of the University of Delaware.

ELNORA RIGIK (1942-   ), associate professor of English at Brandywine College of Widener University, is the director of the first Honors Program there. A native of Coos Bay, Oregon, she received the Lindback Award for Excellence in Teaching.

Black American literature, the Harlem Renaissance, and literature of the women's movement are among the subjects GLORIA T. HULL (1944-   ) teaches in the University of Delaware English department, which she joined in 1971. Hull has written articles on black American women poets, including the Delaware writer ALICE MOORE DUNBAR-NELSON, whose diary (published 1984) Hull edited. She edited a regional anthology, *A Delaware Sampler* (with RUTH J. KAPLAN). Hull edited *All the Women Are White, All the Blacks Are Men, But Some of Us Are Brave: Black Women's Studies* (with BARBARA SMITH and PATRICIA BELL SCOTT) (1982), and wrote *Color, Sex, and Poetry: Three Women Writers of the Harlem Renaissance* (1987). She received an award from the University of Delaware for outstanding contributions and service to minority students. A native of Shreveport, Louisiana, Hull graduated from Southern University with highest honors and received her doctorate from Purdue University. From 1984 to 1986, she had a Fulbright Senior Lectureship at the University of the West Indies, Kingston, Jamaica.

Gloria T. Hull

Women can be found in most areas of college teaching. SUZANNE K. STEINMETZ (1941-   ) is an authority on domestic violence who has written several articles and books on the subject. She wrote *Behind Closed Doors: Violence in American Families* (1980) and the foreword to "Facing Crises," a pamphlet published by the Delaware Commission for Women. Steinmetz is co-author (with Marvin Sussman) of the forthcoming *Handbook on Marriage and the Family*. On the faculty at the University of Delaware since 1973, the New Jersey native received a bachelor's degree from the University of Delaware and earned master's and doctoral degrees from Case Western Reserve University. Steinmetz was a member of the Human Resources Panel of Distinguished College Faculty in 1980.

SANDRA HARDING (1935-   ) returned to graduate school at age thirty-two after ten years in business, teaching school, and having two children. She is a professor of philosophy and sociology at the University of Delaware, where she is also director of women's studies. Harding serves on editorial boards for feminist journals and on the board of directors for the Society for Values in Higher Education.

FLORENCE L. GEIS (1933-   ), professor of social psychology at the University of Delaware since 1982, has combined teaching with research on differences in behavior of the sexes. With her students, she has researched unconscious factors in social situations that influence people's behavior and treatment of each other. Geis's recent publications focus on such issues as how male and female students, faculty, and administrators are perceived and treated in American colleges and universities and whether personality traits commonly assumed to be "naturally" masculine or feminine depend on one's sex or on cultural assumptions about appropriate roles of the sexes. In 1972 she was the first faculty member to conduct an interdisciplinary women's studies course. Geis has been invited to speak in England, Norway, Germany, and India as well as at universities and research conventions across the United States. She has received the University of Delaware Excellence-in-Teaching award.

MARGARET L. ANDERSEN, who has taught sociology at the University of Delaware since 1974, specializes in sex and gender/women's studies and race and ethnic relations. She won the Outstanding Young Scholar Award of the Delaware AAUW in 1979 and the Excellence-in-Teaching Award of the University of Delaware in 1980. At the university, Andersen was director of women's studies and faculty consultant to the Rape Crisis Center and served on the Commission on the Status of Women.

Women are becoming prominent in college administration in Delaware. HELEN GOULDNER (1923-   ) has been dean of the College of Arts and Sciences, University of Delaware, since 1974. She earned a doctorate in sociology at the University of California, Los Angeles, and taught at Washington University, St. Louis, from 1963 to 1973. Before she became dean, Gouldner was chair of the University of Delaware sociology department, a post she also held at Washington University. Her research and

Helen Gouldner

teaching have focused on interdisciplinary approaches to human interaction, sociology of education, and culture and personality. Her book *Speaking of Friendship* was accepted for publication in 1985. *Teachers' Pets, Troublemakers and Nobodies: Black Children in Elementary School* (1978) received the Educators' Award of Delta Kappa Gamma Society International in 1979. Gouldner has served on the National Committee on Education and Utilization of the Engineer and the Council of Colleges of Arts and Science. She is on the boards of directors of the Medical Center of Delaware and the World Affairs Council.

Now dean of development, Delaware Technical and Community College, Georgetown campus,

Charlotte Hedlicka Purnell

CHARLOTTE HEDLICKA PURNELL considers her most important achievement the development and direction of Del Mod, a program designed to improve science education and to encourage a larger number of high-school graduates to enter the field of science. The Del Mod program, which has been emulated by state school systems throughout the country, is still in use.

A native of rural New Castle County, Purnell's career in science resulted from a combination of misfortune and curiosity. Stricken by bulbar polio as a teenager, she became interested in the transmission of bacteriological diseases. To overcome her disability, she became an avid swimmer and excelled in collegiate competition. After earning a degree in biology at the University of Delaware, Purnell worked as a bacteriologist. She taught science courses in Millsboro and Georgetown high schools while caring for her children and earning a master's degree in education. From 1967 to 1971, prior to the development of Del Mod, Purnell was the nation's only female state science supervisor.

GWENDOLYN W. SANDERS has been dean of student services, Delaware Technical and Community College, Stanton and Wilmington campuses, since 1973. She directs guidance and vocational testing services there. Sanders is a consultant to the U.S. Office of Education, the Department of Justice, Community Relation Services, Headstart/Follow Through, the Methodist Action Program, and the Educational Testing Service. Sanders has been a member of the Delaware Human Relations Commission and the Delaware Manpower Planning Council. She is vice-chair of the Brandywine Professional Association and a member of the Delaware Library Council and the Delaware Humanities Forum Council. Sanders earned a master's degree from St. Louis University and a doctorate from Nova University. Before coming to Delaware in 1969, she was a master teacher in the St. Louis Public Schools and directed the Head Start Program in the Lincoln, Nebraska, public schools. From 1969 to 1972, she served as an education consultant-planner for the City of Wilmington.

CAROLYN A. THOROUGHGOOD (1943-   ) is dean of the College of Marine Studies, University of Delaware, and director of the university's Sea Grant College Program. She received a bachelor's degree in food science and nutrition from the University of Delaware in 1965 and M.S. and Ph.D. degrees in nutritional biochemistry from the University of Maryland. In 1968 Thoroughgood returned to the University of Delaware as a faculty member in her former department. She complemented teaching activities with research on diverse topics, including the nutrition education needs of elementary-school children and the study of "organically" versus "non-organically" grown foods.

Because of Thoroughgood's interest in extension education, she joined the College of Marine Studies and the Sea Grant College Program as director of the Marine Advisory Service in 1974. She was responsible for planning and managing statewide marine extension programs. Thoroughgood was the first woman elected president of the National Council of Sea Grant Directors and she reviews sea grant proposals as a member of the Sea Grant Site Team. She was appointed associate dean in 1980 but has remained an active faculty member. Among her professional publications are *The Delaware Approach to Coastal/Oceanic Awareness Studies K-12* (with R.W.

Carolyn Thoroughgood

Stegner) and *A National Policy for Marine Education* (with H.L. Goodwin and J. Schaadt).

Delaware has one female college president. In 1979 AUDREY K. DOBERSTEIN (1932-   ) became the second president of Wilmington College. She joined the college as a consultant soon after it was founded in 1967 to help attain accreditation and design the M.B.A. program. Doberstein improved the image of the college and public awareness of it; encouraged financial stability and growth of the student curricula; and developed centers in Dover, Georgetown, and downtown Wilmington.

Doberstein holds a degree from the University of Delaware and a Ph.D. from the University of Pennsylvania. She taught in Claymont and in Louisville, Kentucky, and worked for the Delaware Department of Public Instruction. In 1969 she established a consulting firm that served colleges in Delaware and nearby states. Doberstein is a member of the board of the Chesapeake Bay Girl Scout

Council and was on the Greater Wilmington Development Council.

As women entered the job market in increasing numbers, colleges began to give them specialized help. MAE RIEDY CARTER (1921-   ) was appointed special assistant to the provost and executive director of the Commission on the Status of Women at the University of Delaware in 1978. When Carter retired in 1986, she had established a supportive environment for women on campus; assembled a data bank of relevant information; and maintained a collection of university and community resources for women. She prepared a yearly evaluation of university progress toward providing equity for women along with numerous other publications, including the Research on Women Series.

Carter counseled women without marketable skills in the Continuing Education Services Department of the university beginning in 1968. She was president of the AAUW, Newark Branch, and of the Friends of the Newark Public Library. Carter holds a B.S. degree from the University of California, Berkeley, where she was born. In 1976 she won a

Audrey K. Doberstein

68

Fulbright Award to study changing sex roles in India. After seventeen years of fighting for women's issues, she is still working to raise student awareness. "A lot of students think the battle is over," she says. "I know it is not."

PAMELA BAILEY MORRIS (1935-   ) is a co-founder and co-coordinator of the Women's Center, University of Delaware and Delaware Technical and Community College, and assistant director of the Division of Continuing Education, Delaware Technical and Community College. Her major interest and contribution is in adult education and career development. The Women's Center was begun to meet the needs of women who wanted to work for the first time or to re-enter the job market. The Center has provided information, referral, and career services to several hundred women free of charge as well as furnishing resource materials on subjects of interest to women. Morris also founded the Delaware Women's Conference, sponsored by the Women's Center, the Delaware Commission for Women, and the Junior League of Wilmington. The conference was begun to encourage networking among women from all walks of life.

Morris has chaired the Human Services Committee of the Intergovernmental Task Force and has chaired an associate degree program in human services and directed a remedial program for status offenders. She holds B.A. and M.A. degrees in American studies from the University of Delaware and an M.S.Ed. in educational research from West Chester University. Morris recently earned a Ph.D. in psychological studies at Temple University and has completed a philosophical book on womanhood.

To help women get the education they need to achieve, DOLORES FENIX-SAPIENZA (1933-   ) of Dover created a position for herself as director of continuing education for Delaware State College. Born in Shamokin, Pennsylvania, Fenix-Sapienza began her career as a manager and writer with the Lancaster (Pennsylvania) Newspaper, Inc., after graduating from Syracuse University with a B.S. degree in journalism and sociology. She interrupted her career to marry and be a mother. Fenix-Sapienza returned to the job market as a program developer at Delaware Technical and Community College, Terry Campus, while completing a master's degree in adult community education at Indiana University, Pennsylvania.

Governor Pierre S. du Pont IV appointed her human relations commissioner. She was recognized as one of five Kent County Wonder Women for her "service to mankind" and received a citation by Kent County Big Brothers/Big Sisters. Fenix-Sapienza was recognized by the Correctional Superintendent of Delaware Youth Center as a Woman Volunteer of "integrity, grit, initiative, and humanistic commitment."

NANCY ARMSTRONG ALDRICH and LOUISE THOMPSON CONNER (1918-1983) worked to establish the Academy of Lifelong Learning of the University of Delaware. The program, which began in 1980, provides intellectual and cultural exploration and development to men and women fifty-five years or older. Aldrich also developed the Summer Youth Campus, an enrichment program for students in grades three through twelve.

Conner was a state senator from 1964 to 1972 and chair of the Delaware Advisory Committee to the U.S. Civil Rights Commission from 1981 to 1983. In 1981 the Delaware State Bar Association gave Conner its Liberty Bell Award for lay contributions to justice. She received the Humanitarian Award of the NAACP and the J. Thompson Brown Award from Family Service of Northern Delaware in recognition of her "outstanding contributions to family life in Delaware." Conner was inducted into the Hall of Fame of Delaware Women in 1985.

Preschool and kindergarten are relatively recent developments. From 1945 to 1978, ANNA R. GRINNAGE operated one of the earliest private kindergartens in her home in downtown Wilmington. At a time when education for blacks was scarce, she helped black children get a good start. Born and reared in Spartansburg, South Carolina, Grinnage taught in Maryland and Pennsylvania before she came to Wilmington. She organized and directed the choir of Bethel A.M.E. Church and performed as a radio soloist. In 1979 her church honored her for forty-five years of contributions to the people of Wilmington.

GERALDINE McKINLEY ("GERRY") GARVIN (1922-   ) is typical of the generation of well-educated women (she was a Phi Beta Kappa graduate of Wellesley College) who served their community while their children attended local schools. A pioneer in preschool education and a leader in the drive to establish public kindergarten in Wilmington suburbs, she was administrator of the Delaware Preschool Association from 1949 to 1977.

In 1966 Garvin joined the faculty of the newly established Brandywine College, Wilmington, where she was an associate professor of psychology and director of the child psychology student internship program until her retirement in 1985. She became president of the Mental Health Association of Delaware in 1986. Garvin has also been active on the Junior Board of the Wilmington Medical Center and in the AAUW, Chesapeake Bay Girl Scout Council, Delaware Humanities Forum, United Way, and her church. She was a graduate of Leadership Delaware in 1986 and was honored by the United Way as an outstanding volunteer. A native of Petoskey, Michigan, Garvin was the first recipient of the AAUW Mather-Smyth scholarship for graduate study at the University of Delaware in 1958. She has written for *New Directions for Women.*

EMILY GEORGE MORRIS (1934-   ) of Dover left her position as secretary to the deputy superintendent in 1970 to direct the troubled Capitol Green Day Care Center in Dover. She revitalized the school and expanded it to form the Dover Educational and Community Center. When Morris was a secretary at Jason High School, she conducted a successful fundraising campaign for the school band. She was the first black secretary at Legislative Hall and at the Department of Public Instruction in the mid-1960s.

In 1980 Morris was elected prothonotary of Kent County on the Republican ticket, making her the first black woman elected to county-wide office in Delaware. Her awards include Order of the First State, the highest honor that can be given to a Delaware citizen, the Susan B. Anthony Cup, and the Wonder Woman Award from the Kent County chapter of the National Organization for Women. Morris was one of ten people chosen from more than two thousand applicants to be a National Rural Fellow. Under the program, she pursued a master's degree in regional planning at the University of Massachusetts.

When RENEE O'LEARY, a kindergarten teacher at Wilmington Manor Elementary School, New Castle, was named Delaware Teacher of the Year in

Emily G. Morris

1982, she had been teaching for thirty-one years. She helps children "learn to express what love is. They can learn that giving love gets love, and they can translate love of the teacher into love of the school." A resident of Newark, O'Leary has led storytelling workshops and taught creative dramatics at the University of Delaware and Cabrini College. She is vice-president of the Brandywiners and performs with the Wilmington Opera Society and the Chapel Street Players of Newark. O'Leary is president of the Brandywine Motorsport Club and was the highest-ranked female rally driver in the nation.

Although not strictly speaking in the teaching profession, librarians are educators. Librarians contribute to education from a person's earliest years on. KATHRYN STURGIS HOWIE (1915-1978), librarian and district coordinator of libraries for the Alexis I. du Pont Special School District from 1947 to 1977, helped books come alive for children. In 1951 alert young readers spotted an inconsistency between the number of robbers mentioned in the text and the number shown in the illustrations of Robert McCloskey's *The Case of the Sensational Scent.* With Howie's encouragement, the children wrote

70

the author, beginning an exchange of letters with authors on various topics.

After earning degrees at De Pauw and Purdue universities, Howie taught school in Ohio, Indiana, and her native state of New Jersey before arriving in Delaware. An authority on American children's literature, Howie contributed articles to professional publications. In 1971 the Delaware State Library Association honored her as the Outstanding Librarian of Delaware. Howie collected more than two hundred original illustrations for children's books, which she housed in the library in each school district. Following her death, the Author's Room Collections were accepted on permanent loan by the Wilmington Institute Libraries for readers of all ages to enjoy. The Howie Library at Henry B. du Pont Middle School was named for Howie and her husband, Thomas.

GRACE HUSTED (1931-   ) developed the public library in Hockessin from a bookmobile stop. She began in a vacated building with two bookcases on each side of a fireplace in June of 1977 and had the first floor ready to open by Labor Day. In 1980 the second floor was renovated and developed into a children's section. Before coming to Hockessin, Husted worked as head of the circulation department at Newark Free Library. From 1979 to 1980 she was president of the Public Library Division of the Delaware Library Association.

SUSAN CLAPP JAMISON (1929-   ) is director of the Corbit-Calloway Memorial Library, Odessa, and an English faculty member of Wilmington College. Jamison is president of the Delaware Library Association. In nine years at Corbit-Calloway she has instituted automated cataloguing and searching and greatly increased library hours, membership, circulation, and the size of the collection.

Jamison has directed local history projects that produced slide-tape programs, exhibits, and booklets on Kent and southern New Castle counties and the state as a whole. In 1983 Jamison was nominated for the Allie Beth Martin Award for outstanding public librarianship in the United States. She represented Delaware at the National Archives Conference on Women's History in 1976. Jamison graduated *summa cum laude* from the City University of New York and has earned three master's degrees, in history and English from the University of Delaware and in library science from the University of Maryland.

Susan Clapp Jamison

SUSAN BRYNTESON (1936-   ), director of libraries for the University of Delaware since 1980, has held increasingly responsible positions in the libraries of the University of Massachusetts, Amherst; the University of Tennessee, Knoxville; and Indiana University, Bloomington. She received her B.A. in philosophy and M.A. in library science from the University of Wisconsin, Madison. Brynteson has been active in the American Library Association (ALA) and is a member of the ALA Council and chair of the ALA Publishing Committee. She was president of the nine-thousand-member ALA Resources and Technical Services Division and chair of the Association of College and Research Libraries Legislation Committee. Brynteson has served as a consultant to academic institutions and regularly

71

Susan Brynteson

serves on teams that accredit institutions of higher education. She has also served on five different local League of Women Voters boards around the country, including that of Newark, and was twice elected a member of the Amherst (Massachusetts) town meeting.

Library patrons were impressed by the efficiency and devotion of GAIL W. JOHNSTON, former librarian of the Rehoboth Beach Public Library. "We couldn't pay her for what she's worth," a library board member admitted. Johnston was attracted to a career in libraries by her love for people and reading.

BARBARA BEAMAN, former library supervisor at Hercules, Inc., began her career as a librarian assistant in 1947. She attended Drexel Institute twice a week for three years to earn a library degree. At Hercules, Beaman established on-line searching for reference information. She is active in library associations, the AAUW, and the Libraries in New Castle County System, which facilitates borrowing and lending among school, public, and special libraries.

Concerned citizens also contribute to education. ALICE LEARNED WILSON (1913-1984) was cited

by the AAUW in 1981 for significant contributions to the quality of life in the community through her work for education. In 1955, under her chairmanship, the education committee of the Wilmington AAUW cooperated with the University of Delaware to sponsor a teacher recruitment program. In 1966 a grant award in Wilson's name was offered by the Wilmington chapter to the National Educational Foundations Program of the AAUW.

Because she believes that books and libraries are the "backbone of education," CARMEN GUEFFROY NELSON of Newark has worked in support of Delaware libraries for thirty years. When she was a child, her family lived in a small Oregon town that had no library and her parents' home became the lending library for the community. After Nelson moved to Delaware in 1952, she organized a fund drive and the first summer library program for the Brookside Elementary School Library. She was a trustee of the Newark Free Library for fifteen years, started its friends group, and chaired the committee for a new building.

Appointed to the first New Castle County Library Advisory Board in 1975, Nelson served six years, three as chair. She was on the steering committee of the Governor's Conference on Libraries and Information Services. As a member and chair of the State Advisory Council on Libraries, 1981-85, Nelson helped pass legislation that tripled state funding for libraries. A former teacher, Nelson was president of Delaware Guidance Services for Children and Youth and of the AAUW, from which she received a fellowship in 1967. She was president and a board member of the League of Women Voters, an officer of the PTA, and a member of the State Committee on Teacher Recruitment. In 1985 Nelson received the Delaware Library Association Distinguished Service Citation. County executive Rita Justice appointed her to the New Castle County library task force in 1986.

Education advisor to Governor Michael Castle, HELEN KNISKERN FOSS (1939-) works to promote human relations in education. She coordinates the Wilmington-area Green Circle program, which promotes pluralism. She is a consultant from the program to the state Department of Public Instruction and wrote a manual used by the national program. Foss also developed a human relations program for secondary-school students. She serves on the Human Relations Advisory Council to the schools. Foss

Jennie Smith

73

is on the board of managers of the Citizens Alliance for Public Education. She chairs the State Board of Education Desegregation Advisory Committee and leads a group of community leaders concerned with implementing desegregation peacefully. Foss was executive director of the Delaware Region, National Conference of Christians and Jews, for nine years and now serves on the board. She developed the curriculum for Leadership Delaware and is on the Women's Center Advisory Panel. In 1985 Foss received the World of People award of the Chesapeake Bay Girl Scout Council.

MARTHA G. BACHMAN (1924-   ) has headed the Delaware Advisory Council on Career and Vocational Education since her appointment by Governor Russell W. Peterson in 1969. She had previously served on the New Castle County Vo-Tech board and was the first woman elected chair of the Marshallton-McKean board of education. Co-chair of the Berndt/

Bachman Committee on people with special needs, Bachman makes use of the experience she has gained from years of volunteer service to the community.

A member of the board of directors of Jobs for Delaware Graduates, Inc., Bachman has served on the State Employment Training Council and the National Advisory Council on Vocational Education and has worked with the Delaware Council on Crime and Justice to study law enforcement agencies. Bachman was appointed to the Delaware Council on Services to Children and Youth and to the Governor's Council on Education by Governor Sherman Tribbitt. In 1979 Governor Pierre S. du Pont IV named Bachman a Distinguished Delawarean.

Women continue to make contributions to education in Delaware as teachers, school-board members, librarians, and concerned and committed members of the public.

74

FOR THE PUBLIC GOOD:

Women In
Government, Politics,
and Military Service

Elizabeth La DuLake

Women in Delaware have been active in politics since they participated in the drive to win the vote for women. The Woman's Suffrage Party was organized in Delaware in 1869. FLORENCE BAYARD HILLES (1865- ?), MABEL VERNON (1884-1975), EMMA BELLE GIBSON SYKES (1885-1970), and VERA GILBRIDE DAVIS (1894-1974) were among the Delaware women who were active in the female suffrage movement. In 1898 the state legislature allowed women to vote in school elections only if they paid a school tax in their district. Full voting rights did not come until 1920, with the Nineteenth Amendment to the United States Constitution. Forty thousand Delaware women registered to vote in the two days left to register before the 1920 election, even though the state House had failed to ratify the amendment.

Delaware women were first involved in community action, political parties, and campaigns and later as legislators and executives of state and local government. They also serve in the military.

MARGARET BURTON WHITE HOUSTON (1864-1937), a native of Milton, was a prominent local leader and a pioneer in the women's suffrage movement. She was also an active Prohibitionist. Houston admonished women not to waste their time on trivial pursuits. She discouraged excessive tea drinking and straining the eyes and nerves over useless fancy work. Houston founded the New Century Club of Georgetown and was third president of the state-wide organization. In 1897 she addressed the Delaware Constitutional Convention on behalf of the Equal Suffrage Clubs of Sussex County to urge them to allow women to vote under the new state Constitution. Houston was also active in the civic and political activities of her husband, U.S. Representative Robert Houston.

BELLE EVERETT (1898-) of Kenton has been involved in Democratic Party politics since 1928, when she was a volunteer worker for Al Smith's presidential campaign. She came to know all the major figures in Democratic politics in Delaware and many national candidates. Everett, who was born in Marydel, Maryland, was a Kent County Democratic committeewoman for twenty-five years, county party vice-chair for eighteen years, and a national committeewoman from 1956 to 1972. Everett's election as state treasurer in 1958 made her the first woman elected to state office in Delaware; she served for eight years. Everett also served on the boards of the state Department of Public Welfare, the state chapter of the American Cancer Society, and her church. Her husband, Levi L. ("Boots") Everett, Jr., shared her love for politics and held county offices. Belle Everett officially retired from politics soon after he died in 1968 but she still advises both male and female candidates.

75

Belle Everett with President and Mrs. Johnson

PEARL HERLIHY DANIELS was chosen for the Hall of Fame of Delaware Women in 1981 for forty years of civic and community service. She helped write the home-rule charter for Wilmington as part of Mayor James F. Hearn's City Government Commission and was a member and officer of the Civic League of New Castle County. As chair of the Delaware Labor Commission, Daniels supervised enforcement of child and women's labor laws. She served on national committees on children, youth employment, and community relations and served two terms as president of Community Action of Greater Wilmington. Daniels has been a member of the Committee of 39 and of the Greater Wilmington Development Council. Governor Pierre S. du Pont IV appointed her to the Intergovernmental Task Force and the Council on Administration of Justice. She was the first non-lawyer who served as a trustee of the Legal Aid Society.

Vivian A. Houghton

VIVIAN A. HOUGHTON (1943-   ) has managed three successful political campaigns. They include MARY C. BOUDART's election to New Castle County Council over the candidate backed by the Wilmington Democratic machine. Houghton has been vice-president of the Wilmington chapter and Delaware coordinator of the National Organization for Women, lobbyist in the Delaware Assembly for women's issues, and Democratic president of the Delaware Women's Political Caucus. Houghton, who was born in Wilmington, worked as a bartender to support herself and her child after she was divorced.

She first attended college full time at age twenty-eight and then went on to Delaware Law School. Houghton founded the Women's Law Caucus as a support system for women, who made up only ten percent of the student body. She is a lawyer in private practice and was interim trustee for the U.S. District of Delaware. Houghton has been attorney for register of wills for New Castle County, assistant public defender in Family Court, and attorney for New Castle County Council. She received the Delaware Business and Professional Women's Club Woman of the Year award in 1982. Houghton has served on the executive committee, White House

Conference on Families (1980) and the board of the American Civil Liberties Union.

As a national committeewoman since 1978, MARILYN HUTHMACHER (1930-   ) helps set the policies and convention rules for the national Democratic Party and helps raise campaign money for national candidates. Huthmacher has participated in three Democratic national conventions. In 1980 she was a Edward Kennedy delegate and was an advocate for the losing open convention rule. This rule would have freed delegates pledged to candidates by the results of state primaries and caucuses to support any candidate they chose.

Huthmacher has long been involved in women's rights and issues. She formed the Committee for Gubernatorial Conscience to pressure Governor Sherman Tribbitt (governor 1973-77) to appoint women to his cabinet. At the mini-conventions she attended from 1978 to 1980, the big issue being debated was passage of the "50-50" rule, which said that any committee within the Democratic Party had to be 50 percent male and 50 percent female. The rule lost in 1976, but passed in 1980. Huthmacher has served as vice-chair of the Women's Caucus of the Democratic Party and is active in the Eleanor Roosevelt Fund, which raises money for women involved in critical political races. Consuming though politics is, Huthmacher considers it her hobby. She works for the Life Underwriter Training Council in Washington, D.C., and was part owner of Artisans III, a store in Wilmington, from its establishment until 1981. She was born in Trenton, New Jersey, and lives in Newark, Delaware.

A longtime worker for the Republican Party, PRISCILLA BRADLEY RAKESTRAW has served on the Republican National Committee and chaired the ELISE DU PONT '84 Committee. Rakestraw has been a member of state Republican committees and the State Federation of Republican Women Executive Committee. She was named Newark Republican Woman of the Year in 1975. Rakestraw has been a delegate to three Republican national conventions and has held leadership positions in several political campaigns during the seventies and eighties. An employee relations coordinator for the Du Pont Company, she served on the executive board of Community Services in Newark, the Commission on Presidential Scholars, Governor Russell W. Peterson's

1984 Delaware Alliance of Professional Women's Dinner; seated l. to r.: Priscilla Rakestraw, Vivian Houghton, Elise du Pont, Tanya Copeland, Karen Peterson; standing l. to r.: Delores Alfano, Rita Justice, Mimi Boudart, Margo Ewing Bane, Janet Rzewnicki

son's Council on Women, and a non-partisan Committee to Stimulate Interest in Newark Elections.

PAULA SEGAL LEHRER (1936-   ) is administrative assistant to the Democrats in the state House of Representatives. She chairs two committees of the National Conference of State Legislatures. A Dover resident, Lehrer is also owner of People to People Communication and is a lobbying consultant with particular expertise in legislative reapportionment. She was chief of staff of the Delaware House

of Representatives, Democratic campaign manager during the state elections in 1978, and state press coordinator for the Carter-Mondale campaign in 1980. In 1984 she was deputy chair of the Walter Mondale presidential campaign in Delaware and served on Mondale's staff at the nominating convention. Lehrer served on the executive committee of Democrats '86, which coordinated legislative races for the party.

Her community service includes membership on the boards of the National Conference of Christians and Jews, the Delaware State Human Relations Commission, and the Delaware Council on Transportation. She has been assistant to the director, Delaware Humanities Forum; executive director, Delaware Nurses' Association; and, since 1981, director, Jewish Federation of Delaware. Lehrer, who was born in Albany, New York, was educated at the State University of New York and Brandeis University.

Women began running for elective office soon after they won the right to vote. In 1947 a woman held office in each house of the state legislature for the first time. WILFREDA J. HEALD LYTLE (1896-   ) (R-suburban Wilmington) served in the House and VERA GILBRIDE DAVIS (1894-1974) (R-Dover) was the first woman elected to the Senate. Since then many women have made important contributions as state and local legislators. Women have many reasons for running for office. Some were "born to it," having grown up in political families; some moved into politics through involvement in community and volunteer groups.

The political career of NANCY W. COOK (D-Kenton) began in 1974 when she won the state Senate seat held by her late husband, Allen J. Cook. After her election, which made her the first Democratic woman in the Senate, Cook became a strong voice in the Democratic Caucus, especially as chair of the Joint Finance Committee. She was Senate Minority Whip from 1977 to 1978. Cook is also a member of the Delaware Economic and Financial Advisory Council. In 1984 she waged an unsuccessful contest in the Democratic primary for lieutenant governor.

MYRNA NORTH BAIR (1940-   ) (R-suburban Wilmington) had a strong interest in an issue, energy conservation. After graduating from the University of Wisconsin in 1968 with a Ph.D. degree in inorganic chemistry, she taught chemistry at Beaver College. She resigned when her children were born, but she continued to teach part-time in the New Castle County public schools and at the University of Delaware. Bair, who was born in Huntington, West Virginia, helped start Delawareans for Energy Conservation and served as president of the group. It provided the impetus for creating the Governor's Energy Commission in 1977. In 1978 Bair became

Myrna North Bair

assistant director of public information for the Delaware Energy Office.

When the General Assembly thwarted efforts at energy-saving reforms despite Bair's frequent lobbying, she ran for the state Senate in 1980, determined to influence policy on energy conservation. Although her previous political experience had been with candidates and issues rather than with the party itself, Bair became Senate minority leader in 1984. She has been co-chair of the Senate Committee on Services to Children and Youth and serves on the Education, Community Affairs, and Administrative Services/Energy committees. Bair has coordinated environmental quality and energy study groups for the AAUW and the League of Women Voters. Her interest in the environment led her to become chair of the executive committee of the Delaware Lung Association. She also serves on the board of trustees of Wesley College.

In 1986 MARGO EWING BANE (1949-   ) (R-suburban Wilmington) retained in the general election the state Senate seat she won six months before in a special election. Bane was born in Wilmington and earned a degree in education and communications from the University of Delaware. A former Miss Delaware, she owns Image Work Shop, a communications and confidence-building business. She was the first woman elected prothonotary (clerk of Superior Court) for New Castle County, in 1984.

RUTH ANN MINNER (D-Milford) was elected to the state senate in 1974 after serving three terms in the House. In 1980 she earned media attention when she voted against the popular drunk driving bill, asserting that parts of the law were unconstitutional. Her stand was upheld when the state Supreme Court ruled the law unconstitutional in 1983. Minner is also credited with legislation on environmental concerns. The daughter of a sharecropper, Minner was born in the district she now represents. She left school after the tenth grade and married when she was sixteen. As a widow with three sons, Minner attended Delaware Technical and Community College and the University of Delaware. She became active in community organizations and politics, including the Democratic State Committee and the National Conference of State Legislatures Natural Resource Committee. She is also affiliated with the State Federation Assembly Rural Development Committee and the Eastern Regional Conference Natural Resources Committee.

Women are also prominent in the state House of Representatives. HENRIETTA RICHARDSON JOHNSON (1914-   ) of Wilmington made political history in 1970 as the first black woman elected to the state House. During the eight years she served, Johnson sponsored and co-sponsored legislation for financial support of senior citizen centers, community-based social service agencies, increased welfare benefits, and general-obligation bonds for school renovations. Johnson worked as a nurse for twenty years and as a volunteer for the YMCA and the Layton Home for Aged Persons. In 1980 a multipurpose medical facility was named for her. Although she is retired, Johnson remains active in city politics.

EVELYN K. PEELE ("TINA") FALLON (1917-   ) (R-Seaford) was first elected to the state House of Representatives in 1978; she ran unopposed in 1986. Fallon is a member of the Agriculture Committee and the Governor's Task Force on Farmland Preservation and vice-president of the Seaford Republican Women's Club. Fallon taught in the Seaford junior and senior high schools for more than twenty-seven years. She is a strong supporter of public schools and serves on the National Retired Teacher's Association, the National and Governor's task forces on Education for Economic Growth, the executive board of the Delaware State Education Association, and the Governor's Library Task Force. Fallon was born in Dudley, North Carolina, and holds a master's degree from the University of Delaware. She chaired the AAUW state legislation and scholarship committee and is a member of the Delaware Federation of Republican Women and the Seaford Chamber of Commerce.

GWYNNE P. SMITH (1924-   ) (R-suburban Wilmington) sought public office as a means to promote conservation and other issues. Since she was elected a state representative in 1974, she has served on the Governor's Select Commission on Energy Conservation, as chair of the House Natural Resources and Agriculture Committee, and as co-chair of the Advisory Committee on Water Resource Conservation Management. Smith is serving her second term on the Joint Finance Legislative Committee. She sponsored the Bottle Bill and legislation for drought emergency powers, energy-efficiency standards in public buildings, preservation of natural areas, the tax check-off for non-game wildlife, and natural areas preservation. On other concerns, Smith sponsored legislation on voting rights and for the elderly and handicapped.

Before she entered the legislature, Smith helped organize Delaware Citizens for Clean Air and helped write the Delaware Environmental Protection Act with the guidance of Representatives Andrew G. Knox and William Poulterer. Smith subsequently helped write the Coastal Zone Act; in 1979 Watch Our Waterways presented her with the Coastal Zone Award. In 1986 she received the Delaware Audubon Society Conservation Achievement Award and the Delaware Parks and Recreation Society Legislative Award. The Chesapeake Bay Girl Scout Council honored her with its World of the Out-of-Doors Award. Smith also serves on the Sea Grant Board of the College of Marine Studies of the University of Delaware and on the Joint Sunset Committee. She has worked for the Delaware Food Bank and the women's shelter and was appointed to the Blue Ribbon Task Force to examine New Castle County government and future directions in 1985.

JANE P. MARONEY (R-Wilmington suburbs) has been co-chair of the House Human Resources Committee. Since she was first elected in 1978, she has focused her efforts on child welfare and mental and physical health issues. Maroney was instrumental in passing the law requiring automobile seat restraints for children and in setting regulations for hospices. She is working for shelters for runaway children and tax relief for senior citizens. Maroney is a native of Boston and a graduate of Radcliffe College. Long active in community affairs, she has served on the Pediatrics Committee of the Junior Board of Delaware Hospital and the executive committee of the Holly Ball Foundation.

ADA LEIGH SOLES (D-Newark) was elected to the Delaware House of Representatives for the first time in 1980. She has established the reputation of a good-government proponent. As an active member of the Joint Finance Committee, Soles is a leader in the movement to reform the state grants-in-aid pro-

Karen Peterson

cess. She is an academic advisor at the University of Delaware.

Women serve in elected and appointive positions in local, state, and federal government. RITA JUSTICE,* a Republican, was elected New Castle County executive in 1984 after serving as register of wills. Also a well-known bowler, she was the first woman in the state to record a 300-point game. In 1982 she won her third consecutive News-Journal Bowling Tournament title.

KAREN E. PETERSON (1950-   ) is the president of New Castle County Council and administrator of Labor Law Enforcement for the State of Delaware. She was elected council president in 1980, the first woman, the first Democrat, and the youngest person ever elected to that office. In the 1984 election she ran unopposed. Peterson, who grew up in Wilmington, was born in Chester, Pennsylvania, into a political family. Her grandfather was involved in Republican politics in Delaware County, Pennsylvania, and her father was chair of the New Castle County Democratic Committee for many years. She believes that Delaware's small size and population enable

Ada Leigh Soles

candidates to "take their beliefs and ideas directly to the people" rather than relying on the communications media, which are "often slanted for or against certain candidates."

Peterson has worked for passage of the Equal Rights Amendment. She has introduced and supported legislation aimed at providing equal pay for men and women in similar jobs and at prohibiting county funding of establishments that discriminate against women. Peterson has helped provide county funding to social service agencies, including senior centers, the Emmanuel Dining Room, Mary Mother of Hope Houses, and the Salvation Army Emergency Housing Shelter. Peterson was named Woman of the Year by the Delaware Federation of Professional Women's Clubs in 1983. In 1984 she received the Outstanding Young Woman of the Year award from both the Wilmington and Delaware Jaycees.

ELISE WOOD DU PONT (1935-   ) ran for the U.S. House of Representatives in 1984, the first Delaware woman to do so. She has also worked in state and national government. Du Pont, a Repub-

Elise Wood du Pont

lican, was a member of the Delaware State Board of Health during Governor Russell W. Peterson's administration, 1969-73. She chaired the Governor's Council on Public Health under Democratic Governor Sherman Tribbitt, and was an author of the state's nursing home regulations. A strong advocate for Delaware's senior citizens and the state hospice program, du Pont worked to improve neighborhood housing projects.

In 1979 du Pont received a law degree from the University of Pennsylvania and joined the law firm of Montgomery, McCracken, Walker and Rhodes. The first woman member of the Delaware World Affairs Council, she led the state's first trade mission to the People's Republic of China the same year. From 1981 to 1984 du Pont, an assistant administrator of the U.S. Agency for International Development, directed the Bureau for Private Enterprise, a two hundred million-dollar program designed to encourage and safeguard private investment in developing countries. When her husband, Pierre S. du Pont IV, was governor, Elise du Pont opened the governor's residence, Woodburn, to thousands of members of the public on special occasions and inaugurated celebrations of Children's Day, Senior Citizens' Day, and the annual Governor's Fair.

LOIS McDONNEL PARKE (1935-   ) of Wilmington is director of intergovernmental and congressional affairs for the Delaware region of the Department of Health and Human Services (HHS). As deputy regional director, Parke also assists in managing HHS programs in the six-state mid-Atlantic region. Parke, a native of Jamaica, New York, holds a bachelor's degree in economics from Mount Holyoke College. Her interest in good government began in 1968, when she was a member of the Delaware Committee of 39.

In 1972 Parke was elected to New Castle County Council, the first woman elected to a governing position in the county. As a council member until 1981, she concentrated on emergency medical care, the library system, open space preservation, and water resource management. Parke played a leading role in county legislation that removed architectural barriers to the handicapped. Under her chairmanship, which began in 1978, the Taxation and Finance Committee of the National Association of Counties produced a national policy for a balanced federal budget and worked toward passage of a revenue-sharing bill. Parke has served as president of the Delaware Tri-County Commission, as a campaign aide to U.S. Senator William V. Roth, Jr., and as a lobbyist for the Delaware Restaurant Association.

The first female secretary of finance for the state of Delaware was MARNA CUPP WHITTINGTON. She was raised in Pennsylvania, attended the University of Delaware, and holds a Ph.D. in quantitative methods from the University of Pittsburgh. After seven years with a market research firm, Whittington began working in government, as deputy secretary of education for the Commonwealth of Pennsylvania. She moved into Delaware state government as secretary of administrative services, and straightened out the state's computer system. Later, Whittington was promoted to state budget director. She was secretary/treasurer of the National Leadership Conference for Women Executives in State Government and served on the boards of Jobs for Delaware Graduates and Goldey Beacom College.

Other female state secretaries are MARCIE BIER-LEIN, LYDIA BOYER, and FRANCES WEST.

State treasurer since 1983, JANET RZEWNICKI has received national attention for introducing the use of book-entry municipal bonds in state bond issues. Born in Akron, Ohio, she earned a bachelor's degree with distinction from the University of Delaware while working part-time for the Du Pont Company. Rzewnicki, the first certified public accountant to hold the treasurer position, is a former director of the accounting firm Whisman & Associates and serves on the board of directors of the American Society of Women Accountants. She is a columnist for *Delaware Business Review*. Rzewnicki, a Republican, was instrumental in organizing the Delaware Alliance of Professional Women. She has served on the boards of directors of Wilmington Women in Business, the United Way, and the March of Dimes.

Other Delaware women have worked for their government in the armed forces. In World War I, more than 10,000 Army nurses served overseas, in addition to more than 100,000 civilian women who worked in munitions factories, as furnace stokers, and in many other jobs for which they would not have received training during peacetime. During World War II, the Women's Army Auxiliary Corps

Janet Rzewnicki

(WAAC) was established when manpower shortages made it clear that the military could not function efficiently without women.

Responding to the call for volunteers, MARY SAM SMITH WARD (1911-   ) signed up immediately. Of the thousands of applicants from her native state of Missouri, she was one of eight to be sent to Fort Des Moines, Iowa, in June 1942 for the first Women's Officer Candidate training in the United States. After she graduated as a third officer (the equivalent of a second lieutenant), she classified and assigned thousands of women to military duties such as motor pool, cooking and baking, and clerical work, in order to relieve men for combat duty. Ward was promoted to captain and later reassigned to the Pentagon on a special G-2 (intelligence) assignment.

In 1943 LILLIAN FOX COBIN also joined the WAACs. Commissioned as a third officer, she was

Mail Call 1942: Mary Sam Ward in center

Lillian Fox Cobin

Grace Knopf Paul

assigned to Civilian Personnel in Daytona Beach and then to the Adjutant General's School for additional training. She served in the WAAC Administrative School, Denton, Texas, until she was commissioned a second lieutenant. Assigned to the Classification and Replacement Branch in the Pentagon, Cobin did personnel research and occupational analysis.

When she married serviceman Herbert L. Cobin, she asked to be stationed near him and was sent to Las Vegas Army Air Base, an aerial gunnery school. There Lillian Cobin became both a legal officer investigating courts-martial and a member of the Discharge Board. Since many of her investigations required interviews of witnesses, she often started work at midnight and visited casinos and jails to look for witnesses and take depositions. Cobin was interviewed for an overseas assignment but chose to serve at Fort Bragg, North Carolina, as a separation officer until she and her husband were discharged to return to civilian life in Wilmington in 1945.

Following the Army's example, other services established similar groups for women. Rehoboth Beach resident ETHEL MYER FINLEY, who grew up on a farm in Minnesota, was the first female pilot to teach Air Force cadets to fly during World War II.

She was accepted into the first class of the WASPs (Women's Air Force Service Pilots) and was sent to Sweetwater, Texas, for basic training in 1943. Ranked male pilots were freed for combat duty when one thousand WASPs assumed the less hazardous jobs of the ferry command, moving airplanes and non-flying personnel around the country.

During World War II, more than 73,000 women served as nurses, some of whom were killed or taken prisoner. CAROL MAE PERRY PFEIFFER of Lewes and GRACE KNOPF PAUL were among the Delaware nurses in the military. Pfeiffer became chief nurse in Aukland, New Zealand. Paul continued her nursing career after the war. She was a nursing instructor at Memorial Hospital School of Nursing, Wilmington, and a nurse at Delaware State Hospital, New Castle, and Riverside Hospital, Wilmington.

Civilians helped the war effort in many capacities. ALINE NOREN EHINGER (189?-1984) was a woman of action who served her country in World War I, World War II, and the Korean War. In 1919, when two of her brothers were stationed in France, she worked at the canteen in Besançon. For the next three years she was program director for the Chautauqua System in New Zealand and Australia. During World War II, Ehinger was a volunteer director of Dover Civil Defense, airplane spotter, board member of the USO, and chairman of Senior Hostesses. For the first two years following the war, she was president of the American Legion Auxiliary in Delaware. When the Korean War began, she helped re-establish the USO in Dover and was chair of the operating committee from 1954 to 1960.

Ehinger was an English teacher at Dover High School for twenty-three years. She was Delaware Mother of the Year in 1958, Dover Woman of the Year in 1969, and was commended for her outstanding lifelong service by Governor J. Caleb Boggs and other Delaware statesmen.

During World War II, when enemy submarines were spotted in the ocean and bay near Rehoboth Beach and Lewes, many women and men served as watchdogs of the Delaware River, one of the longest and most perilous channels in America. MADALYN ELLIS of Lewes tracked ships on the Delaware Bay for the Pilots Association from 1928 to 1981. From atop the C.W. Ellis & Co. building on the banks of the Lewes-Rehoboth Canal, she and her husband, Clayton H. Ellis, identified ships approaching the Delaware Breakwater, communicated with the ships' officers by two-way radio, called ships' owners in Philadelphia and Chester, Pennsylvania, and filled requests for supplies.

The United States Armed Forces Institute was established in 1944 to help patients in hospitals on military bases recover more quickly from operations and accidents through educational reconditioning. RUTH BELL EGAN was assigned to the program to establish an education center. After her own discharge from the Army, Egan continued to work at the Veterans Administration. In 1965 she was the first woman in the nation to be elected department commander of the American Legion. Under her guidance the department continued to grow in membership and to participate in all national American Legion programs.

CAROLE L. CARRICK, one of only three women in the American Legion to hold the position of department service officer, processes the entire range of Veterans Administration benefits for veterans. During her tour of duty, 1973-78, Carrick learned to speak Mandarin Chinese and graduated with hon-

Carole Mitchell

ors in a voice training specialist course and was first in her class in a personnel specialist program.

In 1962 the Delaware National Guard appointed women in the field of medicine and in 1972 and 1973 opened its ranks to women in other career fields. Women now comprise 14 percent of the Delaware Army National Guard and 10 percent of the Delaware Air National Guard.

The first woman to attain the rank of colonel in the Delaware Army National Guard, CAROLE MITCHELL is a registered nurse and a clinical specialist in the Emergency Department of the Medical Center of Delaware. After receiving a nursing certificate from Delaware Hospital School of Nursing, she earned B.S. and M.S. degrees in nursing. Since she joined the National Guard in 1967, she has been promoted to chief nurse in the state surgeon's office of the state area command and has served as chief nurse with the 116th Combat Support Hospital. Mitchell has been decorated with the Civil Authorities

Ribbon, the Medal for Military Merit, and the Army Commendation Medal.

LINDA A. MORELLI of Hockessin became the first female military pilot in the Delaware National Guard and Delaware's first female helicopter pilot.

PRISCILLA FUTCHER of Lewes was the first female graduate of the U.S. Naval Academy from Delaware. Her study of ocean engineering enables Futcher to design and build jetties, oil rigs, and coastal construction projects. She acknowledges that women at the Naval Academy (approximately sixty-five in a class of just over one thousand) still struggle with the problem of male acceptance, with the rituals and exercises, and with the Navy position that, after more than five years, training women at the academy remains an experimental program.

Because of the service and contributions of these women, opportunities in the military will continue to expand and women in all branches of the service, whether on active duty or in the reserves, will continue to broaden their skills and increase their areas of responsibility.

Women have become leaders in both major parties in Delaware. They have been elected to serve at almost all levels of state and local government; others serve in appointive executive positions for local, state, and national government. Delaware women also help defend our nation as members of the armed forces.

TOWARD SOUND MINDS AND BODIES:

Women in Health Care

Emily P. Bissell U.S. Postage Stamp

In their nurturing role, women traditionally have overseen the health of their families and neighbors. In Colonial times, medicinal literature was second only to the Bible in popularity with the few women who could read. When medical care became institutionalized, women formed Junior Boards to raise funds for hospitals. As medical technology has evolved, women have entered the field as technicians and administrators, as well as doctors and nurses.

Delaware has a tradition of distinguished female physicians. The first woman to practice medicine in Delaware was JOSEPHINE MARGARET REBECCA WHITE (DE LACOUR) (1849-1929). Her great-uncle encouraged her to follow the example of her cousin, a Dr. Wilson of Lancaster, Pennsylvania, one of the early woman doctors in the United States. After attending Wesleyan Female College in her native Wilmington, White graduated from the Women's Medical College of Pennsylvania in 1878. She was one of the founders of the Physicians and Surgeons Hospital in Wilmington, which became Wilmington General Hospital. White was a charter member of Eastern Star and was active in the women's suffrage movement. She practiced medicine for fifty-one years and at the time of her death was the oldest member of the state medical association.

MARGARET I. HANDY (1890- ?) was a beloved doctor who cared for four generations of Wilmington children. After attending Goucher College and Johns Hopkins University School of Medicine, she started her practice during the devastating influenza epidemic of 1918. Handy worked in the children's ward of the People's Settlement and, in the 1940s, helped establish the Mothers Milk Bank for premature ba-

89

Margaret I. Handy

Dr. Elizabeth Bucke Miller

bies, the second in the nation. Among her many honors was the Josiah Marvel Cup of the Delaware Chamber of Commerce, conferred for outstanding service to the state and the community.

CATHERINE CROSS GRAY (?-1978) was the second woman to complete a two-year course at the medical college of the University of North Carolina. She graduated from the Women's Medical College of Pennsylvania in 1925 and did her residency at Beebe Hospital in Lewes. Gray established a private obstetrics practice in the Bridgeville area in 1931 and traveled by horse and buggy to deliver hundreds of babies. She was an active staff member of Nanticoke Memorial Hospital in Seaford, Milford Memorial Hospital, and on the courtesy staff of Beebe Hospital, Kent General Hospital, and Peninsula General Hospital in Salisbury, Maryland. Gray belonged to medical societies, her church women's group, and the DAR. She was honored by the Medical Society of Delaware and the Bridgeville schools for her work with girl athletes.

After almost thirty years in private practice in Wilmington, ELIZABETH BUCKE MILLER (1901-1983) and her husband, Edgar, became medical missionaries. They served in the United Mission Hospital in Kathmandu, Nepal, for almost ten years and

in Haiti for three months. Born in Oldwich, New Jersey, Elizabeth Miller was a graduate of Dickinson College and of the Women's College of Pennsylvania. Medical careers run in the family. Her grandmother was a midwife; her mother was a nurse; her son and granddaughter are physicians; and her daughter, ELIZABETH MILLER JENKINS, teaches nursing at the University of Delaware.

MILDRED BRYNBERG FORMAN (1904-   ), born in Elsmere, is descended from Delaware's first doctor, Tymen Stidham. Forman attended Wilmington Friends School and the University of Delaware. Her father had been unable to attend medical school for financial reasons, but encouraged his daughter to go. She was one of three women in a class of ninety-four at the Medical College of Virginia but was unable to study urology there, as she wanted, because female students were not allowed in that department. Years later, Forman worked in the urology clinic at Delaware Hospital. She had a private practice in general medicine for over fifty years in Wilmington before retiring in 1986.

ETHEL FRIEDMAN PLATT (1916-   ) earned a medical degree from Women's Medical College of Pennsylvania and pursued an internship in her native Philadelphia. In 1942 she started a family prac-

Mildred Forman

tice in Wilmington with her husband, David. The group has since expanded to six physicians. Ethel Platt has been active in national and Delaware medical societies.

As barriers were removed, more women became doctors. KATHERINE L. ESTERLY, one of the outstanding and admired female physicians in Delaware, has touched three generations. Born in Norristown, Pennsylvania, she specializes in neonatology, the care of newborn children. Esterly is director of the Neonatology Division at the Medical Center of Delaware, one of the largest such units in the country. She is also attending chief of the Department of Pediatrics at the medical center and a clinical associate professor of pediatrics at Jefferson Medical College. Esterly is medical director of the Children's Bureau of Delaware. She serves on the boards of agencies for child development and guidance.

MARJORIE JANE McKUSICK (?-1976) was a member of the class of 1949 at Harvard Medical School, the first time women were included. She joined her husband, Blaine, in a private pediatric practice in Wilmington. In 1974 she left the practice to become director of student health services at the University of Delaware, where she instituted a daily telephone consultation hour and placed greater em-

phasis on preventive health measures. McKusick helped establish a clinic for adolescents at Wilmington Medical Center and served as its director for three years. Later she founded and served as chair of the Delaware Adolescent Program, Inc. (DAPI), which helps pregnant adolescents.

EDITH INCABABIAN was born in New York City, spent her early years in Sweden, and came to Wilmington as a small child. She is in private practice as an osteopath in Wilmington. Incababian was president of the Quota Club of Wilmington, a professional women's service club, and is the only Wilmington member who has been president of Quota International. She also served as president of the Delaware Osteopathic Association.

LOUISA S. BATMAN (1933-   ), a native of Roanoke, Virginia, spent the first four years after she received an M.D. degree from the Medical College of Virginia as a housewife, mother, and editor. She returned to medicine and established a general practice, but left it in 1970 to join the University of Delaware Student Health Services as a physician. Two years later, she began pursuing a residency in obstetrics and gynecology at the Wilmington Medical Center and established a private practice in Wilmington in that field. Batman has served on the board of directors of the American Cancer Society and as president of its Newark branch. She is also an assistant clinical professor at Thomas Jefferson University Hospital, Philadelphia.

ELIZABETH MUFFET CRAVEN (1936-   ), originally from Camden, New Jersey, is director of Pediatric Ambulatory Services at the Medical Center of Delaware. Her job involves teaching and supervising medical students and pediatric, family practice, and emergency medicine residents. She is an attending physician there, acting director of the Pediatric Pulmonary and Cystic Fibrosis Center of the medical center, and an attending physician at a center of the same name at St. Christopher's Hospital for Children in Philadelphia. Craven has served on the editorial review board of the *Delaware Medical Journal*. In 1983 she was appointed to the Governor's Council on Services to Children, Youth and Their Families.

PATRICIA PURCELL (1944-   ), a pediatrician in Wilmington, answers WILM radio listeners' questions on "Doctor's House Call." She has lived in Delaware since 1966, when the Du Pont Company recruited her as a chemist after she graduated from college. However, because that career did not allow Purcell to work with people, she decided to go to medical school at Hahnemann University. A native of Henderson, North Carolina, Purcell believes that one should "reach back and help somebody else." She served on the boards of the United Way, Delaware Guidance Service for Children and Youth, and the Delaware Adolescent Program, Inc. (DAPI). Purcell is on the March of Dimes Medical Advisory Committee and is a trustee of the Medical Center of Delaware.

JANET PHILLIPS KRAMER (1942-   ), from Pottsville, Pennsylvania, is an internist with a subspecialty in adolescent medicine. She is also interested in clinical toxicology and sports medicine. To help new physicians cope with the emotional hardships that strenuous work loads impose on their personal lives, Kramer initiated a group therapy program for residents at the Medical Center of Delaware. She maintains a private practice in Wilmington, but also has devoted herself to helping adolescents in trouble to live full, happy, and successful lives.

Kramer originated the adolescent clinic at the Medical Center of Delaware and has been medical director of the State Office of Drug Abuse. She is a consultant to the American Institute of Clinical Toxicology and to the Joint Commission on Accreditation of American Hospitals on drug-abuse facilities. Kramer was an active member of the task force on sexuality training for the Chesapeake Bay Girl Scout Council and has been an advisor and/or board member of the Drug Information Action Line (DIAL); Sodat-Delaware; Duncan Road Academy; the Children's Home; Mental Health Association of Delaware; Child, Inc.; and the Task Force on Family Violence.

DIANA DICKSON-WITMER (1949-   ) is one of the first female surgeons to practice in Delaware. She has a private practice and does peripheral vascular surgery in Wilmington. Dickson-Witmer is also on the staff of the Medical Center of Delaware and St. Francis Hospital. She is a member of the trauma team at the medical center and is an instructor at Jefferson Medical College. After receiving a B.A. from Sarah Lawrence College, Dickson-Witmer did graduate study in embryology at the

M. Constance Bilotta Greeley

University of California, Berkeley, before studying medicine at the University of Florida. She came to Wilmington to do a surgical residency at the Wilmington Medical Center. Dickson-Witmer serves on the board of directors of Planned Parenthood of Delaware.

Among the few women practicing orthodontics in Delaware is M. CONSTANCE BILOTTA GREELEY (MUTERSPAW) (1945-   ). A native of Carbondale, Pennsylvania, she obtained a bachelor's degree in pharmacy from Temple University before continuing for a degree in dentistry and further study in orthodontics. Pharmacy training enabled her to earn money during graduate school and also to write articles and give lectures on the pharmaceutical aspects of dentistry. Greeley taught pediatric dentistry at the University of Maryland and orthodontics at Temple University before entering private practice in Wilmington. She lectures and appears in magazine, radio, and television interviews to educate the public about good dental practices and about dentistry as a career, especially for women. Greeley is on the staff of the Medical Center of Delaware and is a consultant to the Delaware State Cleft Palate Clinic.

BERNADINE Z. PAULSHOCK, a family practice physician, takes special interest in medicine related to women and is noted for her moral and educational support of female medical students and physicians. She was a Phi Beta Kappa graduate of the University of Pennsylvania School of Medicine and spent her internship and residency in internal medicine at Delaware Hospital. Paulshock is an associate program director of the Department of Family Practice at the Medical Center of Delaware, where she guides medical students through their family practice residencies. She is also an associate clinical professor at Jefferson Medical College. Paulshock has published articles on health care in both medical journals and medical publications for a more general audience. She serves on advisory committees of the American Cancer Society, Delaware Curative Workshop, and Brown Vocational High School.

REBECCA JAFFE is a family practice physician with a special interest in sports medicine. She was a founder of the Delaware Sports Medicine Program and is a volunteer physician for the U.S. Olympic Committee. Before she established her private practice, Jaffe cared for elderly patients at Eastside Medical Center in Wilmington. She is active in Doctors Ought to Care (DOC), a program in which health-care professionals speak to young people about the dangers of tobacco and other drugs.

Women physicians who serve the residents of smaller towns and rural areas include ELVIRA PAMINTUAN in Seaford and ROBERTA BURNS in Bridgeville. ROSALINDA DE JESUS-JILOCA (1938-), an obstetrician-gynecologist, comes from Manila, Philippines. She received an M.D. in the Philippines but trained for her specialty at the Wilmington Medical Center. De Jesus-Jiloca practices medicine in Seaford and is on the staff of Nanticoke Memorial Hospital.

As assistant medical examiner for Kent and Sussex counties, JUDITH GEDNEY TOBIN (1926-) is available twenty-four hours a day in case of deaths that require an autopsy. Since 1960 Tobin has been associate pathologist at Nanticoke Memorial Hospital, where she is past president of the medical staff.

She is a graduate of Columbia University College of Physicians and Surgeons. From 1947 to 1977, she taught in the Division of Health Studies at the University of Delaware. Tobin has served on the board of directors of the Sussex County unit of the American Cancer Society, Blood Bank of Delaware, and Turnabout Counseling Center. She was given the Delaware Association for Public Administration's award for outstanding contributions to public service in 1976 and was chosen Delaware Mother of the Year in 1984.

Although relatively few women are physicians, the nursing profession has always been a female-dominated field. Many Delaware nurses have made important contributions to their profession and the community.

AMELIA KATHERINE BEEBE (1896-1982) was born in Charlotteville, New York, and earned a registered nurse certificate in 1922. She began her nursing career at a health spa in New York State, where she met Dr. James Beebe, Sr., co-founder of Beebe Hospital in Lewes. After their marriage, Amelia Beebe discontinued her career to raise a family, but was active in many Sussex County groups, including the Rehoboth Art League and Sussex County Gardeners. During World War II, she returned to nursing as a volunteer at Beebe Hospital, helping victims of U-boat attacks. Beebe was honored by the American Red Cross for her service.

At Alfred I. du Pont Institute near Wilmington, MARILYN BOOS, patient care coordinator, developed a home traction program for infants with hip dislocations. Families take training from the staff and have access to a nurse on twenty-four-hour call. Boos visits each patient periodically. This program, which has drawn national and international attention, enables many families to avoid long and expensive hospital stays for their babies and has improved morale for the families as well as the children.

In recent years, many women have chosen to give birth outside hospitals, in a more informal, home-like setting. The Birth Center of Delaware, founded in Wilmington in 1982 by EDITH BALDWIN WONNELL (1931-), is such an institution. A Connecticut native, Wonnell graduated from the first certified nurse-midwife program in the nation, at Columbia University. The midwifery service she es-

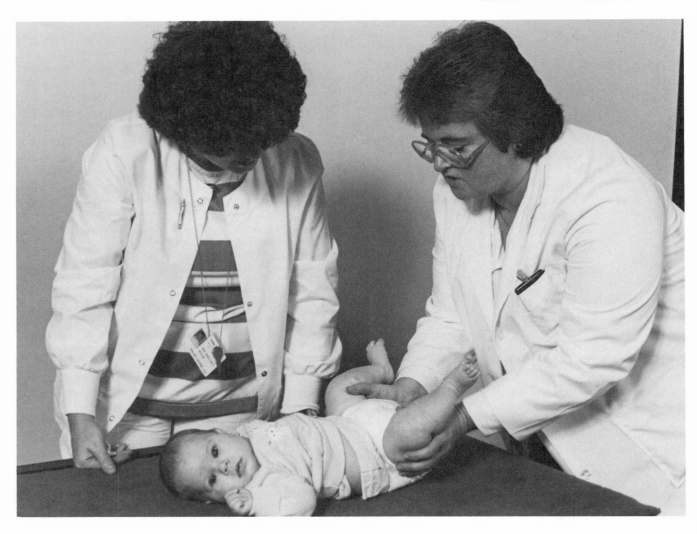

Marilyn Boos (on right)

tablished at Kings County Hospital in Brooklyn, New York, is still in existence. For thirteen years, Wonnell directed a nationally recognized parent and childbirth education program at the Wilmington Medical Center. In 1978 she was dismissed from her job after a remark she made that was critical of physicians was published in the local newspaper. After differences with some physicians and struggle with the medical establishment, Wonnell opened the birth center, which operates independently, but in conjunction with consulting obstetricians.

Many Delaware nurses work in hospitals and hos-

pital administration. GRACE LITTLE moved from a nursing background to become administrator of two hospitals. She was born in Pennsylvania and received nurse's training at Memorial Hospital, Wilmington. After working as a school nurse and serving for one year as director of nursing at Memorial Hospital, in 1942 Little became hospital administrator, a position she held for fourteen years. When Eugene du Pont Memorial Hospital (Pelleport) opened near Wilmington in 1957, Little became the first administrator there. After she retired, her portrait was hung in the hospital lounge to honor her fourteen years of service. The Red Cross and the Blood

94

Bank of Delaware are among the beneficiaries of Little's volunteer efforts. She was president of State Nurses, the League of Nursing, and the State Board of Nurse Examiners.

Before she retired in 1979 as director of nursing at Delaware State Hospital, JANE E. MITCHELL made many positive changes in psychiatric care there. She also helped break down resistance to black nurses. A native of Coatesville, Pennsylvania, who grew up in Wilmington, Mitchell at first was refused a hospital nursing job in Delaware despite her education. She found work in a Jewish hospital in Philadelphia and earned master's degrees in nursing and psychology. In 1949, when the Governor Bacon Health Center opened, Dr. M.A. Tarumianz hired Mitchell over the protest of other nurses, making her one of the first black Registered Nurses to practice in a Delaware hospital. Since her retirement, Mitchell has recruited minority students for the University of Delaware College of Nursing, volunteered for the American Cancer Society, and served as president of the Delaware Board of Nursing. She is also studying painting. Mitchell was given the World of Well-Being Award of the Chesapeake Bay Girl Scout Council in 1985.

ELIZABETH L. DUGGINS (1923-   ) has been administrator for nursing at what is now the Medical Center of Delaware since 1971. She was raised in Swedesboro, New Jersey, but went to North Carolina to study at the Duke University School of Nursing, where she worked and from which she later received the Distinguished Alumna Award. Duggins has served her profession and community on the boards of the Nursing School of Wilmington and the Delaware division of the American Cancer Society and as an advisor to Delaware Technical and Community College Nursing program and the Delaware division of the March of Dimes.

JOANNA E. McCABE (1923-   ) of Selbyville has been director of nursing in the Division of Mental Retardation at Stockley Center, Georgetown, since 1957. She has dedicated herself to preventing mental retardation and developmental disabilities through parent education and prevention of teenage pregnancy and birth defects. McCabe was president of the Delaware Board of Nursing and has served on the Governor's Advisory Council for Exceptional Citizens since 1976. She was a consultant to the state of

New Jersey and the Republic of Panama and was a member of a study team on the developmentally disabled in Costa Rica and Panama under the auspices of the Organization of American States. McCabe has received an award from the Delaware Association for Retarded Citizens and was chosen Delaware Nurse of the Year in 1977 by the March of Dimes for her work in the prevention of mental retardation.

After working for several years as a public health nurse, EDITH H. ANDERSON (1927-   ) earned master's and doctoral degrees from New York University in order to teach nursing. There, she helped establish one of the earliest clinical specialist programs in parent-child nursing in the early sixties. For the Children's Bureau of the U.S. Department of Health, Education, and Welfare, Anderson helped set up master of science programs in parent-child nursing, midwifery, and similar fields. For seven years she was dean of the School of Nursing at the University of Hawaii and a consultant on nursing in American Samoa, Okinawa, Guam, and Taiwan. In 1976 she returned to the East Coast to be near her ailing mother and became dean of the College of Nursing, University of Delaware. Anderson, who is a native of Elizabeth, New Jersey, and a resident of Wilmington, is a fellow of the American Academy of Nursing. She has served on the Delaware Health Council and the State Health Coordinating Council.

As chair of the Nursing Department, Delaware Technical and Community College, LOIS M. STUDTE (1940-   ) of Milford has been able to combine nursing and teaching. Studte, who was born and raised near Philadelphia, worked as a nurse in hospitals, a doctor's office, and a school and taught nursing courses at the Sussex County Vocational-Technical Center. At Delaware Technical and Community College, Georgetown, Studte added three degree programs in nursing. She also helped develop the nursing degree program at Wilmington College.

For SANDRA WHEATLEY KRAFFT (1943-   ), summer employment in a hospital during high school reinforced her childhood ambition to be a nurse. After earning a nursing degree, she worked in hospitals and as a coordinator of mental health services. She also chaired the nursing department at Delaware Technical and Community College. In 1985 she joined Wilmington College as director of the bachelor of science in nursing program. Krafft, who was born in Saginaw, Michigan, lives in Media, Pennsylvania. She has held offices in Delaware, regional, and national professional associations. In 1986 Krafft received the award for Excellence in Nursing Practice of the Delaware Nurses Association.

Women are also active as medical technologists and physician assistants. ELIZABETH F. PHILLIPS was the first woman in Delaware to have a full-time optometric practice, which she operated in Georgetown for thirty-nine years before retiring. Phillips was president of the Delaware Optometric Association and a member of the State Board of Examiners in Optometry. She has been active in the Business and Professional Women's Club, DAR, American Red Cross, and on the board of directors of the Delaware Society for Crippled Children and Adults.

HELEN KUO-HU LIANG TANG (1936-   ), a native of Chekiang, China, has worked in the medical field for twenty-six years as a technologist, supervisor, educator, and administrator. She is now an assistant professor and education coordinator in the medical technology program of the University of Delaware. In 1979 Tang was elected Medical Technologist of the Year by the Delaware Society for Medical Technologists.

PEGGY M. HULLINGER is a physician's assistant and administrator in a private practice for cardiology and internal medicine. In her work, she develops support groups for cardiac patients and group therapy for corrective surgery patients and for women in transition. She is particularly interested in helping slightly and severely impaired geriatrics develop social skills and in promoting women's growth and self-help. Hullinger studied human services at Delaware Technical and Community College in Dover and behavioral science and clinical psychology at West Chester University. For twelve years, she has served on the board of directors of Nativity Day Care Center, helping employ behavioral management techniques for children. Hullinger has also played an active role in Democratic Party politics, serving as a delegate to the state Democratic convention and campaigning for party candidates.

Other women, both physicians and non-physicians, have worked to improve public health in Delaware.

One of the most famous is EMILY PERKINS BISSELL (1861-1948), the Wilmington native who introduced the Christmas seal in the United States in 1907 to raise money for a tuberculosis clinic. She helped found the Delaware Chapter of the American Red Cross in 1904 and was president of the Delaware Anti-Tuberculosis Society (now Delaware Lung Association) for forty years. Bissell also started the West End Reading Room, the first free kindergarten in Wilmington, and the first public playground. Her interests included the arts, too, for she wrote poetry and was one of the founders of the Wilmington Society of the Fine Arts, which has evolved into the Delaware Art Museum. Bissell was posthumously inducted into the Hall of Fame of Delaware Women in 1986.

MARTHA L. WOODFOLK was born and reared in Farrell, Pennsylvania. She came to Delaware in the early 1940s and worked for the Division of Public Health for almost thirty-five years before her retirement in 1981. Woodfolk worked in country schools throughout the state until 1970, when she moved into administration, coordinating all dental activities of the division. She has been president of the National Dental Hygienist Association, commissioner of the state Board of Optometry, member of the Migrant Health Committee, board member of Delaware Rural Ministries, and charter member of the Delmarva Peninsula chapter of the National Council of Negro Women.

After earning a B.A. in journalism and operating gift shops, MAE HIGHTOWER-VANDAMM (1926-   ) decided to study occupational therapy in 1954. In 1958 she moved from her native Georgia to Wilmington to become chief occupational therapist at the Delaware Curative Workshop. At that time, the facility served about thirty-five physically and neurologically handicapped patients per day.

Since then, Hightower-Vandamm has become executive director, and the center's daily caseload has increased to more than three hundred. Under her leadership, the workshop has expanded physically, pioneered programs for handicapped children, started a preschool, implemented programs in cooperation with other institutions, and obtained funding to reduce its dependence on United Way funding. Hightower-Vandamm has served on state and national committees in her field, including the president's and Delaware governor's committees on mental re-

Mae Hightower-Vandamm

tardation and the National Association of Rehabilitation Facilities. She was president of the American Occupational Therapy Association. Hightower-Vandamm also holds awards for needlepoint.

LULU MAE NIX directed Delaware Adolescent Program, Inc. (DAPI), a program started by the Junior League that counsels pregnant teenagers and other adolescents. In 1978 she took a job with the Department of Health, Education, and Welfare in Washington, D.C. There she was the first national director of the Office of Adolescent Pregnancy Programs, which coordinates national efforts to counsel teenagers, provide programs for their parents, and offer health education and treatment for venereal diseases. Nix now heads a program headquartered at Temple University that is aimed at reducing teenage pregnancy. Nix was named Woman of the Year by the Wilmington Chapter of the AAUW.

PATRICIA C. SCHRAMM was secretary of the Delaware Department of Health and Social Services for more than six years. The department, the largest cabinet agency in state government, employs more than four thousand people. To increase their effectiveness, Schramm sponsored development of a data processing system that is a national model. She saw her role as one of leadership: motivating and helping others to achieve their greatest potential in their jobs. Many of her efforts were focused on moving elderly, mentally retarded, and mentally ill people from institutions to be cared for in their own communities. Before entering state government, Schramm earned a Ph.D. from Bryn Mawr College and worked for seven years in Wilmington city government.

BARBARA B. ROSE was director of the state Division of Public Health from 1977 until she retired. A native of Canada, she studied medicine at McGill University and was one of seven female physicians who served as lieutenant commanders in the Royal Canadian Navy, which she entered in 1944. Rose moved to Wilmington with her husband Stuart, a surgeon, having chosen Delaware for a home over other Eastern seaboard states. She worked at Delaware State Hospital and in part-time private practice while raising her two children. Rose decided on a career in public health and earned a master's degree in that field from Johns Hopkins University in 1967. After working in virtually every area of the state public health division, she served as New Cas-

Barbara B. Rose

tle County health officer for six years. Rose is on the board of directors of Planned Parenthood of Delaware.

As state nursing director for the Division of Public Health since 1972, TERESA A. ("TERRY") DUPUIS (1929-) is responsible for establishing policy, guidelines, and procedures for all public-health nurses in the state. Although she had an intense interest in medicine as an adolescent, she settled on nurse's training in her hometown of Berlin, New Hampshire, because of lack of money for college and her father's resistance to a woman attending college. Once she became a nurse, Dupuis was able to work her way through college and master's degrees in public health from Johns Hopkins University and in business administration from Wilmington College.

After doing all types of nursing, Dupuis finds public health the most stimulating because "we are working on the patients' turf" rather than in an institution. She was chief public health nurse in South Vietnam under the U. S. Agency for International Development from 1966 to 1971. Dupuis has been president of the Delaware Public Health Association and vice-president of the Delaware Home Health Agency Association. She serves on the State School Health Advisory Committee; the Commission on Nursing Education, Delaware Nurses' Association; the state branch of the American Cancer

Society; and the Kent County Hospice Advisory Board.

In 1982 VIRGINIA DAVIS came to Delaware as care center administrator of HMO of Delaware. She participated in all phases of setting up the new health maintenance organization. After two years, Davis became vice-president of health center administration of the HMO Corporation, the only woman and youngest person to hold that position. By drawing on her past experience as a nurse and a manager, she has made innovations at HMO. One is the professional provider model, under which patients receive health care from matched teams of physicians and certified nurse practitioners. This system gives members improved access to cost-effective health care. Davis has also designed a versatile physical examination table for children that is more efficient and safer than the usual model. She is a doctoral student in urban affairs at the University of Delaware.

ANNE SHANE BADER has been executive director of the Medical Society of Delaware since 1964. As one of only two female executive directors of state medical societies in the United States, she is responsible for administering programs and policies developed by the board of trustees of the society. Bader coordinates the work of the society's many committees, assists in planning continuing medical education activities and programs on current medical topics, and provides information and resources for the membership of the society as well as for members of the public. She serves as business man-

ager of the *Delaware Medical Journal*. Bader has also been executive director of the Delaware Academy of Family Physicians since 1965. She is a board member of the Blood Bank of Delaware, the Delaware Commission on Crime and Justice, the Wilmington Visiting Nurse Association, Medical Society of Delaware Insurance Services, Inc., and the Delaware Epilepsy Association.

AMY BLATCHFORD HECHT of Hockessin was the driving force in establishing Delaware Hospice, Inc. In 1982, after five years of work, Hecht became the first president of the agency, which enables terminally ill patients to die at home with the support of their doctors, families, and community volunteers. Hecht holds a B.A. in political science, bachelor's and master's degrees in nursing, and an Ed. D. in higher education administration. After teaching nursing and serving as assistant dean of the University of Delaware College of Nursing, Hecht was appointed director of the Department of Nursing, Temple University, in 1985. She was president of the Delaware Board of Nursing and a member of the board of the Visiting Nurse Association. In 1984 the Chesapeake Bay Girl Scout Council gave her its World of Well-Being Award.

Delaware women continue to make important contributions in medicine as nurses, physicians, public health workers, and administrators. As the nature of health care changes in response to medical advances, demographic changes, cost pressures, and technology, women continue to find innovative solutions to problems and to provide quality medical care to the residents of Delaware.

PRESERVERS OF OUR HERITAGE:

Women In History

Louise du Pont Crowninshield

Women have studied, recorded, and celebrated history in Delaware since the Native Americans passed along their legends through the oral tradition. NORA THOMPSON DEAN (Touching Leaves Woman) (1907-1984), a full-blooded Lenape Indian, was born near Bartlesville, on an Indian Reservation, Oklahoma, where her ancestors had settled after they were forced from Delaware by European settlers. Because she was one of the few remaining Lenapes who spoke the language fluently, she was called upon to teach her people the religious ceremonies, dances, crafts, herbal medicines, and language of the tribe. She also taught the ways of the Indians from Delaware to historians, anthropologists, and others who studied Indian ways of life.

ELIZABETH MONTGOMERY (1778-1863) published an early history, *Reminiscences of Wilmington in Familiar Village Tales, Ancient and New*, in 1851. Another important history is *Wilmington, Delaware: Three Centuries under Four Flags* (1937) by ANNA T. LINCOLN (McCREA) (1870-1942). The book is significant because of its data on economic and governmental developments. Lincoln wrote

monographs on several aspects of Delaware history. She was the curator and librarian at Old Town Hall for a decade beginning in 1930, two years after the Historical Society of Delaware made the building its headquarters. Lincoln recatalogued, classified, and repaired the society's documents, rare books, and maps, making them more accessible to historians, genealogists, and the public.

As director of the Delaware Writers' Project beginning in 1936, JEANNETTE ECKMAN (1882-1972) supervised historical publications under the Works Progress Administration (WPA) during the Great Depression. She edited the WPA guide *Delaware: A Guide to the First State* (1938). In 1951 Eckman, a Delaware native, was director and historian of the New Castle Tercentenary Celebration of Dutch settlement. She was a charter member of the Delaware Swedish Colonial Society. In 1958 the American Swedish Historical Museum in Philadelphia gave Eckman its annual award for her book *Crane Hook on the Delaware, 1667-1699* (1958), a religious, political, and military history of Swedish

Nora Thompson Dean (Touching Leaves Woman)

settlement in the area from southeast Wilmington toward the Delaware Memorial Bridge.

Most Delaware women of Lincoln's and Eckman's day who were involved with history worked to save historic buildings and organized historical organizations. As a founder and president of the State Archives Commission, MABEL LLOYD FISHER RIDGELY (1872-1962) helped preserve thousands of public documents. Ridgely, who was born in Washington, D.C., founded Friends of Old Dover and was a member of the Society of Colonial Dames and of Friends of the John Dickinson Mansion. *The Ridgelys of Delaware and Their Circle: What Befell Them in Colonial and Federal Times* (1948), gleaned from twenty-four baskets of family letters written between 1751 and 1890, depicts life in eighteenth- and nineteenth-century Delaware. Ridgely also worked for women's suffrage and supported public libraries in southern Delaware. She succeeded her husband, Henry, as a member of the board of trustees of the University of Delaware. In 1957 the university awarded her an honorary degree in recognition of her contributions to the state. Ridgely entered the Hall of Fame of Delaware Women in 1982.

ANNE READ RODNEY JANVIER (1873-1940) worked to preserve historic buildings in New Castle, her hometown. She started "A Day in Old New Castle" and helped save Amstel House and the Old Dutch House when they were endangered. Janvier wrote *Stories of Old New Castle* to raise money for the Amstel House museum. She was an original member of the state Historical Markers Commission and a member of the State Archives Commission. Thanks to Janvier's leadership and inspiration, New Castle citizens became aware of its history. They continue to work together to perpetuate their town's colonial heritage.

MARY WILSON THOMPSON (?-1947) was a major figure in organizing the Delaware Society for the Preservation of Antiquities. She helped save the Old Dutch House in New Castle and the former Bank of Delaware building in Wilmington, now the headquarters of the Delaware Academy of Medicine. Thompson spoke out against the women's suffrage campaign and was influential in blocking Delaware from ratifying the Nineteenth Amendment in 1920. Thompson started the mosquito control program in Rehoboth Beach and other parts of Sussex County.

Her memoirs were published in *Delaware History* magazine in 1978 and 1979.

LOUISE DU PONT CROWNINSHIELD (1877-1958) became active in preserving historic buildings and in collecting Americana after she moved from Delaware to Marblehead, Massachusetts, following her marriage in 1900. She encouraged her brother, Henry Francis du Pont, in his antique collecting, the fruits of which became Winterthur Museum. Crowninshield restored and landscaped her grandparents' former home, Eleutherian Mills. She gave the homestead she had loved as a child in trust to the Hagley Museum and Library upon her death. She also helped preserve and furnish historic houses for museums in Massachusetts and Virginia. Crowninshield played a major role in the organization of the National Trust for Historic Preservation and served as trustee, vice-chair, and board member. The organization named its major award in her honor.

LYDIA CHICHESTER LAIRD (1895?-1975) and her husband, Philip D. Laird, bought and restored the George Read II House in New Castle and gave it to the Historical Society of Delaware. She was awarded a citation by the National Trust for Historic Preservation in 1971 for her efforts to restore New Castle's Colonial atmosphere.

The impetus behind the preservation and improvement of Brandywine Village in Wilmington was HARRIET CURTIS REESE (1903-1971). When she heard that the surviving residences of the original Brandywine millers were to be razed for a parking lot, Reese called a meeting of public-spirited citizens and authorities on history which led to the incorporation of Old Brandywine Village in 1962. She was a national vice-president of the DAR from 1960 to 1965, a national officer of the Society of Colonial Dames of America, and a regent of Gunston Hall.

In 1964 MARGUERITE DU PONT DE VILLIERS BODEN (1907-1977) received the Award of Merit from the American Association for State and Local History for the preservation of historic buildings in Pennsylvania, New Jersey, and Delaware, including Old Saint James Episcopal Church in Newport and the Hale-Byrnes House in Stanton. Boden was on the program planning committee for the World Conference on Records, honorary chair of the British-American Society of America, and was active in the

Alliance Française of Wilmington. Founder and first state president of the Diamond State Branch, National League of American Pen Women, Boden was responsible for bringing distinguished lecturers of the literary world to colleges in Delaware.

ELIZABETH ROBELEN ("LIB") SCHIEK (1907-1981) was a native Delawarean who lived most of her life in the Claymont house built by her father. She and her husband, Dr. Allen G. Schiek, saved many old and historic buildings in Brandywine Hundred and throughout the state that were threatened by bulldozers and photographed those they could not save. Their extensive collection of slides of artifacts was an important resource for all who were interested in history of the area. They spent several summers with the archaeological team of the University of Pennsylvania, digging in ruins of Central America and at the Caleb Pusey House in

Elizabeth Robelen Schiek

Upland, Pennsylvania, but their chief interest was in Delaware.

The Schieks were active in preserving Fort Delaware, for which they spent three years building a large scale model of Pea Patch Island in their garage with the help of MARY ANN and JIM ACKERMAN and ADELE and JOHN RAY. Lib Schiek was president of the Archaeological Society of Delaware and was director of the Delaware Society for the Preservation of Antiquities when they were restoring the Hale Byrnes House in Stanton.

CATHERINE M. C. IRVING, a lifelong promoter and patron of historical institutions and colleges, participated actively in fundraising, ceremonials, and historic preservation projects both in Delaware and in other states. She established a fellowship in the University of Delaware-Winterthur Museum graduate study program in memory of her husband, A. Duer Irving, a direct descendant of Washington Irving. Catherine Irving was also active with Sleepy Hollow Restorations as an honorary trustee.

Women founded several local historical societies, the focus of much historical activity in the state. RUTH CHAMBERS STEWART, VIRGINIA ORR, MARJORIE VIRDEN, and DR. and MRS. JAMES MARVIL founded the Lewes Historical Society in 1961. M. CATHERINE DOWNING was the organizer and first president of the Milford Historical Society and served on the Milford, Sussex County, and Delaware American Revolution Bicentennial committees. AURELIA CATE DAWSON and SUE MANLOVE compiled an account of women in Seaford history for the Bicentennial celebration.

The driving force for preserving the heritage of Laurel and surrounding towns in Sussex County is MADELINE ARNOLD DUNN (1915-   ) of Laurel. She founded the Laurel Historical Society in 1977 and served as its president during the formative years. Born in Baltimore, Maryland, Dunn came to Delaware in 1937 as an art teacher. She taught for twenty-eight years, was Sussex County Art Supervisor for two years, and received many awards for her art work and publications. She is an active member of the Delaware Humanities Forum.

CORNELIA TAYLOR JONES (1910-1986) of Dover was founder and first president of Dover Heritage Trail, an organization dedicated to preserve,

M. Catherine Downing

interpret, and offer tours of historic Dover. She was a teacher, journalist, state librarian, legislative reporter, and Wesley College staff member. Jones also shared her talents as a leader in education, church, and political groups. She was Delaware president of AAUW and founded the Dover chapter.

In the course of moving from her native California to Massachusetts and on to Delaware, CLAUDIA LAUPER BUSHMAN (1934-) of Newark acquired an appreciation of American traditions, crafts, houses, and furnishings. She studied literature, history, and women's studies and earned a Ph.D. in American studies from Boston University. Bushman published *Mormon Sisters: Women of Early Utah* (1976), *A Good Poor Man's Wife* (1981), and two volumes of Delaware's legislative papers (with Harold B. Hancock and Elizabeth Moyne Homsey). She founded and edited *Exponent II*, a publication for Mormon women. Bushman wonders why "the 'traditional' female role is [greatly] devalued, when there is so much to recommend it objectively."

Bushman was named Woman of the Year by the University of Delaware Women's Club in 1984 and has taught courses on history, literature, and wom-

en's lives in the university Honors Program. When the Newark Historical Society was established in 1981, Bushman was the first president. She is now executive director of the Delaware Heritage Commission, which is coordinating commemorative activities of the bicentennial of the U.S. Constitution and Delaware's ratification as "the First State."

With a grandfather, Christopher Ward, who wrote books on the American Revolution and a grandmother, CAROLINE BUSH WARD, who was active in the National Society of Colonial Dames, it was natural for CYNTHIA KIMBALL HOAGLAND (1924-) to become interested in history. She has served on the boards of the National Society of the Colonial Dames of America and Gunston Hall in Virginia. In 1985 Hoagland was elected the first female president of the Historical Society of Delaware. She considers community involvement to be the responsibility of living in a small state where every citizen should share in the work as well as the benefits. Hoagland has served on the boards of

Claudia Lauper Bushman

105

Planned Parenthood of Delaware and the University of Delaware Library Associates and was president of Delaware Curative Workshop, with which her mother, ESTHER WARD KIMBALL, was also involved. She is a member of the Design Review Commission and of the Waterfront Advisory Commission for the City of Wilmington and is chair of the Wilmington Planning Commission.

The past that early historians and preservationists sought to document and preserve was primarily that of early white settlers. Not until the mid-twentieth century did historians focus on the history of blacks and various ethnic groups. PAULINE A. YOUNG (1900-   ) was the first woman to write about the black experience in Delaware. She wrote a chapter on the subject for *Delaware: A History of the First State*, edited by H. Clay Reed (1947). Young was born in West Medford, Massachusetts, but came to Delaware after her father died. She attended Howard High School in Wilmington, where her mother and her aunt, ALICE DUNBAR-NELSON, taught.

When Young graduated from Howard High School, she could not attend the University of Delaware because she was black. Not easily discouraged, Young commuted to the University of Pennsylvania, where she was the only black student in the School of Education. Young later earned a master's degree in library science from Columbia University. She taught at Howard High School and started its library, which is dedicated to her. Active in the NAACP for many years, Young participated in the civil rights march from Selma to Montgomery, Alabama. She was a Peace Corps volunteer in Jamaica from 1962 to 1964. Young continues to collect historical material and encourage the study of black history. The Memorabilia Room at Howard Career Center (formerly Howard High School) was dedicated to her in 1979. In 1982 Young was inducted into the Hall of Fame of Delaware Women.

A member of Wilmington's Italian-American community, JUSTINE MATALENO has brought the Italian heritage to public attention. By locating collections of photographs and by mining her own extensive knowledge of her community, Mataleno assembled a traveling exhibit. "Pockets of Italian Settlement," sponsored by Italo-Americans United, toured Delaware in 1983 and 1984.

The history of women and their achievements

was also largely undocumented. Genealogies do not follow female lines, or always include daughters and sisters. History books were usually written by men, who stressed the accomplishments of other men.

MARY SAM SMITH WARD (1911-   ) seeks to promote recognition of women in history. She edited and published *Delaware Women Remembered*, the first book that chronicled the contributions of women in the state of Delaware, and was project director of *A Legacy from Delaware Women*. Under the auspices of the Delaware Humanities Forum, Ward lectures on contributions by Delaware women to the state and the nation. A native of Missouri, Ward taught history to junior-high through college-level students. She holds master's degrees in history and American studies. Ward has been a guide at Hagley Museum in Wilmington for more than twenty years. Another rewarding teaching experience was the development of "Colonial Pathways" for the Girl Scouts. She taught Girl Scouts, selected from every state in the union, how people lived in Colonial times by visiting historic sites and museums in Delaware. The Sons of the American Revolution gave Ward

Hazel Downs Brittingham

the Good Citizenship medal for encouraging young people to become interested in history.

Ward's articles have appeared in *Delaware Today*, *Museum News*, *Antiques*, and local newspapers. Her book *Spiritual Heritage* traces the history of Saint James Episcopal Church, Newport, from the Colonial era to the present. Ward was named Delaware Mother of the Year in 1979.

The scarcity of historical references about women has also meant a lack of role models for women in society. In the 1970s, YETTA ZUTZ CHAIKEN (1922-   ), a history and anthropology teacher at Mt. Pleasant Junior High School in Wilmington, developed a course about women to help her female students look beyond the traditionally female careers. Chaiken, who was born in Wilmington, directed the slide-tape project "Forward Women from Delaware's Past," sponsored by the Governor's Commission on Women. The project documented the role of women in Delaware and their influence in public affairs, business, agriculture, science, and crafts.

Chaiken has been active in the Jewish community and directed the periodical *The Jewish Voice*. For the Jewish Historical Society, Chaiken started an oral history library of the accounts of Delaware Jews. Her research on SALLIE TOPKIS GINNS contributed to Ginns's selection to the Hall of Fame of Delaware Women. Chaiken is a member of the Delaware Humanities Forum.

Slides and tapes, guided tours, books, and other educational devices help inform the general public about history. HAZEL DOWNS BRITTINGHAM (1927-   ) retired as a secretary in the public schools to devote more time to her great love, the history of Sussex County, especially Lewes, her lifelong home. She produced a slide show on the educational history of the area before returning to work in real estate. Brittingham is still actively pursuing history, however. She is a member of the Delaware Humanities Forum and has served on the Lewes Planning Commission.

JUDY ATKINS ROBERTS has followed the examples of her mother, ELIZABETH R. ATKINS, and grandmother, LILLE SUTHARD ATKINS, who were also involved with the history of Lewes and in community service. Roberts is president of the Lewes

Judith Roberts

Historical Society and a member of the Swanendael Heritage Commission, the Delaware Heritage Commission, the planning committee for the Friends of the Fisher-Martin House, and the advisory committee for Delaware First. She has been co-chair of the annual Cape Henlopen Craft Fair and has organized walking tours, produced the slide show "A Bird's Eye View of Lewes," and was an advisor for a film on Lewes.

Roberts is also known for her work with children. She worked with the Girl Scouts for fifteen years and has taught Sunday School in the Lewes Presbyterian Church and conducted its junior choir. In 1975 Roberts designed and helped construct over two hundred Bicentennial uniforms for the Milton

Nancy Churchman Sawin

Junior High School. She has directed the Lewes Junior High School flag corps and pop concert.

Students throughout Sussex County remember DOROTHY WILLIAMS PEPPER of Selbyville as the teacher who made Delaware folklore live for them. With songs, poems, artifacts, and special stories, she skillfully tied the past to the present. After receiving a B.S. in education from the University of Delaware in 1928, Pepper taught in the Sussex County public school system for thirty-six years. The notebooks she filled with stories of her childhood became *Folklore of Sussex County, Delaware* (1976). Pepper has immersed herself in the history and folklore of Fenwick Island, where she and her husband own and operate Pepper's Cottages during the summer. She has communicated her love of Sussex County in *The Town of Selbyville* and *Stories of Fenwick Island, Delaware*, which are filled with witticisms, rhymes, folk customs, and ghost stories.

In her pen-and-ink sketches of local scenes and landmarks, NANCY CHURCHMAN SAWIN (1917-   ) brings Delaware history alive. The illustrations are featured in several books, including *Delaware Sketch Book* (1976) and *Up the Spine and Down the Creek* (1982). Sawin ventured farther afield for *China Sketchbook* (1985).

Although BARBARA DENMAN McEWING (1919-   ) was born in Montreal, she is devoted to

Barbara Denman McEwing

Louise Conway Belden

Delaware history. She worked as a guide at Winter-thur Museum and the Historical Society of Delaware after she retired as merchandise manager of John Wanamaker department store in Wilmington. McEwing wrote *The Witness of Market Street,* a history of First and Central Presbyterian Church, Wilmington. She has developed a massive file of information about the history of the Brandywine Hundred-Concord Pike area of New Castle County from the time of William Penn to the present and wrote *Neighbors of the Wilmington-Great Valley Turnpike* (1982). McEwing also does genealogical research for people throughout the United States who have roots in Delaware. In 1986 she received the Americanism Award of the Cooch's Bridge chapter of the DAR, for an adult naturalized citizen who has given service, leadership, and patriotism to the United States.

As in other areas of expertise, the study of history and management of historical organizations have become increasingly professionalized. HELEN SWAIN FOX (1910-   ) retired in 1985 after twenty-two years as hostess-guide of the University of Dela-

ware's Lincoln Room Collection of Abraham Lincoln memorabilia in Wilmington. In 1986 she attended a seminar about Lincoln in Springfield and was given a flag that had flown over Lincoln's grave, awarded to the student who had made the greatest contribution to the seminar. Fox was a guide at Hagley Museum for more than twenty years. A graduate of the University of Delaware who was born in Milford, Fox served on the President's Advisory Committee for fifteen years. She has served on the board of the Chesapeake Bay Girl Scout Council and as president of the Wilmington branch of the AAUW.

LOUISE CONWAY BELDEN, who has worked at Winterthur Museum for twenty-five years, is an authority on the social history of American entertaining, the way in which people used the tableware and decorations that museums like Winterthur collect. She is particularly interested in silver and has written *Collecting for Tomorrow: Spoons* (1975) (with Michael Snodin), and *Marks of American Silversmiths in the Ineson-Bissell Collection* (1980) on the subject. Belden's most recent book, *The Festive Tra-*

dition: American Table Decorations and Desserts, 1670-1870, puts the objects into context.

As a member of the Junior League when she moved to Wilmington, she did volunteer work for community organizations. When she became involved in organizing guides for Winterthur, Belden, who grew up in Winnetka, Illinois, discovered an interest that has motivated her ever since. She returned to school to earn an M.A. from the University of Delaware at age forty-eight and took a position as a curatorial assistant at Winterthur. Belden eventually became curator and continues as a research associate following her official retirement in 1975. She also lectures in museums and at universities throughout the country.

BETTY-BRIGHT PAGE LOW (1929-   ), a native of Virginia, entered the history field because of her knowledge of French. In 1955 she was part of a team that worked at the Longwood Library in Kennett Square, Pennsylvania, to sort and classify the letters and documents, many written in French, that Pierre S. du Pont had accumulated. The collection became part of the Hagley Museum and Library, Greenville, where Low, head of the research and reference department beginning with the opening of the library, is now membership coordinator. She lectures on sports and recreation at the turn of the century and on French influence on America and conducts historical tours to France.

Low is the author of many historical articles. She and JACQUELINE A. HINSLEY have written *Sophie du Pont, a Young Lady in America: Sketches, Letters, and Diary, 1823-1833* (1987). Hinsley, research associate at Hagley Museum, has contributed to an increased understanding of family life and of the role of women at the early du Pont powder mills and in workers' communities surrounding the mills. She has published articles on the education and intellectual pursuits of the daughters of Eleuthère Irénée and Sophie Madeline Dalmas du Pont.

CAROL E. HOFFECKER (1938-   ) blends respected scholarship with popular appeal in writing and teaching about the history of Delaware, especially Wilmington. She has written about her native city in *Wilmington, Delaware: Portrait of an Industrial City, 1830-1910* (1974) and *Corporate Capital: Wilmington in the Twentieth Century* (1983), among others. Hoffecker also wrote *Delaware: A Bicenten-*

nial History (1977) and *Delaware, Small Wonder* (1984) for the State of Delaware. Her Delaware history text for fourth graders is being published as a Constitution bicentennial project. In the history department of the University of Delaware, from which she graduated in 1960 and where she has taught since 1970, Hoffecker is Richards Professor, a position that honors exceptional ability and scholarship. She was president of the University Faculty Senate from 1981 to 1983 and has been chair of the history department since 1983.

Hoffecker serves on the board of trustees of the Historical Society of Delaware and the state Historical Records Advisory Board. She earned a doctorate from Harvard University but returned to Wilmington in 1968 to be fellowship coordinator at the Hagley Museum. She chose to concentrate on Wilmington history because it is similar to the experience of all northeastern cities and offers a means of studying urban history in microcosm. She communicates her abiding interest in the city her family has lived in for over a century and encourages both undergraduates and graduates in scholarly pursuits. She also teaches in the continuing education program, where she inspires hundreds of local residents to find out more about their own community and state.

In her books, articles, and lectures, SUSAN BURROWS SWAN explores the story of early American women as reflected in their needlework. From a background in home economics, she followed her interests to Winterthur Museum. There she moved from senior guide in 1961 to become associate curator in charge of textiles in 1979. Since 1976 she has been an adjunct assistant professor at the University of Delaware. Swan has written *American Crewelwork* (1970), with Mary Taylor Landon; *Winterthur's Guide to Needlework* (1976); and *Plain and Fancy: American Women and Their Needlework, 1700-1850* (1977).

PRISCILLA MERTENS THOMPSON (1932-   ) calls herself a history contractor. She has used imagination in applying her research skills and interest in history to business. Thompson and her husband, Ames, own the History Store in Wilmington, which provides services such as histories of houses, businesses, and organizations and brochures on historic subjects. After working in travel, retail businesses, and volunteer organizations, Thompson decided to change careers in middle age to work in historic preservation. She went back to school to earn an

M.A. in history in 1978 from the University of Delaware, from which she received an award for research on Irish history the same year. Thompson published articles on local history and was accepted to the Delaware Humanities Forum speakers bureau in 1981. She was co-manager with SALLY O'BYRNE of Project R.O.W. (Reclaim Our Waterfront), an inventory of historical, cultural, and physical resources on the Wilmington waterfront sponsored by Cityside, Inc., and funded by a federal marine preservation grant.

As director of the Historical Society of Delaware library, BARBARA E. BENSON (1943-   ) oversees the acquisition, conservation, and use of books, manuscripts, photographs, and other materials in the library collection, the most important resource on Delaware history. A native of Rockford, Illinois, who lives in Hockessin, Benson holds a Ph.D. from Indiana University. She worked at Hagley Museum from 1973 to 1980, has been managing editor of the journal *Delaware History* since 1977, and has taught at the University of Delaware. Benson worked on oral history projects in Indiana and Delaware. She is on the 350th Anniversary Committee, which is preparing to celebrate the anniversary of the Swedish colonization of Delaware in 1638. Benson was on the selection committee for the Hall of Fame of Delaware Women for two years. She also serves on the Delaware Records Advisory Board, the Delaware Humanities Forum, and the Sister Cities of Wilmington board of directors.

Then Lt. Gov. Mike Castle signing proclamation declaring Women's History Week, 1984. Standing l. to r.: Marsha Koston, Pam Morris, Mary Sam Ward, Frances West, Irene Dardashti, Marna Whittington, Jan Konesey, Kate Marvel, Rona Finkelstein, Ruth Kaplan, Mae Carter.

DOMINIQUE COULET WESTERN (1950-   ) has been curator of historical and visual arts exhibits for the state Division of Museums and Historic Sites since 1977. She is also active with the Milford Historical Museum. Western was born in Casablanca, Morocco, of French and Spanish heritage. At an early age, she immigrated to the United States with her family and now lives in Milford. She received a B.A. in anthropology from the University of Delaware in 1972 and completed master's and doctoral degrees at Boston University. She speaks French fluently and has a working knowledge of Spanish, Swahili, and Kiluba. Western has written or co-authored several books and articles, including *A Bibliography of the Arts of Africa* (1976), *Handbook of French Place Names in the USA* (1974 and 1976), and *Handbook of American Counties, Parishes, and Independent Cities* (with René Coulet du Gard). She has represented Sussex County on the State Human Relations Commission for four years.

Delaware women have contributed to a more complete appreciation and understanding of the many aspects of history, both by recording events as they occur and by studying the past. As anthropologist James Deetz says in *In Small Things Forgotten: The Archaeology of Early American Life* (1977), it is in the "seemingly little and insignificant things that accumulate to create a lifetime [that] the essence of our existence is captured. We must remember these bits and pieces, and we must use them in new and imaginative ways so that different appreciation for what life is today, and was in the past, can be achieved." Reading and researching women's letters, diaries, and journals and talking with three or more generations of women who have kept the records and genealogy of the family give us insight into the "bits and pieces" of our collective past and a new perspective on the cultural values of today and on what can be achieved tomorrow.

PURVEYORS OF FAITH:

Women In Religion

Patricia Pratt Knodel

Women are slowly increasing their numbers and influence as priests and ministers in those religions that permit it. Other women, whether nuns or lay people, help their churches and temples or serve the larger community under the aegis of ecumenical organizations or individual religious groups.

At the age of forty, MARLENE WALTERS entered the ministry and now serves the congregation at Mount Lebanon United Methodist Church, Rockland. After receiving a Master of Divinity degree, *magna cum laude*, at Eastern Theological Seminary, Walters went on to earn her doctorate in medical ethics. During her chaplaincy at the Wilmington Medical Center, General Division, she worked principally with the terminally ill. Aware of the lack of bereavement support, she initiated self-help groups for individuals and families faced with long illnesses, death, and other traumas such as divorce or job loss.

Walters teaches medical ethics at Eastern College and at the Nursing School of Wilmington. She leads seminars and has written articles on death and dying. She helped start the Pastoral Care Program at Elkton

Union Hospital, Elkton, Maryland. Walters appeared in the American Cancer Society film "When the Blues Are Running." The American Red Cross, CONTACT, the Better Business Bureau, and the Easter Seal Society have presented awards to Walters for distinguished service.

Pastor of a growing congregation at Mount Zion Holy Church, Milton, GRACE RUTH BRITTINGHAM BATTEN (1943-   ) is a radio minister, counselor, teacher, and community leader. She has worked in the church since her youth and succeeded her late father, Jacob Brittingham, as the pastor of Mount Zion in 1970. Batten earned an A.A.S. in human services at Delaware Technical and Community College and a bachelor's degree in theology at Burke Bible College.

In addition to her pastoral duties, Batten writes devotional booklets and has published a book of poems, *Refreshing Moments*. A life member of the National Council of Negro Women and vice-president of the Milton Ministerial Association, she has served on the boards of the Milton Chamber of Commerce,

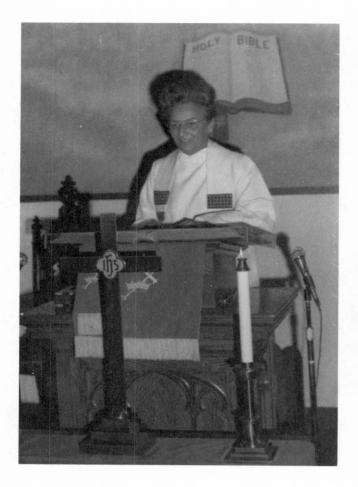

Marlene Walters

Grace Ruth Brittingham Batten

Big Brothers/Big Sisters of Sussex County, Delaware Association of Adult and Community Education, and the Chesapeake Bay Girl Scout Council. Batten was elected to the Milton Town Council in 1982.

Church Women United (CWU) is an ecumenical group of women who work together on matters of mutual concern, particularly church and community service. CWU in Delaware's support of migrant farm workers helped prod President Dwight Eisenhower to initiate a study of their plight. As a result, federal funds were made available for their welfare. In the 1960s, under the leadership of FRANCES TURNER, GERDA LATHAM, and MARIE M. R. HUNTINGTON, CWU aided migrant farm workers

through statewide fund drives. Volunteers established child-care centers and summer-school programs and hired chaplains.

Women of various denominations have spent hundreds of hours listening to the lonely, the troubled, and the suicidal through CONTACT, a twenty-four-hour crisis-intervention telephone ministry. They also counsel rape victims and help the deaf communicate with the outside world via teletype. CAROLYN SLINGLAND ("KELLY") TRUITT (1925-   ) was instrumental in establishing the organization when she returned to Wilmington after living in Sydney, Australia, where she was involved in telephone counseling. In 1976 Truitt was appointed to CONTACT's national board of directors, which she chaired in 1980, and to the Life Line International Secretariat. Truitt, who was born in Paterson, New Jersey, received President Ronald Reagan's Volunteer Action Award in 1982 on behalf of all CONTACT listeners.

114

The following women were in the first training class and have been faithful listeners for at least twelve years: DOROTHY COOKE of Kingswood United Methodist Church, Newark; OLIVE COOK of Aldersgate United Methodist Church, Wilmington; ROSELYN BLISH DECTOR of Temple Beth Emeth, Wilmington; BONNIE HAINES of Limestone Presbyterian Church, Wilmington; SHIRLEY PHILLIPS of Presbyterian Church of the Covenant, Wilmington; and CAROL SHACKLETON of St. John's Episcopal Cathedral, Wilmington. In addition, FRIEDA CUNNINGHAM of St. David's Episcopal Church, Wilmington, MARGARET ("PEGGY") DOSS of First Unitarian Church, Wilmington, and GERDA LATHAM of Second Baptist Church, Wilmington, have logged more than one thousand hours of listening.

Many Delaware church women serve the needs of others far beyond their own religious group. SALLIE TOPKIS GINNS (1880-1976) of Wilmington is considered the most important Jewish woman in Delaware history by the Jewish Federation of Delaware. She was a lifelong member of Temple Beth Emeth who organized the Wilmington Young Women's Hebrew Association in 1913. Ginns founded the Wilmington chapter of the National Council of Jewish Women and led the council in educating immigrants and helping them adapt to American life. She became involved in the women's suffrage movement, as a marcher and as treasurer of the National Women's Party for eight years.

Ginns was convinced that alcohol was at the root of many of the nation's problems and worked hard for Prohibition. She served on the board of Woods Haven-Kruse School for twenty-four years and received the Lammot du Pont Memorial Award for fifty-three years of service as a Red Cross volunteer. Rabbi Herbert E. Drooz observed in his eulogy that Ginns "painted her life spiritually on a vast canvas. . . . Her life was spiritual in its entirety and should serve as a model for this generation and for those that follow." Ginns was chosen for the Hall of Fame of Delaware Women in 1983.

Beginning in 1962, JENNIE ("MOM") MACEY (1915-1983) of Wilmington was the driving force behind the Sharing Christmas Society. Every Christmas she donated her time, her kitchen, and much of her own money—saved from her salary for custodial services at the Wilmington Public Building—to buy,

Gerda Jeksties Latham

cook, and distribute as many as three hundred meals for the city's homeless and poor. Macey called them "her people," because she knew what it meant to be hungry. Macey, a member of the Triumphing Church, received a certificate of commendation from President Richard Nixon in 1972 for "outstanding humanitarian services to the Wilmington community." In 1980 and 1981 she continued the tradition from a wheelchair after her legs were amputated because of circulatory problems.

Born in East Germany and reared in a Lutheran family that moved to Rutherford, New Jersey, in 1923, GERDA JEKSTIES LATHAM (1912-   ) has lived in Wilmington since 1942. Latham began her career of service to others by doing volunteer work for the Junior Board of the Wilmington Medical Center, Memorial Division, and served as a social welfare aid worker for the American Red Cross. At Second Baptist Church, where she was the first woman deacon, Latham led female congregants in folding cancer dressings and visiting hospital patients and shut-ins, and took responsibility for Second Baptist's monthly meal for the Emmanuel Dining Room. She initiated a Community Transportation Service for the elderly. Latham has served as state

115

president of the American Baptist Churches and of American Baptist Churches Women. After trips to the American Baptist Mission Field in Zaire (1971) and Southeast Asia (1973), she shared her findings with groups throughout the state. A leader in the ecumenical movement, Latham has been president of Church Women United and treasurer of the Delmarva Ecumenical Agency.

Latham holds a master's certificate in flower show judging and was a tour guide at Longwood Gardens for fourteen years. A past president of the Wilmington Garden Association, she helped design sixty inner-city gardens in the 1960s. Latham has combined her church work with her interest in horticulture by writing *Gardening in Two Worlds*, a collection of inspirational vignettes on garden themes. She holds a part-time position with the New Castle County Health Unit and received the Community Builder Award of the Delaware Region, National Conference of Christians and Jews in 1986.

Another Baptist, MADALINE BUCHANAN, from Edenton, North Carolina, has been a proponent of the ecumenical movement and of integration of the Delaware public school system. Buchanan has represented the American Baptists on the board of the state Council of Churches. She was one of the founders and early presidents of the state Church Women United (CWU) and of the Dover unit. In 1981 Buchanan was honored for fifty years of dedicated service by the First Baptist Church of Dover, where she was the first and only woman to serve as moderator and where she now serves as deacon.

After the Supreme Court required immediate desegregation of public schools in 1954, Buchanan was the first woman appointed to the Delaware State Board of Education. She served as chair during the difficult months of complying with the decision to integrate Delaware public schools. Her positive public stand also influenced the opening of restaurants and places of amusement to all. After she graduated from Meredith College in North Carolina, Buchanan was director of religious activities and assistant dean of women there before her marriage and move to Dover in 1931. She has been active in garden club projects and in federated women's clubs and serves as historian of Delaware Mothers, Inc. Buchanan is on the advisory board of the Peoples Bank and Trust Co. of Dover and a trustee of Wesley College.

When SUSAN SPRINGER (1914-   ) was con-

firmed in the Episcopal Church, the minister read from Ephesians 6:10, "Put on the whole armor of God." Over the years, those words have given her great spiritual strength. Born on Long Island, she married Wilmingtonian Hal Springer and joined his church, Lower Brandywine Presbyterian, where she taught church school classes and served as deacon. Active in promoting racial equality and justice, Springer invited black people from other churches to social and educational functions at Lower Brandywine. In the 1950s she joined in picketing the Rialto Theater in an effort to open Wilmington's theaters to blacks. She worked with the NAACP and when violence broke out after Martin Luther King's assassination, the Springers were among those who took the risk of underwriting bail money for those who were arrested. After both the Hungarian Revolution and the Vietnam War, the Springers opened their home to refugees for several months. Springer helped the refugees through their struggles with communication, health care, and job hunting.

Since 1964 the Springers have been associated with the Presbyterian Church of Our Savior in a low-income public housing area in Northeast Wilmington. Through the church, Springer started the Price Run Child Center, a day-care center. She affiliated with Pacem in Terris, an organization that supports educational programs for the cause of peace, and joined with thousands of others to march in New York in 1982 against nuclear proliferation. Springer established a food warehouse where surplus or damaged foods from wholesale houses can be received and distributed to food closets. She is persistent in recruiting volunteers to assist her and her work in support of government agencies. Springer has opened her heart, her mind, and her home to serve the needs of others.

Twelve New Castle County Lutheran congregations donate food and money to the largest food pantry system in Wilmington. Through Lutherans Involved in Food Emergencies, RUTH MARIE RASMUSSEN FLEXMAN (1940-   ), who grew up on a farm in Illinois, helped distribute $22,200 worth of food and cleaning products to 5,500 people in 1985. While serving on the Delmarva Ecumenical Hunger Action Task Force and as the first statistician for the Food Closet Study Committee, Flexman discovered that helping people through the church allowed her to emphasize the spiritual aspect of life. She was

116

a member of the first Governor's Council on Volunteer Services and served on the first board of the Delaware Inter-Faith Coalition on Volunteers. Flexman was one of the first trained listeners for CONTACT-Wilmington and the first professional homemaker services specialist for the State of Delaware.

Since she completed a master's degree in education from Indiana University in 1966, Flexman has pursued continuing education in counseling skills, family life, marriage encounter, and aging. Now director of the Martin Luther Foundation, she reorganized the residential management agency into a social and congregational services agency. Flexman is an associate of the Tressler Center for Human Growth.

A three-time delegate to the Lutheran Church of America national convention, PATRICIA PRATT KNODEL is the first woman to serve as president of

Ruth Marie Rasmussen Flexman

the church council at St. Mark's Lutheran Church, Wilmington. Committed to serving her church, she chaired committees and served as a liturgist and communion assistant. Knodel served her community on the Public Assistance Task Force, the Emmanuel Dining Room Steering Committee, the Human Services Information Exchange, the Delaware Alliance for Better Housing, and the Food Closet Study Committee.

As director of the Wilmington Lutheran Urban Cluster, Knodel supervised educational and spiritual growth programs, administered the major food pantry system in New Castle County, fostered extensive volunteer recruitment, and developed means to address social injustice issues. She was project manager of the Food Bank Study sponsored by the Office of Economic Opportunity and the Delmarva Ecumenical Agency in 1981 and now works with Brother Ronald Giannone in the Ministry of Caring.

Concern and loving care for the elderly poor in a home-like atmosphere is the mission of the Roman Catholic religious order LITTLE SISTERS OF THE POOR, founded in 1842 in France. Today, almost 4,800 sisters care for the aged in 280 homes throughout the world. In 1903 the order established St. Joseph's Home for the elderly in Wilmington. Applicants, received without regard to creed or nationality, were required only to be of good moral character, destitute, and over sixty years old. When the building was declared unsafe and obsolete under new state and federal regulations, a new building was constructed in Newark. In 1978 ninety residents moved into the new facility, Jeanne Jugan Home, named for the founder of the order. The Little Sisters of the Poor continue to care for the elderly while preserving their dignity.

SISTER MARY CORDULA BRAND (1906-   ), a Wilmington native, entered the Sisters of St. Francis when she was seventeen years old. After graduating from Villanova University and studying music in New York City, she administered a home for orphans and taught in rural New Jersey, Mahanoy City, Pennsylvania, and inner-city Philadelphia and Marcus Hook, Pennsylvania. When Sister Cordula left teaching, she began a career in social service. In 1976 she was assigned to do social service work in Our Lady of Fatima Parish in Wilmington. Sister Cordula was the first sister to join the staff of Mary

Mother of Hope House, a shelter for homeless and destitute women, in 1977. Since then, she has counseled more than six hundred women.

There is a house on Milltown Road outside Wilmington called the Jesus House. The century-old building was purchased by Christian and ANGELA ROSSI MALMGREN in 1975. When they moved in with their four children, they had two objectives in mind: to provide emergency short-term shelter for people with no other place to go and to serve as a nucleus of study, prayer, and retreat for others who have enjoyed some charismatic experience. Jesus House has served the Veterans Administration Hospital, the Delaware State Hospital, the Child Abuse Prevention Service, Travelers Aid, the Wilmington Senior Center, and Catholic Social Services. Each year, the Malmgrens provide housing and retreat facilities for about 2,500 people, including Spanish-speaking men, women, and children and both Catholic and Protestant youth from Ireland. Malmgren sees in women today a tendency she fights in herself: the "danger . . . that in striving for their own goals, they might lose sensitivity, gentleness, and compassion towards others." She believes that she is keeping pace with the new direction of the Catholic Church through the services she provides at Jesus House.

During her childhood in Baltimore, JANET HOHMAN SALEMI (1928-   ) danced in hospitals, institutions, and homes for crippled children. Over the years, Salemi has continued to reach out to others. She taught in the Baltimore public school system for two years before moving to Wilmington in 1952. One of the first women selected as a special minister of the Eucharist, Salemi serves communion at St. Mary Magdalene Roman Catholic Church. She was narrator at Mass for ten years and also was appointed to the Pastoral Commission of the Catholic Diocese of Wilmington.

Salemi served as state president and as president of the Wilmington unit of Church Women United, encouraging both Roman Catholic and Greek Orthodox women to become active in the organization. Her outreach work has included preparing meals at a senior center and cooking for the Emmanuel Dining Room. She has worked with Cuban refugee children in arts and crafts. As a member of Citizens for Decent Communities, Salemi has worked to pass laws against pornography. She has served as a chapel

Janet Hohman Salemi

escort at the Delaware State Hospital and has participated in programs at the Delaware Correctional Center, Smyrna, and at the Women's Correctional Institution in Claymont.

MARION OWINGS's first exposure to life behind bars occurred during a visit to a prison in 1952. She was so moved by the experience that she became devoted to active prison ministry. A registered nurse and native Delawarean, Owings has brought help and hope to hundreds of inmates at the women's prison in Claymont and at the Delaware Correctional Center, Smyrna. Her leadership has drawn many others to the cause she champions. A member of the board of Church Women United, she rallied support of the Wilmington chapter to organize sewing projects for the Smyrna inmates and to establish a small library for them. Owings also was responsible for the donation of a piano and for improving the surroundings. The pastor and the congregation of her church, Presbyterian Church of the Covenant, now hold weekly services at the women's prison.

Other women's attentions are focused on, although not limited to, their own religious groups. The philosophy of LUCILLE HUNTER MANGUM (1902-   ) is to "hold fast on God with one hand and open the other to your neighbor." She was born in England and grew up in Illinois. Mangum began her religious activities in Wilmington as a member and secretary at St. Paul's United Methodist Church. The Rev. Dr. John Link, Wilmington District Methodist superintendent, admired her fluency and she was accredited as a lay speaker. She has filled pulpits ever since. In the early 1960s, Mangum was a moving force in uniting black and white churchwomen into a single summer school. She served on the Board of Child Care in Baltimore from 1972 to 1980.

Mangum enriches the lives of children by teaching music at the Neighborhood House in Wilmington. She serves as a surrogate mother for them, joining in the fun by dressing in costume for the Halloween parade. Although she does not live at the Methodist Country House, Mangum chaired the Fall Festival fundraiser at the retirement home near Wilmington for three years.

JANE DU PONT LUNGER (1914-   ) has been a leader of the intercessary prayer group and a lay reader at Christ Church Christiana Hundred, Greenville, for the past thirty-five years. She also has supported the Migrant Ministry and has served as devotional chairman for Episcopal Churchwomen and for Church Women United. The chaplaincy service that now functions successfully within the Medical Center of Delaware was begun by Lunger at the Delaware Division in 1965. In 1978 Lunger donated "Oberod," her home for many years, and forty surrounding acres to the Episcopal Diocese of Delaware for use as a conference center. The gift included funds for maintenance of the property. Lunger has been active with the Junior League of Wilmington and as a trustee of Holderness School, Plymouth, New Hampshire. Although she is allergic to horses, Lunger is a devotee of racing. She and her late husband, Harry W. Lunger, founded Christiana Stable, where they bred and trained some of the finest race horses on the East Coast. For her contributions to thoroughbred breeding and racing, Lunger was Honored Lady Guest of the Thoroughbred Club of America in 1980.

Through service to her church and to her community VIRGINIA REBECCA KEITH SMITH

Jane du Pont Lunger

(1916-   ) experiences the spiritual growth that she seeks. A member of Salem United Methodist Church, Selbyville, Smith has served as chair of the Council of Ministries, of worship committees, and of an interdenominational Bible study group. She also participated in Lay Witness Missions in churches in the Mid-Atlantic area. A native of Selbyville, where she owns a business, Smith has taken active roles in the Lions Club, the Chamber of Commerce, the PTA, and the Elks Club Auxiliary. She supervised and promoted the local Farmers' Market and she has been president of the Selbyville Improvement Foundation.

Some women have directed community service agencies for their religious groups. MARY G. WHITE will be remembered as a beloved director of the Neighborhood House in Wilmington, sponsored by the Methodist Action Program. White graduated from the University of Delaware with a degree in education in 1940. She was one of the first teachers at Alfred I. du Pont Institute and later served as director of Christian education at Grace United Methodist Church. When she began her nineteen years at the Neighborhood House, young people's potential was not being developed. By the time White retired

119

Virginia Rebecca Keith Smith

Grace Adolphsen Brame

in 1983, the Neighborhood House had become a full-fledged United Way agency.

For twenty-five years, LENNIE FRISBY LEWIS (1922-   ) was the director of St. Michael's Day Nursery in downtown Wilmington, which is supported by the Episcopal Church. Since her retirement, she has been active on the board of Boy Scouts of America and the YWCA. Lewis was president of Christina Cultural Arts Center, Wilmington, and received its Distinguished Service Award in 1986. She also participates in American Red Cross Home Nursing, sings in the Center City Chorale, and coordinates luncheons for the annual ecumenical Lenten services. Lewis grew up in Mississippi and studied music at Fisk University. She specialized in the study of church music at Juilliard School of music and attended Virginia Theological Seminary. Lewis gives private piano lessons and serves as church organist at both Old Swedes Church, where she is a member, and at St. Joseph's Church. Lewis was elected president of Church Women United of Wilmington in

1982 and was recognized as a Community Builder by the Delaware Region, National Conference of Christians and Jews.

A professional singer who is as well known for her concerts of sacred music as she is for her opera roles, GRACE ADOLPHSEN BRAME is also a writer, lecturer, and leader of meditation groups and retreats. She comes from a Lutheran heritage and her parents, Pastor W. Frederick and KETURAH ADOLPHSEN, were missionaries in India. Brame is a graduate of Wittenburg University and Union Theological Seminary School of Sacred Music. She is a candidate for the Doctor of Religion degree from Temple University. Brame has given lectures and conducted retreats for colleges and hospitals. In 1981 she and her husband, Edward, spent three months in the Soviet Union. After they returned, Grace Brame spoke to many groups about how she found God in the Soviet Union.

Her articles on Christian meditation, written for ministers and lay leaders, have been published in

120

Christian periodicals. She has also written *Receptive Prayer: A Christian Approach*. In the field of religion, Brame has found "male chauvinism to be extreme, unrealized, and deep. . . . [She believes] insensitivity must be met by *groups* of women to be effective, and that groups of women must support individual women."

During the Lenten season in 1961, HELEN LESHER GANGWERE staged the first Religious Festival at St. Andrew's Episcopal Church, Wilmington. For thirty years, she served as Religious Arts chair for Church Women United in Delaware, persuading numerous Delaware artists and churches to exhibit paintings and sculpture with spiritual themes for the festival and for special celebrations in local churches.

In 1972, when KATHLEEN M. GRAHAM became editor of the *Dialog*, the official weekly newspaper of the Catholic Diocese of Wilmington, she was, at twenty-six, the youngest editor in the national Catholic press. The Morristown, New Jersey, native revamped the newspaper, adding regular columns, editorials, hard news, and features, with a freshness of style that assured a steady growth in circulation. The *Dialog* now serves 122,000 Catholics in Delaware and on the Eastern Shore of Maryland. Graham received many honors and awards for her work from the Maryland-Delaware-District of Columbia Catholic Press Association and a first-place award for editorials from Delaware Press Women in 1978. In 1983 she resigned to join the *Baltimore Evening Sun*, but returned to Wilmington in 1986 to edit the *Dialog*.

HALINA WIND PRESTON (1922-1982) worked for Jewish causes, but she never forgot that two Christians had risked their own safety to help her. When the Nazis began slaughtering the residents of the Jewish ghetto in Lvov, Poland, in 1943, Preston and twenty others escaped into a sewer and remained there for fourteen months. Fed and clothed by two Christian sewer workers, ten of the Jews survived in their filthy hideout. As a survivor of the Nazi Holocaust, Preston frequently spoke about it to impress Delawareans with its bitter lesson. Her emphasis, however, was not on blaming, but on forewarning. To that end, she helped develop a comprehensive curriculum on the Holocaust for Delaware schools.

Helen Lesher Gangwere

Born in Turska, Poland, Preston immigrated to the United States in 1947. She was graduated from Hunter College and from the Teachers' Institute of the Jewish Theological Seminary of America. Preston was active as a director of the Jewish Federation of Delaware, Wilmington Gratz Hebrew High School (where she taught Jewish studies until her death), Albert Einstein Academy, and the Jewish Community Center in Wilmington. Throughout the years she remembered the Christians who saved her life. To honor them and others like them, the Garden of the Righteous Gentiles was dedicated in November 1981 at the Jewish Community Center. It is the only memorial outside Jerusalem to non-Jews who helped Jews survive the Holocaust.

Ecumenical emphasis such as Preston's is strong among religious women in Delaware. Through

Church Women United and other interfaith groups, as well as through the efforts of individual religious organizations, Delaware women seek to improve the spiritual and material lives of those around them.

Halina Wind Preston

ON THE CUTTING EDGE:

Women In Science and Technology

Deborah Lynn Grubbe

Many more women are pursuing scientific and technical careers today, although there are still relatively few, compared with women in other fields. Because of chemical firms headquartered in Delaware, most of the women who are prominent in science and technology are chemists or engineers employed by chemical companies. Women have also made contributions in natural and information sciences.

The first female scientist from Delaware who achieved national fame was an astronomer, ANNIE JUMP CANNON (1863-1941). Her mother encouraged Cannon's fascination with astronomy from an early age, when she studied the stars from her home in Dover. Cannon earned bachelor's and master's degrees from Wellesley College and worked at the Harvard University observatory. She was noted for classifying stellar spectra and discovering novae and variable stars. Cannon was an honorary member of the Royal Astronomical Society of Great Britain and

was the first woman to receive an honorary doctorate in science from Oxford University. She was also the first woman officer of the American Astronomical Society. In 1921 she received a doctor of science degree from the University of Groningen in the Netherlands, at that time the highest scentific award that had been granted to any American woman by a foreign university. In 1981 Cannon was among the first inductees into the Hall of Fame of Delaware Women.

A growing number of women are teaching science at the university level. QUAESITA C. DRAKE (1889-1967) was an important influence in science education for women, both as chair of the chemistry department of the Women's College and after it was incorporated into the University of Delaware. Drake retired in 1955 after thirty-eight years of teaching. Quaesita Drake Hall was the first university building named for a female faculty member. The univer-

123

Quaesita C. Drake

sity awards an annual scholarship in her name to a female chemistry major for "academic accomplishment, potential, and excellence in character."

JEANNETTE E. GRAUSTEIN (1892-1982) was Drake's counterpart in the Women's College biology department. After serving as chair for over twelve years, she took early retirement to write on the history of botanists. Her major publication is the biography *Thomas Nuttall Naturalist, Explorations in America 1808-1841* (1967). Graustein earned a B.A. from Mount Holyoke College and a Ph.D., in botany, from Harvard University.

ELIZABETH DYER (1906-   ) taught chemistry at the University of Delaware from 1933 to 1971, becoming full professor in 1951. She taught ele-

mentary organic chemistry to hundreds of non-major students and polymer chemistry to graduate students. Dyer directed the research of over fifty doctoral and master's degree students. Most of her sixty-three technical papers are joint publications with students. She was educated at Mount Holyoke College (B.A. and M.A.) and Yale University (Ph.D.). Dyer received a national award for excellence in teaching from the Manufacturing Chemists Association in 1958 and a University of Delaware teaching award in 1969. She served the American Chemical Society as secretary of the Delaware Section and as a member of the National Women Chemists Committee.

When ROBERTA COLMAN (1938-   ) came to the University of Delaware in 1973, she was the only woman who taught chemistry there. As a professor of biochemistry, she takes pride in guiding graduate students as they pursue research and go on to careers in teaching and industry. After earning a Ph.D. from Harvard University, Colman received fellowships at the National Institutes of Health and Washington University and taught at Washington University and Harvard University before coming to Delaware. She has published extensively and serves on editorial boards of scientific journals. Colman has held office in professional organizations and has served on grant review committees for the American Heart Association and the National Institutes of Health. Her many honors include the Francis Alison Award in 1985, for "that faculty member of the University of Delaware who has made the most outstanding contributions to his/her field of inquiry."

LILA M. GIERASCH (1948-   ) is engaged in research on peptides at the University of Delaware, where she is a professor in the chemistry department. She received a bachelor's degree from Mount Holyoke College and a doctorate in biophysics from Harvard University. Gierasch is a consultant to Merck, Sharp & Dohme Research Laboratories. She has published extensively in the fields of biophysics, peptide membrane interactions, and protein secretions and was given the first Vincent du Vigneaud Award for Young Investigators in Peptide Research in 1984. Gierasch has received an Alfred P. Sloan Fellowship (1984-86), the Mary Lyon Award from Mount Holyoke College (1985), and a Guggenheim Fellowship (1986).

Other scientists have chosen to do research in an industrial rather than a university setting. EMMA-JUNE H. TILLMANNS-SKOLNIK (1919-1984) came to Delaware in 1960 to work for Atlas, a predecessor to ICI Americas, and became supervisor of biomedical information there. She received a Ph.D. from New York University. Tillmanns-Skolnik served on the board of directors of the Drug Information Association and was the first female chair of the Delaware Section of the American Chemical Society. She was on the advisory board of the *Journal of Chemical Information and Computer Sciences*. Tillmanns-Skolnik was chair of the board of Mt. Salem Methodist Church and was a judge and an exhibitor for the American Rose Society.

STEPHANIE KWOLEK made outstanding contributions to research on fibers and polymers in her work for the Du Pont Company. She holds sixteen patents on polymers, polycondensation processes, and liquid crystaline solutions, polymers, and fibers, and has authored or co-authored more than twenty publications. A native of New Kensington, Pennsylvania, she graduated from Carnegie-Mellon University with a B.S. in chemistry and joined Du Pont in 1946. Her current research began in 1965 with the discovery of liquid crystalline solutions of synthetic aromatic polyamides from which rigid-chain, high-strength, high-modulus fibers such as Kevlar® can be produced.

Kwolek has been recognized by the American Society of Metals for her contributions to the development and application of Kevlar,® for which the Du Pont Company received the Engineering Materials Achievement Award in 1978. The Franklin Institute gave her its Howard V. Potts Medal in 1976 for individual and joint contributions toward the development of improved fibers. Kwolek has also received the American Chemical Society Award for Creative Invention in 1980 and the American Institute of Chemists' Chemical Pioneer Award. In 1981 Worcester Polytechnic Institute conferred on Kwolek an honorary doctor of science degree for her contributions to polymer and fiber chemistry.

MARY A. KAISER (1948-   ) supervises the work of seventeen people in the Central Research and Development Department at the Du Pont Company. She joined Du Pont as a research chemist in 1977 following two years of teaching chemistry at Villanova University, where she earned a Ph.D. in analytical chemistry, and a year of postdoctoral research at the University of Georgia. Kaiser's research interests include the analytical and physical chemistry of separation and environmental analysis. She has authored and co-authored many scientific publications, including the book *Environmental Problem Solving Using Gas and Liquid Chromatography*. Kaiser is past president of the Chromatography Forum of the Delaware Valley and has been an officer of the Delaware Section of the American Chemical Society. She served on the staff of the *Del-Chem Bulletin* and on Governor Pierre S. du Pont IV's advisory committees on state laboratories and alcohol testing. She comes from Jenkins Township, Pennsylvania.

UMA DALAL CHOWDHRY (1947-   ) manages a team of chemists, chemical engineers, and materials scientists devoted to the study of heterogeneous catalysts at the Du Pont Company. Her position allows her to engage in research while developing management skills. Chowdhry earned a B.A. from Bombay University in her native India, an M.A. from Cali-

Uma Dalal Chowdhry

Marlene J. Jones

fornia Institute of Technology, and a Ph.D. from M.I.T. Since her husband is in the same field, finding jobs in the same area was a challenge, but it was solved when Du Pont offered positions to both of them.

MARLENE J. JONES (1948-   ), a chemist, has been an internal consultant on applications of Hercules, Inc., products for more than ten years. She holds two patents and also represents the company at trade meetings, where she presents papers to sales and technical representatives on the use of Hercules products. Jones considers herself a suitable role model for black children and works through organizations such as the Educational Resources Association to expose youth to the career opportunities available to them through the proper training and hard work. She has participated in Special Olympics,

the Girls Club, and tennis tournaments for Sickle Cell Anemia, and organized a United Way fair at the Hercules Research Center. Jones has served on the board of directors of Hercules Country Club and as president of the Hercules Research Center Women's Club. The Wilmington YWCA awarded her the Minority Achievement Award in 1974.

Delaware women also work in pharmacology, toxicology, and other sciences. JANET SPENCE KERR (1942-   ) is a senior research pharmacologist with the Du Pont Company. Her research interests are the role of oxygen-derived free radicals in acute inflammation and the effect of nutritional restriction on lung structure and function. She is also an adjunct assistant professor of physiology at the University of Pennsylvania School of Medicine. Previously, Kerr taught at Rutgers University, where she earned a Ph.D. in physiology. She has spoken and published extensively and is a reviewer for the National Science Foundation *Journal of Applied Physiology* and of grants for the Veterans Administration. Kerr serves on the Professional Education Committee of the Delaware Lung Association and is a member of the board of directors of the Delaware-Raritan Lung Association.

RUTH REINKE MONTGOMERY, born in New York City, is an information analyst with the Du Pont Company. She has done experimental toxicological research in skin and eye tests and co-authored papers on various aspects of toxicology. She wrote a chapter on polymers for *Patty's Industrial Hygiene and Toxicology* series and has evaluated material safety data sheets and general toxicity literature. Montgomery also worked in the Du Pont Company's medical emergency information system. She has been an officer and committee chair for the Delaware Section of the American Chemical Society. Montgomery is involved with the University of Delaware Library Associates and Earthwatch.

As a medical reporter for the Du Pont Company, ANN PENNELL MOFFETT (1946-   ), born in Huntingdon, Pennsylvania, translates clinical studies on drugs into reports to the Federal Drug Administration, information for physicians and consumers, and investigative drug brochures used when a product is first marketed. She was formerly a clinical information coordinator for the Stuart Pharmaceutical Division of ICI Americas, Inc. Moffett has been an officer of the Delaware Section and of the Division of Chemical Information of the American Chemical Society (ACS). She is co-editor of a book on the retrieval of medicinal chemical information in the ACS Symposium Series. Moffett works in United Way campaigns. She sees signs of "a greater awareness by women that the way to solve [problems] is to make them issues for both men and women."

A life scientist for the Du Pont Company, FRANCES S. LIGLER (1951-   ) does research on human B-cell tumors. She is also a research associate professor at Hahnemann University. Ligler holds a Ph.D. in biochemistry from Oxford University and has many publications to her credit. She belongs to the American Association of Immunologists, American Association of Pathologists, Association for Women in Science, and Wilmington Women in Business.

Women scientists also work in corporate management positions. JEAN G. MARCALI (1926-   ) is supervisor of administrative services for the Central Information Services Division of the Du Pont Company. She is responsible for coordinating, developing, and monitoring the division's budget, cost control, and office systems. Marcali entered the field of information science in 1960, when she was assigned responsibility for all research divisions of the Organic Chemicals Department. She was one of the first information specialists assigned to design a company-wide indexing service and to operate a computer-aided facility for retrieving technical information for all departments. Marcali served the American Chemical Society as an officer on national and local levels, as well as in its Chemical Information Division. She is on the editorial board of the *Journal of Chemical Information and Computer Sciences*.

A native of Hagerstown, Pennsylvania, BARBARA ANN MONTAGUE (1929-   ) works in the Employee Relations Department of the Du Pont Company. Having started at Du Pont as a chemist in 1951, she took on increasing responsibilities as she moved into supervisory and management positions. She has held a number of offices in the American Chemical Society. Montague has contributed articles to the *Journal of the American Chemical Society* and the *Journal of Chemical Information and Computer Sciences*. She is a deacon of Red Clay Creek Presbyterian Church and has been active in Du

Pont Company musical organizations and the Delaware Symphony Orchestra.

SUSAN ANNE VLADUCHICK (1947-   ), born in Aliquippa, Pennsylvania, spent ten years doing research in exploratory synthetic organic chemistry for the Du Pont Company, where she obtained several patents and published numerous papers. She now works in the Employee Relations Department and enjoys talking with young people about careers in chemistry and industrial research. Vladuchick also has worked for youth as an advisor to Junior Achievement and Boy Scouts, and as a volunteer for a handicapped children's recreation program at the A.I. du Pont Institute.

Female engineers apply their skills to a variety of fields. During World War II, Westinghouse selected A. ELIZABETH RIDER RONAT for an engineer training course for college graduates, even though she had just graduated from high school. After she completed the course, Ronat pursued an engineering degree while she worked for Westinghouse. She left work when her children were young and later taught high-school and college physics and mathematics. Ronat's husband's job transfers interfered with her career path in academia, so in 1974, after her husband had been transferred to the Philadelphia area, she returned to industry. At Hercules, Ronat, who is a licensed professional engineer, worked on the construction of the headquarters building in Wilmington and later was responsible for computer systems and telecommunications for the Hercules Research Center. She is chair-elect of the Delaware Bay Section of the Institute of Electrical and Electronic Engineers.

LESLIE ANN FREEMON BENMARK (1944-   ) is Dacron staple strategist and business analysis manager for Dacron/"Qiana" fibers with the Du Pont Company. She joined Du Pont in 1968 in Nashville and held engineering positions in Planning/Industrial Engineering and Computer Operations. In 1979 Benmark was transferred to a management position in Wilmington. She was the first woman awarded a Ph.D. in system and information engineering from Vanderbilt University, where she served as assistant to the dean of Engineering and director of the Women Engineering Program from 1975 to 1979.

Leslie Ann Freemon Benmark

Benmark earned a degree from the Delaware Law School and passed the Delaware Bar examination in 1985. She was selected Tennessee's Outstanding Young Woman for 1978 and received the State of Tennessee Governor's Outstanding Tennesseean Award the same year. She is interested in assisting young women considering career options in nontraditional fields.

JACQUELINE ANN RICHTER MENGE, a fourth-generation Delawarean from Dover, specializes in ice mechanics. She is a research civil engineer employed by the U.S. Army Cold Regions Research and Engineering Laboratory in Hanover, New Hampshire. Menge goes to Alaska to evaluate the resources and also analyzes ice samples flown from Prudhoe Bay, Alaska, by companies exploiting the oil resources in the area. In 1979, when Menge was working on a master's degree in mechanical and

aerospace engineering from the University of Delaware, she was the first female student named to the university board of trustees.

ROBERTA S. GARRISON BROWN (1951-   ), a native of Alexandria, Virginia, is coordinator of Power Plant Performance for Delmarva Power and Light Company, Wilmington. In this capacity, she monitors the efficiency and reliability of Delmarva's generating stations, establishes cost-effective improvement programs, and prepares and presents written and oral testimony before the three public-service commissions that regulate the company. She has also been project engineer in the Production Planning and Project Control Department, where she prepared planning studies for future generating unit additions and retirements and analyzed production engineering and construction projects. Engineering design and analysis for nuclear and fossil-fuel power plants for Metropolitan Edison Company, Reading, Pennsylvania, gave her experience in the utility field.

Brown graduated from Immaculata College with a B.A. in physics and mathematics while working for Metropolitan Edison Company. She is a registered professional engineer in Pennsylvania, Maryland, and Delaware. Brown has held offices in the Society of Women Engineers, Philadelphia Section. She found being in a nontraditional field for women

Jacqueline Ann Richter Menge

128

was an obstacle early in her life, because many technical schools were not open to women.

DEBORAH LYNN GRUBBE (1955-   ) was lead engineer for construction of the multi-million-dollar Greenewalt Laboratory at the Du Pont Company Experimental Station outside Wilmington and is in charge of a plant being built in Northern Ireland. Originally from Chicago, Grubbe is a registered professional engineer. After receiving a B.S. in chemical engineering from Purdue University, she did postgraduate study in that field at Cambridge University, where she was a Winston Churchill Fellow. She returns to Purdue annually to address the women of the freshman class entering the field of engineering. Grubbe has held offices in engineering organizations and in Wilmington Women in Business, Delaware Alliance of Professional Women, and Zeta

Tau Alpha Fraternity. She received the Trailblazer Award of the Delaware Alliance of Professional Women in 1986. Grubbe credits her mother and one of her high-school teachers with steering her in the direction of her interests and abilities.

In the past decade, women have made progress in the field of science and technology. Their rarity poses challenges in securing technical education and in pursuing their careers. UMA CHOWDHRY notes that women tend to work harder to prove themselves in this male-dominated field. DEBORAH GRUBBE believes that women can make special contributions to engineering because they approach people and situations from a different perspective than men. Chowdhry declares that women are being given more chances to prove themselves. "In the U.S. today, the opportunities are limitless."

129

READY . . . SET . . . GO:

Women In Sports

Gretchen Vosters Spruance

Until the late nineteenth century, most people kept fit by doing hard work and few had either time or need for sports. However, with the growth of sedentary occupations and labor-saving devices for housework and with increasing leisure time, organized sports became popular. Women went beyond the limits of genteel pastimes like backyard croquet and sidesaddle riding to more active sports, and shed their corsets and inhibiting attire in the process.

Individual sports such as riding and tennis were the first in which women excelled. MARION DU PONT SCOTT in 1915 was the first woman to ride horseback astride instead of sidesaddle in competition and MARGARET OSBORNE DU PONT first won the Wimbledon tennis singles crown in 1947.

When STELLA BROWN (?-1986) of Harrington was in her teens, her mother discouraged her from caring for the family horses because it was not ladylike. Brown followed her mother's advice for a few

years and taught school. Then she married a horseman and worked with horses the rest of her life. Brown and her husband followed the harness racing circuit throughout the United States and Canada. Stella Brown specialized in correcting problem horses. She trained and exercised horses before feeding time at the Harrington Race Track.

BETSY REIVER DE MARINO (1950-   ), a native Delawarean, is a veterinarian who lives in Riyadh, Saudia Arabia, where she treats all kinds of animals, including hedgehogs, falcons, ospreys, and racing camels. She is employed by the Equestrian Club, which is headed by Crown Prince Abdullah. De Marino was also a consultant for a new zoo in Taif. Since April 1984, De Marino has been the veterinarian for the Saudi government in the Saudi Customs Dog Detector program. In general, women are not permitted to work in Saudi Arabia, but exceptions are made for doctors and teachers. In these professions,

131

women receive the respect of their western counterparts. De Marino also participates in horse shows and carriage shows. She is active in the International Women's Group in Riyadh and she collects artifacts of Bedouin culture, especially their traditional costumes and jewelry. De Marino has helped manage pageants of Arabian costumes and she sometimes models at fashion shows.

Tennis was another acceptable sport for women in the nineteenth century. When MARION ZINDERSTEIN JESSUP (MACLURE) (1896-1980) came to Wilmington from her native Brookline, Massachusetts, in 1921, she was already a national finalist. Jessup was the first woman from Delaware to compete in the Olympic Games. Jessup and Vinnie Richards won a silver medal for mixed doubles in Paris in 1924. Jessup ranked first in women's doubles for four years and was among the top ten in singles for eleven years. From 1918 to 1948, she won fifteen national and two Canadian titles in singles, doubles, and mixed doubles. When the Delaware Sports Hall of Fame was established in 1976, Jessup was the only woman inducted.

MADGE HARSHAW ("BUNNY") VOSTERS and her daughter GRETCHEN VOSTERS SPRUANCE (1947-   ) are not just getting a light workout when they walk onto a tennis court. Vosters began playing tennis in her hometown, Lansdowne, Pennsylvania. In 1964 she was named captain of the U.S. Federation Cup team. She and Spruance teamed up three years later to win the women's doubles of the Mid-States Clay Court Tournament. By 1983 they had captured twenty-two mother-daughter national titles. Vosters won two more with daughter NINA VOSTERS MOYER. Vosters and Spruance are also eight-time winners of the U.S. National Mother-Daughter Grass-Court Championship and have won the women's doubles in the U.S. National Squash Championship ten times. Vosters won the 60 and Over National Grass-Court Singles title in 1985. In 1980 VOSTERS was inducted into the Delaware Sports Hall of Fame.

Spruance has won nineteen consecutive Delaware women's singles tennis titles beginning in 1965. She is also a five-time national singles champion in squash, as well as a five-time national doubles champion. As chair of the Governor's Physical Fitness Council, Spruance has fostered interest in racquet sports in the state that has encouraged other champions.

A native of Wilmington, JOYCE NIDZGORSKI (1960-   ) set a University of Delaware tennis record for wins in a single season when she compiled an 18-4 record in her freshman year in 1978. She played the number one position on the university tennis team three out of four years and was voted most valuable player. Nidzgorski holds the university record for career wins (42).

CHARLOTTE BALICK's sport is golf, which is becoming more popular with women. She won an unprecedented sixth Delaware Women's Amateur Golf Association victory in 1983. Balick captured her first title in 1967.

PATSY HAHN (1940-   ) is the first woman in Delaware and one of a half dozen in the entire country to become a head golf pro, the position she holds at the Du Pont Louviers course. A winner of the Delaware Women's Amateur Golf Association medal five times since 1954, Hahn was either a champion or runner-up for the next ten years. In 1963 she tied for seventh place in the U.S. Open.

Native Wilmingtonian JOAN SCHIMPF SAMONISKY (1957-   ) excelled at team sports before she took up golf. She earned letters in softball and field hockey at the University of Delaware and the 1979 Outstanding (female) Senior Athlete Award. Samonisky won the Delaware Women's Amateur Golf Association championship in 1979 and 1982. She coaches at Caravel Academy in Bear.

During the late 1960s, the Wilmington 600 Club was organized to recognize women bowlers who reached a 600 scratch series. The club has about four hundred members. GRACE WITTLAND is often credited as the "mother of junior bowling in Delaware" for developing the Wilmington Junior Bowling Association in 1963. She was accorded life membership in the Wilmington Women's Bowling Association after holding a series of club offices. Wittland was the first person inducted into the Delaware State Women's Bowling Association Hall of Fame when it was established in 1979. Women honored since then for "distinguished and meritorious service on behalf of the sport" include ANN CABREY, Wilmington; JAN DANNING, Claymont; and BERNICE McAFEE, Dover.

Laurie Kirkpatrick

BETTY GANTER (1931-   ) has bowled for twenty-five years. She was the third woman in Delaware to record two 300-point games. Still an active bowler, she also manages Silverside Bowling Lanes.

Archery is an individual sport that is often associated with summer camp and has few widely known serious competitors. In 1970 LAURIE KIRKPAT-RICK (1963-   ) took her first aim at the sport. Five years later, she garnered first place in the Delaware State Championship. In 1977 Kirkpatrick placed first in the National Championship, a title she retained for three years. A native of Wilmington, Kirkpatrick was introduced to archery by her father, who used his bows and arrows for hunting. Paul Weisser,

a co-owner of Whitetail Archery, encouraged her to pursue the sport and became her coach and friend. As a teenager, Kirkpatrick struggled to be accepted by her peers, who nicknamed her "Robin Hood," while spending a great deal of time on a sport few appreciated. She traveled and competed for eleven years and won twenty-seven awards.

ROSEMARY YOUNG MILLER (1939-1974) of New Castle began shooting traps competitively in 1965 and in three years was one of the best in the country. As the 1968 Grand American Women's Handicap Champion, Miller won what is called the "Super Bowl" of trapshooting. After the start of her competitive career, Miller dominated the sport in Delaware, winning the state title eight times in nine tries. She was named to the *Sports Afield* Women's All-American first team in 1970, 1972, and 1973 and was named to the second team three other years. In 1973 she had the second-best women's average in the United States. Miller was named to the Delaware Sports Hall of Fame in 1983.

Her mother's support enabled GINGER SMITH (PARKS) (1947-   ) of Washington, D.C., to weather the difficulties of breaking ground for women in track and field in the 1960s. She convinced coaches at Tower Hill School in Wilmington to allow her to train with the boys' track team and developed a girls' track team with girls from other schools. In 1964 Smith proved herself by competing in the prestigious Penn Relays, the first Delaware woman to do so.

As the ranks of women track enthusiasts swelled, SANDY GIBNEY (1961-   ) set her sights on the 1988 Olympic Games. She took up track to strengthen herself for field hockey, in which she excelled. An all-state hockey player in high school (as well as an all-star softball player), Gibney was chosen for national hockey camp, part of the Olympic team selection process. In 1979 she was selected a Mitchell and Ness Field Hockey All-American. Gibney turned her attention to track, and in 1980 she set a University of Delaware record for the 5000-yard run. Later that year, she placed second in the AIAW Cross-Country Championship Division II Eastern Regionals and took first place at the East Coast Conference women's cross-country championships. Gibney placed sixteenth in an AIAW Division II cross-country meet and received national recognition. She topped the

133

Rosemary Young Miller

women's division of the Pepsi Challenge 10,000-meter run and placed seventh in a field of two thousand runners at the Avon half-marathon in 1982.

Delaware also has outstanding master swimmers. JEAN TROY won nine medals at the Mid-Atlantic Masters in 1983, placing either second or third. She was a member of the 200-yard freestyle team which set a national record. Troy, a native of Tarboro, North Carolina, came to Delaware in 1955. She was the aquatics director of the Western YMCA, near Newark, until her retirement in the early 1980s.

In 1984 NANCY CHURCHMAN SAWIN (1917-   ) of Hockessin won each of the five events she entered in the Mid-Atlantic Masters Swimming Championship, the 50-, 100-, and 500-yard freestyle and the 50- and 100-meter backstroke.

Delaware is strong in team sports, especially field hockey and lacrosse, and NANCY SAWIN has been a leader in this area. In 1981 Sawin was inducted into the Delaware Sports Hall of Fame for her contributions to field hockey. She was on the All-American Field Hockey Team for seven years and was president of the United States Field Hockey Association and of the International Federation of Women's Field Hockey Associations. Sawin, a fifth-generation Delawarean, promoted hockey during her ten years as head of Sanford School, which was started by her mother, ELLEN SAWIN.

While at the University of Delaware, SHARON WILKIE was co-recipient of the Pepsi-Cola Scholarship, awarded to the athlete with the highest grade-point average as of junior year. She was selected a Mitchell and Ness All-American for two years and was a member of the United States Field Hockey Squad in 1981, the National Under 21 Team in 1982, and the 1984 Olympic Training Squad. Wilkie was a student representative of the University of Delaware Athletic Governing Board.

CAROL MILLER of East Petersburg, Pennsylvania, was selected for the Mitchell and Ness Field Hockey All-American team in 1981. She was the University of Delaware co-captain in 1980 and 1981 and was a varsity player for four years. Miller ranks as the university's second all-time scorer with forty-six career goals and eight assists for fifty-four career

points. She was a member of the United States national team in 1978 and 1981.

In 1982 ANNE BROOKING (1959-   ) became the first athlete to receive All-American status in two female sports, twice for lacrosse and once for hockey. She was Outstanding Lacrosse Athlete at the University of Delaware for two years and played on the Division II National All-Tournament Team for two years. Brooking was named Outstanding Field Hockey Athlete of the university in 1982, Mitchell and Ness Collegiate All-American, and a nominee for the Broderick Award. Brooking played on the U.S.A. Under 21 Team and the American Cup Team.

In 1972, when the United States women's lacrosse team defeated the English team for the first time, JACQUELIN ("JACKIE") PITTS (1937-   ) was captain. She was captain again while on the U.S. squad from 1960 to 1974, one of the top thirty female lacrosse players in the nation. Pitts was on the team (one of the top eleven players) from 1964 to 1966 and from 1969 to 1973 and was high scorer in 1970. She played on three teams that toured to world championship games and coached two others, including the world-championship team of 1982. Pitts played lacrosse at Sanford School in Hockessin and, inspired by her coach, NANCY SAWIN, returned to the school after graduating from Saint Lawrence University to teach mathematics and coach lacrosse. Pitts directs the Sanford School lacrosse and field hockey camp, which she helped found. She was president of the Women's Lacrosse Association for five years and was inducted into the Delaware Sports Hall of Fame in 1983. Pitts is president of the International Federation of Women's Lacrosse and will preside over the World Cup Tournament in Perth, Australia, in 1989.

In 1984 KAREN EMAS became the all-time leading scorer in NCAA lacrosse (men's or women's) with 310 goals and 111 assists. She holds the Delaware record for most assists and points in a single game and the NCAA and Delaware records for most goals in a season (98). Her scoring helped the University of Delaware team win the NCAA Division I championship in 1983. Emas, a three-time All-American, was the university's outstanding female athlete in 1984, her senior year. She was the East

Sharon Howett

SHARON HOWETT, a native of New Holland, Pennsylvania, won letters in both basketball and tennis for four years at the University of Delaware. She was captain of both teams and was Outstanding (female) Senior Athlete. In basketball, she was the first female athlete at the University of Delaware to score more than one thousand career points and make over one thousand rebounds. She holds the all-time record for rebounds in a game (27).

LORI HOWARD was captain of the University of Delaware basketball team for two years. She broke four records for points scored. Howard was selected an Academic All-American, Outstanding Basketball Player, and Outstanding (female) Senior Athlete (1981). The AAUW named Howard, a native of Basking Ridge, New Jersey, an Outstanding Senior Woman.

Softball player AUDIE KUJALA was the first recipient of the University of Delaware Outstanding (female) Senior Athlete Award in 1977. She was a leading batter and was recruited by the Connecticut Falcons professional team. After the Falcons won the national championship, they were invited to play a series of exhibition games in China. While at the University of Delaware, Kujala was also co-captain of the field hockey team, which reached the national finals.

Behind most superstars or winning teams there is a dedicated coach. Such is the case with Ursuline Academy's swim team coach, GAIL P. GLYNN, an Elizabeth, New Jersey, native now living in Wilmington. In 1983, only the school's third year in varsity competition, Ursuline Academy won the Delaware Girls Interscholastic Swimming Championship. An impressive accomplishment by any standard, it is even more so considering that there is no pool at the school for practice or competition. Glynn rents four different facilities and plans a complicated schedule for daily practice. Although Glynn herself never swam competitively, she learned to swim at age three. She has taught swimming since 1972, five years as a volunteer at the Ursuline Junior School. Her nursing training (she earned an R.N. degree) helps her understand the orthopedic aspect of the sport.

Coast Conference women's lacrosse scholar-athlete in 1983 and was a member of the U.S. Lacrosse Squad.

The success of women's intercollegiate athletics at the University of Delaware is due in large measure to MARY ANN HITCHENS (1945-   ). Although

Mary Ann Hitchens

she was captain of three women's sports teams at Milford High School and broke the one thousand-point barrier in basketball, athletic opportunities at the University of Delaware during her years as a student there were severely limited. Hitchens had a chance to improve conditions for female athletes at the university when she joined the faculty in 1969, the first year of a two-year pilot program in women's intercollegiate athletics. At that time, the women's playing fields were in bad shape, there was only one basketball court available for the female players, and swim meets had to be scheduled away because the home pool was inadequate for competition. Out of dedication to the program, the coaches took on increased responsibility on top of full teaching schedules without additional pay. The sacrifices paid off when the program was made permanent at the end of the pilot period.

In 1970 Hitchens became varsity basketball coach and chair of the Women's Intercollegiate Athletic Council. Her hockey teams earned a 96-39-19 record in the decade following her appointment as head coach in 1973, including a second-place, two third-place, and one fourth-place finish in the Division I AIAW championships. Hitchens's lifetime coaching record as of March 1985 was 138-61-24. Outstanding in her role as coordinator of Women's Athletics, Hitchens was the driving force behind a program that now includes ten varsity intercollegiate sports.

Associate dean of physical education at the University of Delaware, BARBARA J. KELLY (1933-   ) was inspired to pursue a career in physical education by her college field hockey coach. Kelly coached and taught at her high school and earned a master's degree before joining the University of Delaware faculty in 1962. She taught while she completed a Ph.D. in behavioral sciences. Kelly specializes in stress management and tension control and is researching the important contributions of Delaware women physical educators. She was a member of the New Castle County Health Advisory Committee. Kelly chaired the University of Delaware Commission on the Status of Women and the United Way campaign at the university.

BARBARA VIERA (1941-   ) was the first University of Delaware field hockey coach. Now, as the first and only volleyball coach at the university, she enjoys an immensely successful career. Viera's lifetime coaching record as of March 1985 was 333-169-2. A highlight of her volleyball career came in 1979, when she coached the Blue Hens to the Eastern AIAW championship. That same year, her team was a participant in the Division II national tournament. Viera's consistently high level of coaching has led to the participation of all of her teams in Eastern AIAW championship tournaments. She has also contributed to the university as the men's volleyball club advisor and as director of the Olympic Development Volleyball Camp. A graduate of the University of Massachusetts and Springfield College, she is a past president of the Delaware Association for Health, Physical Education, Recreation and Dance (DAHPERD).

JANET SMITH, a graduate of Ursinus College and West Chester University, is best known for making sports history three years after she became coach of the women's lacrosse team at the University of Delaware in 1980. Her coaching strategies helped the team retain the national title in 1983 even though its status had been upgraded by a division. No team, in any men's or women's college sport, has yet matched that feat. Before she came to the university, Smith coached at Tatnall School, Wilmington, and Sanford School, Hockessin. She also coaches hockey at the University of Delaware.

ELIZABETH H. ("BETTY") RICHARDSON (1930-   ) has been honored for outstanding educational and personal leadership toward students at Tower Hill School, Wilmington, by receiving the William Lloyd Kitchel II Endowed Faculty Chair. A dedicated faculty member for nearly three decades, Richardson has made a profound impact on the students she taught and coached in hockey. A native of Brain-

Christine Ann Talley

tree, Massachusetts, she has been girls' athletic director since 1963. Richardson has also won five Delaware state amateur golf championships.

In 1981 CHRISTINE ANN ("CHRIS") TALLEY (1959-   ) received a degree in physical education with an emphasis in adaptives (meeting the needs of the handicapped) from the University of Delaware. She began teaching adaptive physical education at the Pilot School in Talleyville the same year. Inspired by the sports women in *Delaware Women Remembered*, she researched current Delaware sports women for her master's thesis in 1983. Since 1985, Talley has taught adaptive physical education at the Richardson Park Learning Center in the Red Clay Consolidated School District. Talley, a native Delawarean, coaches mentally retarded adults to participate in the Delaware Special Olympics and

138

Dorothy Baker

serves as secretary of the Delaware Association for Health, Physical Education, Recreation and, Dance (DAHPERD).

Through the Olympic Games, the best athletes from Delaware are given the opportunity to compete beyond their state and their nation. DOROTHY BAKER (1929-   ) helped Delaware raise the most Olympics money per capita of any state. Baker, who was born in Boston, was appointed to the U.S. Olympics Committee in 1975 and in 1976 became the first woman in the country appointed state chair. She is now chair of the national committee.

In the twentieth century, doors have opened to allow women to achieve in areas of sports that at one time were limited to men. As a result of changing female roles, the increasing popularity of individual and team sports, and the passage of Title IX legislation to prohibit discrimination against women's sports programs, women have shown increased interest and achievement in athletics. They are no longer limited to participating in the genteel sports of the twenties. Consequently, women of the eighties are beginning to participate in many sports that men have enjoyed for years. They are also competing with men for scholarships, publicity, and education.

SIGNIFICANT DATES
IN THE HISTORY
OF DELAWARE WOMEN

Women in Delaware have excelled in many different fields of life and work and have been a positive influence on those around them and after them. Despite numerous barriers and limited resources, they have demonstrated what it means to be successful. This often involved balancing an active public life with the obligations of a family.

It is clear that progress toward equality of opportunity and responsibility in society is still needed. Though women have worked hard in the community (agencies and church groups, schools and corporations) few have attained policy-making positions. Yet opportunity lies ahead. In the next decade or so, more women will become executive directors, ministers, and presidents. At the same time, they will continue to be daughters, wives, and mothers and, thus, bring a distinctly feminine orientation with them as they extend their influence in society.

The following partial chronology of women's achievements is a visual presentation of the historical contributions of Delaware women.

1642   Johan Printz, appointed governor over the colony New Sweden, was knighted. His daughter, Armegott, 16 years of age, was excited about coming to the New World.

1643   On the 15th day of February, Armegott Printz stepped ashore on American soil after a 3½-month journey across the Atlantic.

1683   12 women from Lewes were selected as jurors in a murder trial.

1698   Old Swedes Church, Wilmington, was built of stone that was carried by women of the colony.

1776   Mary Vining so charmed General Lafayette with her wit, beauty, and delightful conversation in French that he wrote to Queen Marie Antoinette of France, "This beautiful woman would be at home in your Court." Mary Vining, cousin of Caesar Rodney, was his official hostess when he was president of Delaware State.

1814   Victorine du Pont Bauduy, assisted by her sisters Sophie and Eleuthera, helped develop the Brandywine Manufacturers Sunday School for the children of workmen employed at the mills along the Brandywine.

1827   Elisabeth Margaret Chandler, a native Delawarean, became the editor of the first woman's magazine in the United States, *The Ladies' Repository*. Active in the abolitionist movement, she wrote essays to arouse the sympathies of women for the plight of slaves.

1850   The Fugitive Slave Law was passed and Mary Ann Shadd of Wilmington urged black Americans to immigrate to Canada.

Mary Ann Shadd Cary

1854　Mary Ann Shadd Cary established *The Provincial Freedman*, the first anti-slavery weekly newspaper, in Canada West.

1860　Dr. Frances Treadwell, Delaware City, was noted as the first woman dentist in Delaware.

1863　Mary Ann Shadd Cary was appointed recruiting officer by special order to enlist colored black volunteers in the Union army in Indiana.

1872　Six women attended lectures at Newark College as freshmen.

1876　Edwina Kruse was named the first black principal of Howard High School, where she served for 45 years. A reform school for girls in Belvedere was later named for her.

1878　Dr. Margaret White received a medical degree. She practiced in Wilmington for 50 years, caring for more than 3,000 maternity cases.

1881　Mary Ann Shadd Cary from Wilmington became a member of the National Women's Suffrage Association. Two years later she received an L.L.B. degree from Howard University.

1889　Emalea Pusey Warner helped organize the Wilmington New Century Club.

1899　Mary A. Moran worked to have a law passed in Delaware to license professional registered nurses.

1904　Ella Middleton Maxwell Tybout published *Poketown People*. Her short stories chronicled Delaware folklore of her neighborhood.

1906　Carolyn Bockius, Wilmington, married Newell Convers Wyeth. He and their five children, Henriette, Nathaniel, Carolyn, Ann, and Andrew Wyeth became one of America's leading families of artists.

1907　In the lobby of the Wilmington post office, Emily Perkins Bissell raised $3,000 to care for tuberculosis patients by selling Christmas Seals, inaugurating an annual yuletide institution in this country.

1914　Mary A. Mather promoted an Americanization program in Wilmington for the foreign-born.

　　　Emalea Pusey Warner helped establish the Women's College in Newark.

1917　Delaware women in the famous White House Picket Line for Women's Suffrage were An-

Carolyn Bockius Wyeth

142

nie Arneil, Naomi Barrett, Catherine Boyle, Mary E. Brown, Sallie Topkis Ginns, Florence Bayard Hilles, Annie J. Magee, and Mabel Vernon.

Sallie Topkis Ginns was a founder and first president of the Wilmington chapter of the National Council of Jewish Women.

1918 Alice Moore Dunbar-Nelson helped to bring about the equalization of salaries of black and white teachers when she served as head of the English department of Howard High School.

1919 Jean Kane Foulke du Pont was a founder of the Prisoners' Aid Society, which later became the Delaware Commission on Crime and Justice.

1920 Etta J. Wilson became the first executive secretary of the PTA in Delaware. She had been named to a commission to evaluate the state school system.

1921 Mabel Lloyd Fisher Ridgely was the first president of the Delaware League of Women Voters.

Gertrude Kruse joined the staff of the Greenwood Book Shop in Wilmington and promoted books by Delaware authors.

1922 Julia Hays Tallman became the state's first policewoman due to her interest in highway safety. She was also the first woman to serve on the board of the Delaware Safety Council.

1923 Cecile Long Steele of Ocean View was the founder of the multi-billion-dollar Delmarva broiler industry.

1925 Anne Parrish's novel *The Perennial Bachelor* won the Harper's prize.

1926 Julia Tallman became Republican National Committeewoman, a position she held for twenty-six years.

May B. Leasure was awarded a teaching medal from President Calvin Coolidge and was a guest in the White House.

1928 Dr. Elizabeth Miller came to Wilmington as a general practitioner. Later she received international praise for her medical missionary service in Nepal.

1930 Marie Munis was the first blind person to graduate from a New Castle County high school. In 1982 she was named president of the Delaware Association for the Blind.

1931 Annette Reese was a charter member of Planned Parenthood in Delaware, which was the ninth state to have a birth-control league.

1938 Jeannette Eckman supervised *Delaware: A Guide to the First State*, a WPA writers' project. She was also one of the founders of the Delaware Swedish Colonial Society.

Lydia Chichester du Pont established the Children's Beach House in Lewes to provide care, maintenance, and recreation for handicapped children.

Louise Chambers Corkran founded the Rehoboth Art League, a cultural and community center in Sussex County.

1939 Deaconess Marian Brown of Talleyville began her missionary work with the Arapahoe Indians in Arizona.

1940 Dorothy Banton joined the staff at Kruse School. Later, as superintendent, she insti-

Louise Chambers Corkran

143

Wilfreda Heald Lytle

tuted many innovative training procedures to aid the black girls who were committed to her care.

1941   Evelyn W. Dickey became leader of the Wilmington Federation of Teachers Union (AFL-CIO).

1944   Mary Clark Keyser was the first woman in Delaware to graduate from veterinary school and to be licensed to practice.

1946   Vera Gilbride Davis became Delaware's first woman in the state Senate. Wilfreda Heald Lytle was elected to the state House of Representatives.

1947   Ednah D. Leach was appointed by Governor Walter W. Bacon as Delaware's first poet laureate.

1948   Mary Ann Wright formed the Mancus Foundation in Wilmington to help handicapped persons lead fuller and more interesting lives. She received a Distinguished Service Award for outstanding leadership in 1976.

1952   Sarah Bulah took action so that her black daughter could attend an all-white school in Hockessin, two years prior to the Supreme Court decision ordering integration of schools nationwide.

Elsie Williams, Millsboro, became the first Delawarean elected president of the Congressional Club, Washington, D.C.

1953   Mary Fraim was named Woman of the Year for her service to education for women, cancer research, beautifying the highways, and helping to establish Family Court.

Louisa Spruance Morse was appointed acting wing commander of the Delaware Civil Air Patrol, the first woman to serve in that capacity.

1954   Mary C. Dennison, as president of Soroptimists International Club of Wilmington, organized the first Girl's Club in Delaware.

The lawsuit of a black Claymont girl, Ethel L. Belton, was part of *Brown v. the Board of Education of Topeka, Kansas*, the landmark desegregation case decided by the U.S. Supreme Court.

Dr. Anna Janney de Armond, the first woman professor in the English department at the University of Delaware, received the first Excellence-in-Teaching Award from the university. In 1977 she became the first faculty member to receive the award a second time.

1955   Quaesita Drake Hall was the first University of Delaware building named for a woman faculty member.

1963   Sister Aloysius (Mother Peach), Ursuline Academy, was named poet laureate of Delaware. The next year, she received the Freedom Foundation Medal and the Valley Forge Teacher's Award.

Dorothy Elston ("Dottie") Kabis served as president of the National Federation of Republican Women from 1963 to 1967. In 1969 she was appointed treasurer of the United States.

1966   Dr. Hilda Andrea Davis became the first black faculty member of the University of Delaware with a full-time contract. In 1982 she became the first woman senior warden of a mission in the Episcopal Diocese of Delaware.

1967   Rosemary Miller received an award as Delaware's highest-ranking woman trapshooter.

Mother Peach

Margaret Osborne du Pont was voted into the National Lawn Tennis Hall of Fame; in 1947 she won the Wimbledon Singles Crown in tennis. She won the U.S. National Tennis Championship three times and the national doubles title 13 times.

1969　The Golden Age Center in Wilmington was dedicated in memory of Julia Tallman.

1970　Helen R. Thomas helped to organize the Council for Women (now the Delaware Commission for Women) at the request of Governor Russell W. Peterson and served from 1970 to 1975.

1971　Roxana Cannon Arsht was installed as a judge in Family Court.

1972　Louise Conner, the Republican senator from Delaire from 1964 to 1972, sponsored the Equal Rights Amendment ratification bill. Delaware was one of the first states that voted to ratify the amendment.

Margaret R. Manning became the first female Majority Whip in the General Assembly.

Arva Jean Jackson became the first black member of the University of Delaware board of trustees. She was the administrative assistant for urban affairs during the term of Governor Russell W. Peterson and received the University of Delaware Merit Award in 1982.

1974　Edith Kendall retired after serving the Red Cross for 30½ years as nursing director and director of the Office of Volunteers.

145

Sally Monigle

Sally Monigle was appointed the first woman to direct Wilmington's downtown YMCA.

Delores J. Baylor was the first warden to supervise a Delaware prison for both males and females, at Price's Corner. She was awarded a commendation from the state Senate in 1979.

1975 Dorothy Baker was appointed a member of the United States Olympic Committee and was the first woman in the country to be appointed state chair.

Miriam E. Howard was the first woman elected mayor of Rehoboth.

1976 Mary Duggan Jornlin was elected New Castle County executive.

Roslyn Rettew organized the first chapter of the National Organization for Women (NOW) in Delaware.

Jean T. Conger, national secretary of NOW, organized "Teachers' NOW" to draw attention to sexism in the schools.

Marion Jessup (MacLure) was the first woman inducted into the Delaware Sports Hall of Fame. She won the women's doubles in the U.S. National Tennis Championship, 1919-1920.

The Rev. Jymmie L. McClinton received the Distinguished Service Award for her work among prison inmates and the elderly and for raising foster children.

Beatrice Ross ("Bebe") Coker received a Distinguished Service Award for her contribution to education and the arts.

1977 The University of Delaware board of trustees honored Dean Bessie B. Collins by renaming the Kirkbride Room in the Student Center in her honor.

The Delaware Art Museum mounted a retrospective exhibition of the work of Eugenia Eckford Rhoads in recognition of her 50 years of participation in the museum's activities.

1978 Through the efforts of Martha Verge du Pont, crusader for the rights of children, legislation was passed preventing juveniles from being treated as criminal offenders.

Audrey K. Doberstein was appointed president of Wilmington College.

Lulu Mae Nix became the first director of the new federal Office of Adolescent Pregnancy Programs. Previously, she administered a Delaware teen counseling program.

1979 As a fellow of the American Institute of Architects, Victorine du Pont Homsey helped restore The Octagon, where President and Dolley Madison lived after the White House was

Marion Jessup MacLure

146

Eugenia Eckford Rhoads

burned during the War of 1812. She also aided in restoring Dumbarton Oaks in Washington.

Nancy Garvin Shor, a graduate of Tower Hill School, Wilmington, became the first executive director of the National Organization of Social Security Claimants' Representatives, a nationwide organization established to assist disabled and handicapped persons.

The Pauline A. Young Memorabilia Room in Howard Career Center was dedicated to a teacher, historian, journalist, and community leader noted for her work in black history.

E. Jean Lanyon was named poet laureate of Delaware.

1980   Gertrude Lowell received the Outstanding Citizen Award from the U.S. Department of Health, Education, and Welfare.

Emily George Morris was the first black woman to be elected to countywide office in Delaware (prothonotary).

1981   Catherine ("Kappy") Hanke, who developed the American Competitive Enterprise System (ACES) for teachers in-service program received the Freedom Foundation Award.

1982   Kathryn S. Andersen was awarded the Mary Marsh Award for her support in the Wilmington Garden Center.

The first Delaware woman graduate of a U.S. military academy was 2nd lieutenant Priscilla Anne Greene of Wilmington, who was graduated from West Point.

Judith McCabe was appointed a member of the Advisory Committee on the Arts by President Ronald Reagan.

Karen Peterson, president of New Castle County Council, became the first Democrat, the first woman, and the youngest person to hold the position.

Cynthia Hoagland became the first female president of the Historical Society of Delaware, founded in 1864.

Antonia Laird published her fourth volume of poetry, *Echo of My Heart*.

Estella Hillersohn Frankel introduced

Estella Frankel

147

Delaware to the Suzuki method of teaching violin playing after teaching for six decades in the Wilmington public schools.

1984   Eugenia Eckford Rhoads was honored with

the Governor's Award for the Arts by the Delaware State Arts Council.

1985   Jean Statts, Wyoming, was the Delaware winner of the Bob Evans Quarter Horse Weanling.

In this photograph taken October 16, 1959, Past Presidents of the Wilmington Branch of AAUW who served in the years from 1924 to 1960 assembled for a formal portrait. Seated in the front row, l. to r., are Mrs. Earl S. Ridler and Mrs. Charles B. Paschall. In the second row, l. to r., are Mrs. T. Muncy Keith, Dr. Quaesita C. Drake, Mrs. George W. Rigby and Mrs. Robert M. McAdam. Standing, l. to r., are Mrs. Arnold Goldsborough, Mrs. Frank R. Swezey, Mrs. S. Marston Fox, Mrs. Lawrence V. Smith, Mrs. W. Clayton Lytle, Mrs. Ellsworth K. Ellingboe and Mrs. Bert S. Norling. Mrs. Paschall, Mrs. Keith, Mrs. Goldsborough and Mrs. Fox are University of Delaware alumni and Dr. Drake was a longtime Professor of Chemistry at the University. The Wilmington Branch established a major scholarship fund in memory of Mrs. Keith at the time of her death in 1961.

Hall of Fame of Delaware Women

Dr. Ruth Mitchell Laws

Mary Ann Wright

1981　Annie Jump Cannon
　　　Pearl Herlihy Daniels
　　　Dr. Ruth Mitchell Laws
　　　Mary Ann Wright

1982　Vera Gilbride Davis
　　　Mabel Lloyd Fisher Ridgely
　　　Emalea Pusey Warner
　　　Pauline A. Young

1983　Esther Schauer Frear
　　　Sally Topkis Ginns
　　　Edith J. Newton
　　　Cecile Long Steele

1985　Louise T. Conner
　　　Norma B. Handloff
　　　Mary Askew Mather
　　　Mary Jornlin Theisen

1986　Roxana Cannon Arsht
　　　Emily P. Bissell
　　　Dr. Hilda Davis
　　　Mabel Vernon

1987　Marguerite Hill Burnett
　　　Florence Bayard Hillis
　　　Gertrude M. Lowell
　　　Elizabeth Ryan

Emalea Pusey Warner

Pauline A. Young

Esther Schauer Frear

Sally Topkis Ginns

Cecile Long Steele

Louise T. Conner

Norma B. Handloff

Mary Jornlin Theisen

Roxana Cannon Arsht

Mabel Vernon

150

DELAWARE AMERICAN MOTHERS

In 1950 Governor Elbert N. Carvel appointed Jane Ennis as chair of the Delaware American Mothers, Inc., Committee. In 1953 Ruth Cann followed Ennis as chair, and continued until 1980.
Delaware American Mothers are as follows:

1950 Mrs. Jonathan S. Willis (Huldah) - Milford
1951 Mrs. W. Reily Brown (Mattie) - Wyoming
1952 Mrs. William Shallcross (Elizabeth) - Odessa
1953 Mrs. Samuel Stein (Fannie) - Seaford
1954 Mrs. Edgar J. Boggs (Lettie) - Cheswold
1955 Mrs. Morris L. Zurkow (Esther) - Dover
1956 Mrs. George Seitz (Margaret) - Wilmington
1957 Mrs. Edgar F. Isaacs (Delma) - Lincoln
1958 Mrs. George Ehinger (Aline) - Dover
1959 Mrs. W. Edward Thompson (Hannah) - Lewes
1960 Mrs. Harry Mayer (Bessie) - Dover
1961 Mrs. William H. Aydelotte (Anna) - Delmar
1962 Mrs. Frank Hall Davis (Vera) - Dover
1963 Mrs. Robert F. Lewis (Emily) - Seaford
1964 Mrs. Francis J. O'Neil (Margaret) - Smyrna
1965 Mrs. John Freeman (Catherine) - Lewes
1966 Mrs. William Tierney (Helen) - Clayton
1967 Mrs. Samuel Stewart (Elizabeth) - New Castle

1968 Mrs. Melvin Kershaw (Florence) - Newark
1969 Mrs. Park W. Huntington (Marie) - Wilmington
1970 Mrs. Cummins Speakman (Marge) - Smyrna
1971 Mrs. David J. Conly, Sr. (Sadie Mae) - Wilmington
1972 Mrs. Douglas F. Milbury (Lillian) - Dover
1973 Mrs. William B. Mitten (Jean) - Dover
1974 Mrs. J. Edwin Lewis (Doris) - Dover
1975 Mrs. Raymond Townsend (Pearl) - Frankford
1976 Mrs. Millard Biddle (Hattye Mae) - Dover
1977 Mrs. Richard J. Cannon (Goldie) - Lincoln
1978 Mrs. Granville W. Lambden (Mable) - Georgetown
1979 Mrs. George Ward (Mary Sam) - Wilmington
1980 Mrs. J. Allen Frear, Jr. (Esther) - Dover
1981 Mrs. Archie B. Brittingham, Sr. (Virginia) - Lewes
1982 Mary Jornlin Theisen - Wilmington
1983 Mrs. James Homan (Elizabeth) - Milford
1984 Dr. Judith G. Tobin - Seaford
1985 Mrs. Beverly Walter La Dage (Zenobia) - Wilmington
1986 Dr. Ruth M. Laws - Dover
1987 Stephanie Hawke

SCHOOLS NAMED FOR WOMEN EDUCATORS IN DELAWARE

Marguerite H. Burnett Junior High School
37th and Franklin Streets, Wilmington

Carrie Downie Elementary School
Frenchtown Road, New Castle

Misses Hebbs School
Wilmington

May B. Leasure Elementary School
Delaware #7 and U.S. #40, Bear

Maclary School (named for R. Elisabeth Maclary)
St. Regis Drive, Chapel Hill, Newark

Anna P. Mote Elementary School
Edward Avenue and Kirkwood Highway, Wilmington

Myers Building, Tatnall School (named for Josephine Myers)
Wilmington

Sarah Webb Pyle Elementary School
5th and Lombard Streets, Wilmington

Lulu M. Ross Elementary School
310 Lovers Lane, Milford

Jennie E. Smith Elementary School
Brennen Drive, Todd Estates, Newark

Margaret S. Sterck School (special school for hearing-impaired)
Chestnut Hill Road and Cherokee Drive, Newark

Nellie Hughes Stokes Elementary School
Camden-Wyoming Avenue, Camden-Wyoming

Tatnall School (founded by Frances Swift Tatnall)
Wilmington

Warner Elementary School (named for Emalea Pusey Warner)
18th and Van Buren Streets, Wilmington

Mary C.I. Williams School (demolished)
4th and Adams Streets, Wilmington

Etta J. Wilson Elementary School
Forge Road, Newark

INDEX

Abel, Becky Paul 18
Ableman, Peggy 29
Ackerman, Maryann 104
Adelman, Alice Caffrey 13
Adolphsen, Keturah 120
Aldrich, Nancy Armstrong 69
Alfano, Delores 78
Allman, Margo 11
*Andersen, Katherine 51, 52, 147
Andersen, Margaret L. 66
Anderson, Edith H. 95
Anderson, Mary Lowenstein ix
Andruk, Marjorie Dean 14
Angstadt, Ginger 7
Antongiorgi, Norma Ivonne 63
*Arnell, Annie 143
*Arsht, Roxanna 28, 145, 149
*Atkins, Elizabeth R. 107
*Atkins, Lille Suthard 107
*Aydelotte, Anna 151

Bachman, Martha G. 74
*Bader, Anne Shane 99
Bair, Myrna North 79
*Baker, Dorothy 139, 146
Baker, Sharon Kelly 39
Balick, Carol 12, 15
*Balick, Charlotte 132
*Balick, Helen Shaffer ix, 28, 29
Balick, Lillian Rosen 5, 6
Bane, Margo Ewing 78, 80
*Banton, Dorothy 144
*Barrett, Naomi 143
Barsky, Evangilyn 28
Bass, Mary Owen 48
Batman, Louisa S. 91
Batten, Grace Ruth Brittingham 113,
    114
*Bauduy, Victorine du Pont 141
Bayard, Martha ix
Baylor, Delores J. 43, 146
Beaman, Barbara 72
Beebe, Amelia Katherine 93
Belden, Louise Conway 109
Belton, Ethel L. 144
Benmark, Leslie Ann Freeman 127,
    128
*Bennethum, Ann 7
Benson, Barbara x, 111
Berenice, Sister 2
Beresin, Constance G. 49

Bernardi, Rosemarie 11
Biddle, Hattye Mae Betts 47, 151
Biden, Janine Jacquet ix
Bierlein, Marcie 83
*Bissell, Emily Perkins 24, 89, 96,
    142, 149
*Bissell, Georgina 51
*Blish, Carolyn Bullis 9, 10
*Boden, Marguerite du Pont de
    Villiers xi, 103
*Boggs, Lettie 151
*Bohning, Elizabeth E. 64
Boos, Marilyn 93, 94
Bosworth, Gina C. 8
Boudart, Mary C. 77, 78
*Boyd, Betty 7
Boyer, Lydia 83
*Boyle, Catherine 143
Boyer, Lydia 83
*Boyle, Catherine 143
*Brame, Grace Adolphsen 120
Brand, Sister Mary Cordula 117
*Breslin, Wynn 14
Brittingham, Hazel Downs ix, 106
Brittingham, Virginia Lodge 48, 151
Brooking, Anne 135
*Brown, Marian 144
*Brown, Mary E. 143
Brown, Mattie 151
Brown, Roberta S. Garrison 128
Brown, Stella 131
Brynteson, Susan 71, 72
Buchanan, Madaline 116
*Buck, Polly 1
*Bulah, Sarah 144
*Burnett, Marguerite Hill 149, 153
Burns, Roberta 93
*Burroughs, Betty ix, 34
Bushman, Claudia Lauper ix, x, 105

Cabrey, Ann 132
Callahan, Evelyn 28
*Callahan, Margaret 7
Campbell, Nan Kennedy Fooks 44
*Cann, Ruth xii
*Cannon, Annie Jump 123, 149
Cannon, Goldie 151
*Cary, Mary Ann Shadd 141, 142
Carey, Teresa G. 60
Carnell, Helen ix
Carothers, Martha 11

Carrick, Carole L. 86
*Carter, Mae Riedy ix, 68, 111
Carter-Pierce, Cheryl 21
Cason, June 5
Chaiken, Yetta Zutz 107
*Chambers, Doris ix, xii
*Chandler, Elisabeth Margaret 141
Chase, Kathryn S. xii
Chowdhry, Uma Dalal 125, 129
Church, Isabel ix
*Ciesenski, Katherine 3, 4
Ciesenski, Kristine 3, 4
*Clark, Nancy Kissel 12
Clendaniel, Anne Evans 38
*Cobin, Lillian Fox 83, 85
Cohen, Sally W. 13
*Coker, Beatrice Ross 146
Colbert, Jean 54
Coleman, Jereline 25
Collins, Bessie B. 146
*Colman, Roberta 124
*Conger, Jean T. 146
Conly, Sadie Mae 151
*Conner, Louise Thompson 69, 145,
    149
Cook, Nancy W. 79
Cook, Olive 115
Cooke, Dorothy 115
Cope, Penelope Bass ix, 35
Copeland, Pamela, 54
Copeland, Tatiana Brandt 24, 78
Corkran, Louise Chambers xii, 8, 143
Corty, Suzanne Pisko 35
Craig, Eleanor Duguid, 24
Craven, Elizabeth Muffet 91
Cronin, Betty ix
*Crosby, Muriel 61
*Crowninshield, Louise du Pont xi,
    51, 101, 103
Cunningham, Freida 115

*Daniels, Pearl Herlihy 76, 149
Danning, Jan 132
Dardashti, Irene ix, 49, 111
*Davis, Elizabeth 7
*Davis, Hilda Andrea 64, 144, 149
Davis, Lizette xi
Lewis, Emily 151
*Davis, Vera Gilbride 75, 79, 144,
    149, 151
Davis, Virginia 99

Dawson, Aurelia Cate 104
*Dean, Nora Thompson xii, 101, 102
de Angeli, Marguerite 34
*De Armond, Anna Janney 64, 65, 144
Dector, Roselyn Blish 115
de Jesus-Jiloca, Rosalinda 93
de Luz, Lozelle 20, 22
de Marino, Betsy Reiver 131
Demsey, Christine 30
*Dennison, Mary C. 144
De Reimer, Dixie Jane Thompson 22
Devine, Bessie, Margaret, Sarah 61
Dickey, Evelyn W. 144
Dickson-Witmer, Diana 92
Doberstein, Audrey K. 68, 146
Donofrio, Harriet Beach 62
Donoghue, Moira Katherine 28
Doss, Margaret 115
Downie, Carrie xii, 153
*Downing, M. Catherine xi, 104, 105
Drake, Linda C. 27
*Drake, Quaesita 123, 124, 144
Duggins, Elizabeth L. 95
*Dunbar-Nelson, Alice Moore 60, 65, 106, 143
Dunn, Madeline Arnold 104
du Pont, Elise Wood 77, 78, 82
*du Pont, Emily x
du Pont, Genevieve Estes 51
*du Pont, Jean Kane Foulke 41, 143
*du Pont, Lydia Chichester 143
*du Pont, Margaret Osborne 131, 145
*du Pont, Marka Truesdale 43
*du Pont, Martha Verge 42, 146
Dupuis, Teresa A. 98
Dyer, Elizabeth 124

*Eckman, Jeanette 101, 143
*Edinger, Mildred 7
*Edwards, Jeanette Slocum xii, 7, 38
Egan, Ruth Bell 86
Egri (Holden), Ruth 1, 8
*Ehinger, Aline Noren 85, 151
Ellis, Madalyn 86
Emas, Karen 135
Esterly, Katherine L. 91
Evans, Mary Page 9
Everett, Belle xi, 75

Fallon, Evelyn K. Peele 80
Farrand, Amy Guest Lloyd 61
Fausnaugh, Carolyn J. Mann 24
Fenix-Sapienza, Dolores 69
*Findlay, Violet 52
*Finkelstein, Clara 17
*Finkelstein, Rona ix, 111
Finley, Ethel Myer 85
Fleming, Blanche Miles 61, 62

*Fleming, Lorraine M. 52
Flexman, Ruth Marie Rasmussen 116, 117
Forman, Mildred Brynberg 90, 91
Foss, Helen Kniskern 72
*Fox, Helen Swain ix, 109
*Fraim, Mary 41, 144
*Frankel, Estelle Hellersohn 147
Frazier-Hedberg, Ann ix, 37
*Frear, Esther Schauer 149, 151
*Frederick, Nancy 52
*Freeman, Catherine 151
*Frelick, Jane Hayden 53
Frinck, Lynne 52, 53
Futcher, Priscilla 87

*Gangwere, Helen Lesher 121
Ganter, Betty 133
*Garvin, Geraldine McKinley ix, 69
Gause, Catherine D. 61
*Geis, Florence L. 66
Gibney, Sandy 133
Gierasch, Lila M. 124
*Ginns, Sallie Topkis 107, 115, 143, 149
Giovino, Marie ix
Glynn, Gail P. 136
Gore, Genevieve x, 20, 21
Gouldner, Helen 66
Graham, Anne Krohn 13
Graham, Kathleen M. 121
Grant, Hilda ix
Graustein, Jeanette E. 124
Gray, Catherine Cross 90
Gray, Eugenia ix
Greeley (Muterspaw), M. Constance Bilotta 92
Greene, Priscilla Anne 147
Griffith, Helen V. 33, 34, 35
Grimes, Bertha 50
*Grinnage Anna R. 69
Gross, Joanne 8
Grubbe, Deborah Lynn 123, 129
Gruber, Annette 47

*Hahn, Patsy 132
Haines, Bonny 115
Hallman, Carol ix
Hamilton, Phyllis ix
*Handloff, Norma B. 149
*Handy, Margaret Irvine xi, 89, 90
*Hanke, Catherine ix, 147
Harding, Sandra 66
*Harker, Christine McDermott 31
*Harrison, Arrie J. 61
Hawke, Stephanie 151
Hawkins, Sally Vandecar 39, 40
Hayes, Florine Huger 7
Hayward, Ethel Luella Jones xii

Hebb, Ruth, Elizabeth, Mary 153
Hecht, Amy Blatchford 99
Heenan, Barbara T. 51
Held, Christine ix
*Henry, Mabel Clough Wright 61
Henry, Margaret Rose 46
Herndon, Lin ix, x
Herr, Barbara Chase ix, 48
Hibbard, Mollie ix
Hightower-Vandamm, Mae 96, 97
*Hilles, Florence Bayard 75, 143, 149
*Hinsley Jacqueline A. ix, 110
Hitchens, Mary Ann 136, 137
Hoagland, Cynthia Kimball 105, 147
Hoffecker, Carol E. x, xii, xiii, xiv, xv, 110
Homan, Elizabeth 151
*Homsey, Victorine du Pont, 19, 146
Hoopes, Judith Heckroth 1
*Horowitz, Shirley Graeff 49
Houghton, Vivian A. ix, 77, 78
Houston, Margaret Burton White 75
Howard, Lori 136
*Howard, Marion 7
*Howard, Miriam E. 146
Howett, Sharon 136
Howie, Katherine Sturgis 70
Hudson, Ivy M. 45
Hukill, Jay H. 42
Hull, Gloria T. 65
Hullinger, Peggy M. 96
Huntington, Marie M. R. 114, 151
Husted, Grace 71
Huthmaker, Marilyn 77

Incababian, Edith 91
Irvin, Jean Battles 11
Irving, Catherine M. C. 104
Isaacs, Delma 151

*Jackson, Arva Jean 145
Jaffe, Rebecca 93
Jameson, Jorene 49
Jamison, Susan Clapp ix, 71
Jankus, Lynn 54
*Janvier, Anne Read Rodney 103
Jenkins, Elizabeth Miller 90
Jessup, Jan 23
Jessup (Maclure), Marion Zinderstein 132, 146
*Johnson, Ella Weldin xi
Johnson, Henrietta Richardson 80
Johnson Joyce P. 46
*Johnson, Marion F. T. 9
Johnson, Ruth Petit 54
Johnston, Gail W. 72
Jones, Cheryl Yvonne 61
Jones, Cornelia Taylor 104
Jones, Dorothy D. W. 45

Jones, Ethel Luella Hayward xii
Jones, Marlene J. 126
Just, Judith x
*Justice, Rita 78, 81

*Kabis, Dorothy Elston xi, 144
Kaiser (Dybowski), Mary A. 125
Kaminski, Vera E. 13
Kane, Peggy 9
Kaplan, Ruth J. ix, 65, 111
*Keane, Marie J. Santora 9
Kelly, Barbara J. 137
*Kendall, Edith 145
*Kent, Patricia ix
Kerr, Janet Spence 126
Kershaw, Florence 151
Keyser, Mary Clark 14, 15, 144
Kimball, Esther Ward 106
Kincannon, Margaret Scott 12
Kirkpatrick, Laurie 133
Knodel, Patricia Pratt 113, 117
Konesey, Jan 111
Koston, Marsha 111
Krafft, Sandra Wheatley 95
Kramer, Janet ix, 92
Kressman, Annabelle x
*Kruse, Edwina B. 60, 142
*Kruse, Gertrude 143
*Kujala, Audie 136
Kwolek, Stephanie 125
LaDuLake, Elizabeth 75
LaDage, Zenobia 151
*Laird, Antonia Bissell 33, 147
*Laird, Lydia Chichester 103
Lambden, Mabel 151
Lane (Hooper), Rosemary 11
Lanyon, E. Jean 147
La Porte, Susan Moerschel 54
Larsen, Wanda Blazejewski 46
Latham, Gerda Jeksties ix, 114, 115
*Laws, Ruth Mitchell 63, 149, 151
Layfield, Sandra 17, 18
*Leach, Ednah Deemer 33, 34, 144
Learned, Terry 22
Leasure, Elizabeth May B. 60, 143, 153
Lehrer, Paula Segal ix, 78
*Lenher, Irene 7
*Lewis, Doris 151
*Lewis, Emily 151
Lewis, Lennie Frisby 120
Ligler, Frances S. 127
*Lincoln (McCrea), Anna T. 101
*Little, Grace 94
Little Sisters of the Poor 117
Lomax, Flora xi
Longhi, Betty Helen 13
Lorenz, Marjorie, 43

Loven, Marjorie K. 48
*Low, Betty-Bright Page ix, 110
Lowell, Gertrude M. 43, 147, 149
Lunger, Jane du Pont 119
Lynch, Alva 41, 42
Lynch, Nancy Bartoshesky ix, 1, 2
*Lytle, Wilfreda J. Heald 79, 144

*MacArtor, June D. 55
Macey, Jennie 115
Maclary, R. Elizabeth 153
Magee, Annie J. 143
Malmgren, Angela Rossi 118
Mangum, Lucille Hunter 119
Mankin, Ruth L. ix, 25, 26
Manlove, Sue 104
Manning, Margaret R. 145
Marcali, Jean G. 127
Marcial, Ann ix
Maroney, Jane P. 81
Marquisse, Eleanor Ann Betting 39
*Marsh, Mary 51
*Martyn, Annie Lu ix
Marvel, Kate 111
*Marvil, Mrs. James 104
Mason, Helen 14
Mataleno, Justine 106
*Mather, Mary Askew 142, 149
Mayer, Bessie 151
McAfee, Bernice 132
McBride, Candida Diaz 46
McCabe, Joanna E. 95
McCabe, Judith 15, 147
*McClennan, Janet ix
*McClinton, Jymmie L. 146
McDonough, Mary M. 30
*McEwing, Barbara Denman 108, 109
*McKusick, Marjorie Jane 91
Menge, Jacqueline Ann Richter 128
Mertz, Ann Mary ix
Mervine, Margaret 19, 20
Meyer, Kathleen M. ix, 23
*Michel, Sandra Seaton 34
*Milbury, Lillian 151
*Miller, Beth 35
Miller, Carol 135
*Miller, Elizabeth Bucke 90, 143
*Miller, Rosemary Young 133, 134, 144
Miller, Wilhelmina 43
Mingus, Judith 6
Minner, Ruth Ann 80
Mitchell, Barbara 34
Mitchell, Carole 86
*Mitchell, Jane E. 95
Mitchell, Jane T. 56
Mitten, Jean, 151
Mitten, Margaret E. 21

Moffett, Ann Pennell 126
Monet, Marion ix
*Monigle, Sally 146
Montague, Barbara Ann 127
*Montgomery, Elizabeth 101
Montgomery, Ruth Reinke 126
Monty (Leary), Lise 37
Mooney, Karen ix
Moore, Paulette Sullivan 28
Moran, Mary A. 142
Morelli, Linda A. 87
Morgan, Martha 22
Morris, Emily George 70, 147
Morris, Pamela Bailey vii, x, 69, 111
*Morse, Louisa Spruance 144
Mote, Anna P. 153
*Moyer, Nina Vosters 132
Mullen, B. Ethelda 41, 42
Mullen, Nancy Jane 30
Mullen, Regina M. 30
Mullins, Mary Katherine 2
Munis, Marie 44, 143
*Myers, Josephine 153

Naczi, Carolyn B. 62
Naczi, Frances Daily ix, x, 36, 37
Nelson, Carmen Gueffroy 72
Nesbitt, Anne Clayton 38
Newlon, Martha Hart 48
*Newton, Edith J. 149
Nidzgorski, Joyce 132
Nix, Crystal 35
Nix, Lulu Mae 36, 98, 146
*Nolan, Agnes ix
Norling, Nancy M. 55

O'Byrne, Sara Frelick, 53, 111
Okonowicz, Helen Decaire 6
Oldach, Anne Sloan 12
O'Leary, Renee 70
*O'Neill, Margaret 151
*Orr, Virginia 104
Outlaw, Linda 23
Owings, Marion 118

Pamintuan, Elvira 93
Parke, Lois McDonnel 82
Parker, Hilda 41
*Parrish, Ann 143
Passmore, Joanne 55
Patel, Jyotsana Dhiren 17, 21
*Patterson, Shirley ix
Paul, Grace Knopf 85
Paulshock, Bernadine Z. 93
*Peach, Mother M. Aloysius 144, 145
Pepper, Dorothy Williams 108
Peterson, Karen E. 78, 81, 147
*Pfeiffer, Carol Mae Perry 85
*Phillips, Elizabeth F. 96

Phillips, Shirley 115
Pierce, Grace Wagner 53
*Pitts, Jacquelin 135
Platt, Ethel Friedman 90, 91
Ponsell, Irene Carmean Hill 8
Poole, Elizabeth Stroud 42
Pratt, Sara S. 17
Prescott, Patricia Johnson 50
Prest, Grace 52
Preston, Halinda Wind 121, 122
Printz, Armegott 141
Purcell, Patricia 91, 92
Purnell, Charlotte Hedlicka 67
Purnell, Matilda 56
Pyle, Margery 7
Pyle, Sara Webb 153

Rakestraw, Priscilla Bradley ix, 77, 78
Ramirez, Olga 46, 47
Raubacher, Rebecca 15
Ray, Adele 104
Reese, Annette 143
*Reese, Harriet Curtis 103
Reiver, Joanna 31
Rettew, Roslyn 146
*Reynolds, Nancy du Pont xii
*Rhoads, Eugenia 7, 146, 147, 148
*Richardson, Elizabeth H. 138
*Ridgely, Mabel Lloyd Fisher 103, 143, 149
Rigik, Elnora 65
Riggin, Grace xii
Roberts, Judith Atkins ix, 107
Roberts, Thelma xii
Robertson, Emily ix
*Robinson, Battle Rankin 29
*Robinson, Sally 52
*Robinson, Winifred J. 59
*Roedel, Leah ix, 56
Ronat, A. Elizabeth Rider 127
Rose, Barbara B. 98
Ross, Lulu M. 153
*Roth, Jane Richards 29
*Ryan, Elizabeth H. 46, 149
*Rydgren, Ann 52
Rzewnicki, Janet 78, 83

Salemi, Janet Hohman 118
Salter, Florence L. 6
Samonisky, Joan Schimpf 132
Sanders, Gwendolyn W. 67
*Sawin, Ellen 135
*Sawin, Nancy Churchman ix, 108, 135
Schiek, Elizabeth Robelin 104
Schramm, Patricia C. 98
Scott, Edith I. C. 61
Scott, Marion du Pont 131
Scott, Patricia Bell 65

Seitz, Margaret 151
Shackleton, Carol 115
Shadoan, Irene E. 27
Shallcross, Elizabeth 151
Sherr, Bonnie M. 18
Shipe, Martha 45
Shor, Nancy Garvin 147
Slavov, Eugenia M. Hintz 64, 65
Sloan, Helen Farr 7
Sloan, Sonia Schorr 45
Small, Cynthia Sheppard Mitchell 35
Smead, Helen McCauley Barrett 34
*Smigie, Katherine Ward ix, x
Smith, Barbara 65
*Smith (Parks), Ginger 133
Smith, Gwynne P. 80
Smith, Janet 138
Smith, Jennie E. 73, 153
Smith, Virginia Rebecca Keith 119, 120
Soles, Ada Leigh 81
Soltys, Susan Webb x
*Speakman, Marjorie xi, 151
*Spraker, Eileen C. 35
Springer, Susan 116
*Spruance, Gretchen Vosters 131, 132
Stan, Cynthia 15, 16
Statts, Jean 148
*Steele, Cecile Long 17, 143, 149
*Stein, Fannie 151
Steinmetz, Suzanne K. 65
*Sterck, Margaret S. 153
*Stewart, Elizabeth 151
*Stewart, Ruth Chambers ix, xii, 104
Stokes, Nellie Hughes 153
*Storey, Margaret 5
Stratton, Arlene Berger ix, 27
*Stuber, Gloria ix
Studte, Lois M. 95
Sturtevant, Brereton 29
*Swajeski, Marie 3
Swan, Susan Burrows 110
*Swensson, Evelyn Dickenson 3, 5
*Sykes, Emma Belle Gibson 75

Talley, Christine Ann ix, 138
*Tallman, Julia Hays 143, 145
Tang, Helen Kuo-Hu Liang 96
Tansey, Ann Taylor 25
*Tatnall, Frances Swift 153
Taylor, Barbara 43
*Theisen, Mary Duggan Jornlin 146, 149, 151
Thomas Helen R. ix, 145
Thomas, Susan Alexis 59, 63
Thompson, Hannah 151
Thompson, Jennifer 19

*Thompson, Mary Wilson 103
Thompson, Priscilla Mertens 53, 54, 110
Thoroughgood, Carolyn A. 67, 68
Tieman, Nancy B. 56, 57
Tierney, Helen, 151
*Tillmanns-Skolnik, Emma-June ix, 125
Tobin, Judith Gedney 93 ,151
Todd, Patricia 57
Toro, Lucille Ponatoski 63
*Townsend, Pearl 151
Tracy, Marion 6
Traynor, Janice M. 18, 19
Treadwell, Frances 142
Troy, Jean 135
Truitt, Carolyn Slingland 114
*Truman, Dorothy E. 15
Tull, Carol Ann DiSantis ix, x, 38
Turner, Frances 114
*Tybout, Ella Middleton Maxwell xii, 142
*Vernon, Mabel 74, 143, 149
*Viera, Barbara 138
*Vining, Mary 141
*Virden, Marjorie 104
Vladuchick, Susan Anne 127
*Vosters, Madge (Bunny) Harshaw 132

Walker, Charlotte ix
Wallace, Helen 47
Walsh, Carole 57
Walters, Marlene 113, 114
Ward, Carolyn Bush 105
*Ward, Mary Sam Smith vii, x, xi, xii, xiii, 83, 84, 106, 107, 111, 151
Ward, Sybil 28
*Warner, Emalea Pusey 59, 142, 149, 153
Warner, Susan 39
Waserstein (Doroshaw), Aida 30, 31
Webb, Sarah Simpson 48
*West, Frances 83, 111
Western, Dominique Coulet 112
White, Dorothy J. 23
White, Josephine Margaret Rebecca 89, 142
White, Mary G. 119
Whittington, Marne Cupp 83, 111
*Widdoes, Kathleen 3
Wilkie, Sharon 135
Williams, Ellen 44
*Williams, Elsie xii, 144
*Williams, Lynn 57
Williams, Mary C. I. 153
Willis, Huldah 151

Wilson, Alice Learned 72
*Wilson, Etta J. 143, 153
*Winchester, Naomi Gaines 52
Winfield, Linda F. 53
Wingate, Bonnie ix
Wingate, Frances Elma Norris 44

Wittland, Grace 132
Wohl, Faith A. 25, 32
Wonnell, Edith Baldwin 93, 94
Woodfolk, Martha L. 96
*Wright, Mary Ann 144, 149
*Wyeth, Carolyn Bockius 142

*Young, Pauline A. 106, 147,
  149
Young, Toni 2

Zipf, Jeanette ix
Zurkow, Esther 151